Self, Motivation, and Virtue

These chapters summarize the research findings from the incredibly successful Self, Motivation, and Virtue Project. The book is must reading for anyone working in the areas of character and moral psychology.
—*Christian B. Miller, A.C. Reid Professor of Philosophy, Wake Forest University, USA*

This volume features new findings by nine interdisciplinary teams of researchers on the topics of self, motivation, and virtue. Nine chapters bringing together scholars from the fields of philosophy, psychology, neuroscience, and sociology advance our substantive understanding of these important topics and showcase a variety of research methods of interdisciplinary interest.

Essays on Buddhism and the self in the context of romantic relationships, the development of personal projects and virtue, the notion of self-distancing and its moral impact, virtues as self-integrated traits, humility and the self in loving encounter, the importance of nation and faith in motivating virtue in Western and non-Western countries, roles for the self and virtue in eudaimonic growth, overcoming spiritual violence and sacramental shame in Christian communities, and an investigation into the moral self highlight the range and diversity of topics explored in this volume. The concept of deep integration also characterizes this work: each member of the interdisciplinary teams was fully and equally invested in their project from inception to completion. This approach invites teams to examine their disciplinary assumptions, rethink familiar concepts, and adjust methodologies in order to view their topics with fresh eyes.

The result is not only new findings of substantive and methodological interest, but also an interesting glimpse into the thinking of the researchers as they sought interdisciplinary common ground in their research. *Self, Motivation, and Virtue* will be of interest to scholars in philosophy, moral psychology, neuroscience, and sociology who are working on these topics.

Nancy E. Snow is Professor of Philosophy and Director of the Institute for the Study of Human Flourishing at the University of Oklahoma. She is the author of *Virtue as Social Intelligence: An Empirically Grounded Theory*, and more than 45 papers on ethics. She has edited *The Oxford Handbook of Virtue*.

Darcia Narvaez is Professor of Psychology at the University of Notre Dame. One of her recent books, *Neurobiology and the Development of Human Morality: Evolution, Culture, and Wisdom* won the 2015 William James Book Award from the American Psychological Association and the 2017 Expanded Reason Award.

Routledge Studies in Ethics and Moral Theory

Philosophical Perspectives on Empathy
Theoretical Approaches and Emerging Challenges
Edited by Derek Matravers and Anik Waldow

Putting Others First
The Christian Ideal of Others-Centeredness
T. Ryan Byerly

Methodology and Moral Philosophy
Edited by Jussi Suikkanen and Antti Kauppinen

Self-Transcendence and Virtue
Perspectives from Philosophy, Psychology, and Technology
Edited by Jennifer A. Frey and Candace Vogler

Moral Rights and Their Grounds
David Alm

Ethics in the Wake of Wittgenstein
Edited by Benjamin De Mesel and Oskari Kuusela

Perspectives in Role Ethics
Virtues, Reasons, and Obligation
Edited by Tim Dare and Christine Swanton

Self, Motivation, and Virtue
Innovative Interdisciplinary Research
Edited by Nancy E. Snow and Darcia Narvaez

For more information about this series, please visit: www.routledge.com/Routledge-Studies-in-Ethics-and-Moral-Theory/book-series/SE0423

Self, Motivation, and Virtue
Innovative Interdisciplinary Research

Edited by Nancy E. Snow and
Darcia Narvaez

LONDON AND NEW YORK

First published 2020 by Routledge

2 Park Square, Milton Park, Abingdon, Oxon OX14 4RN
605 Third Avenue, New York, NY 10017

Routledge is an imprint of the Taylor & Francis Group, an informa business

First issued in paperback 2021

Copyright © 2020 Taylor & Francis

The right of the editors to be identified as the authors of the editorial material, and of the authors for their individual chapters, has been asserted in accordance with sections 77 and 78 of the Copyright, Designs and Patents Act 1988.

All rights reserved. No part of this book may be reprinted or reproduced or utilised in any form or by any electronic, mechanical, or other means, now known or hereafter invented, including photocopying and recording, or in any information storage or retrieval system, without permission in writing from the publishers.

Notice:
Product or corporate names may be trademarks or registered trademarks, and are used only for identification and explanation without intent to infringe.

Publisher's Note

The publisher has gone to great lengths to ensure the quality of this reprint but points out that some imperfections in the original copies may be apparent.

Library of Congress Cataloging-in-Publication Data
Names: Narvaez, Darcia, editor. | Snow, Nancy E., editor.
Title: Self, motivation, and virtue : innovative interdisciplinary
   research / edited by Nancy E. Snow and Darcia Narvaez.
Description: New York : Routledge, 2019. | Series: Routledge
   studies in ethics and moral theory; 56 | Includes bibliographical
   references and index.
Identifiers: LCCN 2019031983 (print) | LCCN 2019031984 (ebook) |
   ISBN 9780367203177 (hbk) | ISBN 9780429260858 (ebk)
Subjects: LCSH: Self (Philosophy) | Motivation (Psychology) | Virtue.
Classification: LCC BD438.5 .S443 2019 (print) | LCC BD438.5 (ebook) |
   DDC 126—dc23
LC record available at https://lccn.loc.gov/2019031983
LC ebook record available at https://lccn.loc.gov/2019031984

ISBN: 978-0-367-20317-7 (hbk)
ISBN: 978-1-03-217743-4 (pbk)
DOI: 10.4324/9780429260858

Typeset in Sabon
by Apex CoVantage, LLC

Contents

List of Figures and Table vii
Preface ix
Acknowledgments xi

Introduction 1
NANCY E. SNOW AND DARCIA NARVAEZ

1 Self, Motivation, and Virtue, or How We Learned to Stop Worrying and Love Deep Integration 7
MOIN SYED, COLIN G. DEYOUNG, AND VALERIE TIBERIUS

2 Expansive Interdisciplinarity and the Moral Self 25
JAVIER GOMEZ-LAVIN, JESSE PRINZ, NINA STROHMINGER, AND SHAUN NICHOLS

3 The Virtues of Interdisciplinary Research: Psychological and Philosophical Inquiry Into Self, Motivation, and Virtue 43
BLAINE J. FOWERS AND BRADFORD COKELET

4 Virtue and Self-Distancing 63
WARREN HEROLD, WALTER SOWDEN, AND ETHAN KROSS

5 Admiring Moral Exemplars: Sketch of an Ethical Sub-Discipline 85
ROBERT ROBERTS AND MICHAEL SPEZIO

6 Achieving Deep Integration Across Disciplines: A Process Lens on Investigating Human Flourishing 109
CHRISTINE D. WILSON-MENDENHALL, JOHN DUNNE, AND PAUL CONDON

7 Toward an Integrated Psychology and Philosophy of
   Good Life Stories   127
   JACK J. BAUER AND PEGGY DESAUTELS

8 Reflections on Our Sociological-Philosophical Study of
   the Self, Motivation, and Virtue Among LGBTI Conservative
   Christians and Their Allies   147
   THERESA W. TOBIN AND DAWNE MOON

9 Integrating "Cultures of Reasoning": Interdisciplinary
   Research on Motivating the Self to Wisdom and Virtue   167
   RICCA EDMONDSON, MICHEL FERRARI, MONIKA ARDELT,
   AND HYEYOUNG BANG

   List of Contributors   193
   Index   203

Figures and Table

Figures

2.1 Averaged Similarity Map of Musical Genres Generated From Ratings of Our 46 German Participants Produced with the PROXSCAL Algorithm   33

3.1 Common Content for Interdisciplinary Research on Virtue and Eudaimonia   44

Table

3.1 Virtues and Vices of Interdisciplinary Research   49

Preface

The essays in this volume recount the findings and experiences of nine research teams whose work was funded by the "Self, Motivation, and Virtue Project" (hereafter SMV Project), which was, in turn, funded by the Templeton Religion Trust.[1] The project, which began on September 1, 2014, and ended on March 31, 2018, was co-directed by Nancy E. Snow and Darcia Narvaez. It had three aims:

> The first aim is to encourage investigations of the self as the possessor of personality, motivation, and virtue, including views on the development of the moral self. The second aim is to stimulate methodological innovation that incorporates multiple disciplinary perspectives and goes beyond paper-and-pencil measures. Meeting this aim requires that research teams move beyond traditional psychological measures, and that they meet the criterion of "deep integration" by generally being comprised of at least one scientist and one humanities scholar with full and equal investment in specific projects from inception to completion. Ideally, research teams include members from differing scientific traditions.
> (http://smvproject.com/about/overview/)

The project sought to encourage researchers to depart from the personality framework traditionally used by personality psychologists to study traits and to focus more directly on an alternative perspective—that in which the self is taken to be the possessor of traits and virtues. Not only did we think this would open up a new avenue for research on traits and virtues, but we also thought it could be more amenable to studying the development of virtues than the personality framework.

A brief comment on deep integration is in order. Though we realize that deep integration is not new to academic work, we imposed this requirement as a condition of teams' receiving and keeping funding in order to combat a trend that we thought detrimental to truly interdisciplinary research. In our experience, some funded projects tended to be led by a researcher from one discipline, typically a scientist, who then brought on board a humanist in a consultative or advisory capacity. The downside was that sometimes the humanist was never even consulted, or, alternatively, his or her advice was sought but not integrated into the research in a fundamental or impactful way.

Acknowledgments

The editors and contributors to this volume gratefully acknowledge the support for the Self, Motivation, and Virtue Project provided by the Templeton Religion Trust. The views expressed are not necessarily those of the Templeton Religion Trust. The editors would also like to thank Mr. Jonathan Casad for editorial assistance with this volume.

Note

1. One research team was unable to provide a chapter for this volume.

Introduction

Nancy E. Snow and Darcia Narvaez

Many of the most interesting and important questions within scholarship require interdisciplinary approaches. The chapters in this book describe both the process and outcome of research projects addressing self, motivation, and virtue. The projects involved interdisciplinary team members, scholars from both social sciences and the humanities. In their designs, the teams worked to innovate not only theoretically but methodologically. In their chapters, they describe the progress of their efforts and the challenges and compromises as well as findings. Each team to a greater or lesser degree struggled with finding shared language and disciplinary assumptions about constructs. Teams often adopted working definitions of their target constructs, integrated methodological approaches to analyses and interpretation, navigating the challenges of interdisciplinary work. Many reached nuanced understandings of their topics that could not otherwise have emerged from a solitary disciplinary approach.

The first two chapters present reflections on different frameworks within which the self, motivation, and virtue can be studied. We chose these two chapters to lead the volume because of the foundational nature of conceptual frameworks in pursuing work on self, motivation, and virtue, as well as the centrality of the concept of "self," whichever framework is used. Chapter 1, "Self, Motivation, and Virtue, or: How We Learned to Stop Worrying and Love Deep Integration," was authored by Moin Syed, Colin G. DeYoung, and Valerie Tiberius, two psychologists and a philosopher from the University of Minnesota. We chose this piece as the lead chapter because it challenges the entire framework on which the project was built: the "self" framework as a way of understanding the development of virtue and the cultivation of virtuous motivation. Instead, the authors make the case that the personality framework is better suited for understanding self, motivation, virtue, and a range of other concepts. The authors conducted a highly successful project investigating personal projects, well-being, and the development of virtue among college students (see Bedford-Peterson et. al., 2019). Their thoughtful chapter in this volume provides a thorough review of the concepts of self, personality, identity, motivation, virtue, and well-being, with an eye to showing the superiority of the personality to the self framework as an approach to understanding virtue.

Chapter 2, "Expansive Interdisciplinarity and the Moral Self," is by Javier Gomez-Lavin, Jesse Prinz, Nina Strohminger, and Shaun Nichols, three philosophers and a psychologist. Unlike Chapter 1, which challenges the moral self framework, the research presented in Chapter 2 lies squarely within the moral self frame. Chapter 2 articulates and defends the "Moral Self Hypothesis"—the claim that morals matter for identity, more than other constructs such as memory, narrative, and agency—which have been focal points for research on personal identity. The authors offer a brief history of their work on this topic and review aspects of the research they undertook as part of the SMV Project (see also Gomez-Lavin & Prinz, 2019). Of special interest are the empirical revisions they made to their hypotheses, as well as their recognition, based on studies of perceptions of the moral self undertaken among different cultural groups, of the need to obtain more background in the areas of cross-cultural psychology, history, and politics, so as better to understand the multifarious real-world influences on the shaping of moral identity.

Chapters 1 and 2 take up perspectives on the frameworks within which traits and virtues are studied—the personality framework on the one hand and the moral self framework on the other. In contrast, Chapter 3, "The Virtues of Interdisciplinary Research: Psychological and Philosophical Inquiry into Self, Motivation, and Virtue," by psychologist Blaine J. Fowers and philosopher Bradford Cokelet, takes up the topic of traits and virtues. Their interdisciplinary collaboration led them to develop the STRIVE-4 model of traits as a way of guiding research on virtues. Three key features of this model are that virtues come in degrees (are scalar), are role-sensitive, and interact with situational factors (see also Cokelet & Fowers, 2019). Their chapter exemplifies the kind of nuanced work on virtue that can be done when philosophers and psychologists join forces.

The authors of Chapters 4 and 5 address features of the self. Chapter 4, "Virtue and Self-Distancing," by philosopher Warren Herold and psychologists Walter Sowden and Ethan Kross, discusses their empirical investigation of Adam Smith's hypothesis of the perspective of the impartial spectator, or "self-distancing," as they call it. They initially predicted that self-distancing would reduce people's tendency to exaggerate their self-importance relative to others and would increase altruism. Their empirical findings proved them wrong, forcing them to rethink their framework. The data instead revealed aspects the team had not originally considered—that altruistic motivation is complex and depends on a host of factors, including a person's circumstances and her relations with other people.

In Chapter 5, "Admiring Moral Exemplars: Sketch of an Ethical Sub-Discipline," philosopher Robert Roberts and psychologist Michael Spezio extend their solitary disciplinary research on humility to address it in specific contexts. They investigated humility at L'Arche communities and Homeboy Industries to offer reflections on moral exemplarism and roles for admiration in it. L'Arche communities, founded by the late Jean Vanier, are communities in which Core Members, who are intellectually disabled adults, live with non-disabled Assistants. Homebody Industries, based in Los Angeles and founded by Father Gregory Boyle, are groups in which former gang members welcome others into communal life. These communities served not only as sites for the authors' empirical study of humility but also prompted reflection on the nature of exemplarism. Exemplar theory maintains that we can develop morally through admiring and emulating exemplars such as Confucius and Jesus Christ (see Zagzebski, 2017). Roberts and Spezio maintain that Jean Vanier and Father Boyle are clearly exemplars, but so, too, are many ordinary people. Exemplars can be positive or negative, showing us how to be good as well as evils to avoid. The authors also offer insights on the complexities of admiration and emulation, taking their original studies of L'Arche and Homeboy Industries in new and interesting directions (see Spezio, Peterson, & Roberts, 2019).

In Chapter 6, "Achieving Deep Integration Across Disciplines: A Process Lens on Investigating Human Flourishing," Christine D. Wilson-Mendenhall (neuroscience), John Dunne (Asian languages and cultures), and Paul Condon (psychology) share the complex process by means of which careful interdisciplinary interaction enabled them to develop an integrated theoretical framework, bridging Buddhist philosophy and psychology for studying romantic relationships (see also Condon, Dunne, & Wilson-Mendenhall, 2019). They write: "Whereas the balance of wisdom and compassion in Buddhist accounts goes beyond existing constructs in the psychology literature, the context-specific instantiation of wisdom and compassion in close relationships goes beyond discussions in Buddhist accounts" (this volume, p. 118). Their work thus integrated differing conceptual perspectives and achieved conceptual precision, but it did not neglect the empirical side. The authors discuss their empirical approach and their integration of methods toward the end of their chapter.

Chapters 7, 8, and 9 furnish broader perspectives on self, motivation, and virtue. Chapter 7, "Toward an Integrated Psychology and Philosophy of Good Life Stories," by psychologist Jack J. Bauer and philosopher Peggy DesAutels, broadens the perspective by integrating feminist virtue ethics with the psychological study of life stories through the analysis of personal narratives and the study of eudaimonic personality development (see also Bauer & DesAutels, 2019). The qualitative and quantitative analyses of life stories in terms of virtue themes reveal preliminary findings that link virtues with motivation, action, and meaning in the research participants' lives. Also revealed are respects in which social institutions burden and impede the development of virtue, especially for women and others who face non-ideal circumstances.

Chapter 8 opens a window on the experiences of another group—conservative Christians who are lesbian, gay, bisexual, transgender, and intersex (LGBTI) and their allies. In "Reflections on Our Sociological-Philosophical Study of the Self, Motivation, and Virtue Among LGBTI Conservative Christians and their Allies," Theresa W. Tobin (philosophy) and Dawne Moon (sociology), empirically investigate a form of harm that they call "sacramental shame" (see also Tobin & Moon, 2019). Sacramental shame is a form of spiritual violence that is perpetrated on LGBTI Christians by other Christians. The authors study the efforts of a conservative Christian group to end practices of sacramental shame, including what motivates members of this group to see these practices as incompatible with Christian love and to end them. They include a discussion of the methodological limitations of their research and how they tried to address them but argue that combining a philosophical with a sociological approach enabled them to glean nuanced insights into experiences of sacramental shame, as well as to provide empirically grounded accounts of how it is overcome.

Chapter 9, "Integrating 'Cultures of Reasoning': Interdisciplinary Research on Motivating the Self to Wisdom and Virtue," offers the broadest perspective that researchers took on topics pertaining to self, motivation, and virtue (see also Ferrari, Bang, Ardelt, & Feng, 2019). Ricca Edmondson (political science and sociology), Michel Ferrari (psychology), Monika Ardelt (sociology), and Hyeyoung Bang (education) addressed the question, "How do people motivate themselves to behave as virtuously and wisely as they can, and how do nation, religious faith, age, and/or wisdom contribute to this?" The authors' project was to compare Canadians (in a highly Christian country) with South Koreans (in a highly Buddhist country) in four different faith conditions: Christian, Muslim, Buddhist, and atheist. Their paper recounts the interdisciplinary underpinnings and challenges their project faced, and discusses issues of how to approach data collection and interpretation. Their work, they inform us, is still in progress.

In conclusion, the nine research teams uncovered significant findings in a number of areas: how using the personality framework can shed light on the personal projects of emerging adults and their well-being; how the moral self is constituted and develops; the nature of traits and virtues; the factors that unify the self; those that can impact altruistic motivation or fail, despite expectations, to do so; relational aspects of the self, such as exemplarism and admiration; approaching romantic relationships through a lens integrating Buddhist and psychological thought; the impact of non-ideal circumstances on the development of virtue; sacramental shame and how to overcome it through Christian love; and, finally, interdisciplinary work on faith and wisdom across cultures. The findings of these groups were significantly shaped by the highly integrated nature of their research partnerships. Their work was creative, yet challenging, and certainly ongoing. May it continue.

References

Bauer, J., & DesAutels, P. (2019). When life gets in the way: Generativity and development of non-idealized virtues in women's life stories. *The Journal of Moral Education*, 48(1), 126–145.

Bedford-Peterson, C., DeYoung, C., Tiberius, V., & Syed, M. (2019). Integrating philosophical and psychological approaches to well-being: The role of success in personal projects. *The Journal of Moral Education*, 48(1), 84–97.

Cokelet, B., & Fowers, B. (2019). Realistic virtue and how to study them: Introducing the STRIVE-4 model. *The Journal of Moral Education*, 48(1), 7–26.

Condon, P., Dunne, J., & Wilson-Mendenhall, C. (2019). Wisdom and compassion: A new perspective on the science of relationships. *The Journal of Moral Education*, 48(1), 98–108.

Ferrari, M., Bang, H., Ardelt, M., & Feng, Z. (2019). Educating for virtue: How wisdom coordinates informal, non-formal, and formal education in motivation to virtue in Canada and South Korea. *The Journal of Moral Education*, 48(1), 47–64.

Gomez-Lavin, J., & Prinz, J. (2019). Parole and the moral self: Moral change mitigates responsibility. *The Journal of Moral Education*, 48(1), 65–83.

Spezio, M., Peterson, G., & Roberts, R. (2019). Humility as openness to others: Interactive humility in the context of L'Arche. *The Journal of Moral Education*, 48(1), 27–46.

Tobin, T., & Moon, D. (2019). The politics of shame in the motivation to virtue: Lessons from the same, pride, and humility experiences of LGBT conservative Christians and their allies. *The Journal of Moral Education*, 48(1), 109–125.

Zagzebski, L. (2017). *Exemplarist moral theory*. New York, NY: Oxford University Press.

1 Self, Motivation, and Virtue, or How We Learned to Stop Worrying and Love Deep Integration

Moin Syed, Colin G. DeYoung, and Valerie Tiberius

The Self, Motivation, and Virtue Project (Snow & Narvaez, 2015) was developed "to open avenues of inquiry into virtue using the framework of the 'self,' instead of 'personality,' to require deep and ongoing interdisciplinary collaboration, and to stimulate methodological innovation into the study of virtue." But what does this mean to use a "framework of self" instead of "personality"? What do we mean by "self" and "personality"? This is a difficult distinction to make succinctly, as the two terms are not used consistently across psychology and associated disciplines.

In this chapter, we review the major inconsistencies in the use of "self" and "personality," as well as "identity," which is another key concept that is not often clearly distinguished from self and personality. The thrust of our argument is that the concept of personality—when conceptualized as extending beyond personality traits—provides a broad framework for understanding not only self and identity, but also consistent individual differences in motivation and virtue.

Additionally, our own interest in these issues arose out of concerns about how different aspects of personality are relevant for well-being. However, "well-being" is another term that is conceptualized and studied in divergent ways, especially when moving beyond psychological conceptions. We review these different perspectives following our discussion of self, identity, and personality and suggest that understanding well-being in the context of individuals' personal projects (i.e., active goals) provides one possible strategy for finding common ground among different conceptions.

We approach these issues from our individual perspectives as a developmental psychologist, a personality psychologist, and a philosopher. Perhaps because the philosopher among us takes David

Hume as her inspiration, we found that differences between the two psychologists from different sub-fields were as significant as the differences between the psychologists and the philosopher. Hume was an empiricist philosopher who attempted to locate the self, virtue, and indeed all of ethics in a naturalistic picture of human psychology. The Humean tradition in philosophy is, therefore, more amenable to integration with psychology than other philosophical traditions. Nevertheless, we did have three different disciplinary perspectives that led to different assumptions and understandings of self, identity, personality, and well-being. We have not always agreed on all of the issues presented in this chapter, and in some ways still do not, but through collaboration we worked toward a deep integration that has refined our understanding. We highlight some of these challenges to deep integration throughout the chapter.

The Self and Identity

Few concepts in the social sciences are as confused and diffuse as the "self." Even looking within the field of psychology, there is no agreed-upon definition of the self, and thus the term is not consistently used. Accordingly, a critical starting point for understanding the relations among self, motivation, and virtue is gaining clarity on what, exactly, is the "self."

William James (1890), Charles H. Cooley (1902), and George Herbert Mead (1934) are often credited with laying the foundations for psychological understandings of self and identity. Importantly, even these earliest articulations of the self eschewed a singular global concept of "the self" in favor of more specific aspects of the self. For example, James made a distinction between the "me" self and the "I" self. The "me" is the self as object, what is consciously *known* about the self (and which he further divided into the material self, social self, and spiritual self). In contrast, the "I" is the self as subject, the *knower* of who one is.

Although both James and Mead emphasized the role of internal and social/interactional processes, James relatively favored the internal whereas Mead relatively favored the social/interactional. This crude alignment is useful for understanding the subsequent intellectual lineages of these two early influential figures as researchers sought to develop formal theories, experiments, and assessments that followed from their ideas (see Hammack, 2015). Mead's work went on to heavily influence sociological and social psychological concepts of the self, which tend to emphasize the nature of the self within specific social contexts. In contrast, James's work was heavily influential in developmental psychological concepts of the self, which tend to emphasize internal processes of continuity, coherence, and person-environment fit. Herein we briefly review each of these broad perspectives.

Social Psychological Approaches to Self and Identity

Although the self is a concept widely used in social psychology, it is not used consistently or coherently. In their introduction to the *Handbook of Self and Identity*, Leary and Tangney (2012) organize definitions of the self into five categories: 1) self as the total person, 2) self as personality, 3) self as experiencing subject (I self, or self as subject), 4) self as beliefs about oneself (me self, or self as object), and 5) self as executive agent (self as cybernetic system). They reject the first two definitions, largely because those definitions rely on a global "self" that they feel is not specific enough to be useful. The latter three definitions, they argue, can be synthesized into a higher-order process of *reflexive thinking*, or "the ability to take oneself as the object of one's attention and thought" (p. 6), with the self then being defined as "the set of psychological mechanisms or processes that allows organisms to think consciously about themselves" (p. 6).

One confusion that arises with this synthesized definition of the self stems from what seems to be a misunderstanding of two distinct linguistic functions for the word "self." "Self" can refer to a distinct entity, typically a psychological entity such as the conscious experience and understanding of the individual's own being as a coherent agent (encompassing the I and the me, as we have already discussed, and aligning with the aforementioned definitions 3 and 4). However, it can also simply signify reflexivity, as it often does when used as a prefix, as in the terms "self-regulation" and "self-control" (aligning with definition 5). Many social psychologists seem to take the existence of these terms as evidence that the "self" as a psychological entity is somehow necessary for inhibiting impulses—as if it were the "self" that was doing the regulation or exercising control. Instead, however, the prefix "self" here is simply indicating reflexivity. Human beings are systems that regulate themselves, also known as "cybernetic" systems (DeYoung, 2015). From our perspective, therefore, the fifth definition offered earlier should also be excluded from the meaning of "self" because, in fact, the whole person is a cybernetic system.

In the context of this linguistic analysis, the case of "self-esteem" is interesting because "self" in this term can be interpreted either as a psychological entity or as a signifier of reflexivity. In the latter case, the individual esteems (evaluates) itself. In the former, it is precisely the conscious understanding of what one is that is being evaluated. In this case, the two meanings of "self" are largely congruent; however, in many cases (as with "self-regulation" and "self-control") they are not, and we observe that this has given the social psychological definition of self a rather amorphous and confused quality. Many unconscious processes are involved in self-regulation and self-control, and we do not think that these should be considered part of the "self" as that term is typically used in psychology. Thus, from our perspective, the self should be limited to the self as experiencing subject and the self as beliefs about oneself, thereby remaining largely congruent with James's original definitions of the I self and the me self.

One peculiar phrasing commonly used in social psychology is "self and identity." There is the *Handbook of Self and Identity* and also the journal *Self and Identity*, which is the flagship journal of the International Society of Self and Identity. The frequent use of both terms suggests that they are believed to be different in some way, but to the best of our knowledge there is no meaningful distinction between them to be made. In their introductory chapter to the handbook, Leary and Tangney (2012) devote considerable attention to the definitional and conceptual thicket of the self but do not even offer a definition of identity, let alone how it may differ from self.

Social psychological approaches to identity have largely focused on group-based processes, heavily influenced by *social identity theory*. Tajfel (1981) defined social identity as "that *part* of an individual's self-concept which derives from his knowledge of his membership of a social group (or groups) together with the value and emotional significance attached to that membership" (p. 255; italics in original), and the concept has been primarily used to understand situational in-group and out-group behavior (Ashmore, Deaux, & McLaughlin-Volpe, 2004; Verkuyten, 2016).

Tajfel's definition, referenced earlier, is frequently cited in the literature verbatim, often followed by a paraphrase of the contrasting definition of personal identity as the focus on aspects of the self that individuals believe make them unique. But Tajfel did not provide a definition of personal identity and was clear that there was much more to identity than he was considering with social identity. Nevertheless, social psychology has essentially defined the conceptual universe of identity as group memberships (social, or collective, identities) that connect individuals to others, and as personal identities, which are characteristics that make individuals unique (e.g., Ashmore et al., 2004; Brewer, 1991).

Developmental Psychological Approaches to Self and Identity

From the perspective of developmental psychology there is no meaningful difference between self and identity. The lack of distinction between the terms is largely due to convention rather than researchers in the field actively sorting out the differences in the meaning of the terms. When "self" is used by developmental psychologists, it is typically applied to individual reflective processes occurring before adolescence (e.g., mirror self-recognition in infancy; Suddendorf & Butler, 2013). Following Erik Erikson (1950), developmental psychologists tend to understand identity as arising in early adolescence in response to broadening cognitive capacities that facilitate deeper reflective thinking and an expanding social milieu that affords greater social comparison (Habermas & Köber, 2015; Meeus, 2011). Thus, the distinction, if any, corresponds to one of maturity or sophistication rather than conceptually distinct psychological phenomena.

The use of the terms "social identity" and "personal identity" in social psychology is different from how they are used in developmental psychology. Indeed, the whole concept of identity is understood and studied from a very different perspective (Syed, Azmitia, & Cooper, 2011). The developmental perspective on identity is rooted in Erikson's (1950, 1968) psychosocial theory of lifespan development, which as noted, was heavily influenced by William James's conceptualization of the self. In particular, Erikson was taken by the concept of the I self, exploring individuals' efforts to develop a stable internal sense of self, or identity. For Erikson identity corresponds to a sense of inner sameness, coherence, and integration of the self across time and place.

Erikson also used the terms *personal identity* and *social identity*, as well as ego identity, but he used them in a different way than how social psychology has defined them. Erikson conceptualized personal identity as individuals' personal beliefs and goals in relation to culturally relevant roles. Social identity was defined in a similar way, as connections individuals have to various group memberships, but also connects identity processes to larger social structures, taking into consideration how individuals develop identities within a specific cultural context (Way & Rogers, 2015). So both personal and social identities correspond to the me self. Finally, ego identity represents the synthesizing process used to establish and maintain personal continuity, closely aligning with James's conceptualization of the I self. Whereas the social identity perspective largely sets aside the concept of personal identity in favor of exploring social identity, the developmental perspective views the two as closely linked; that personal and social identities can work together to enhance or constrain individual development.

The social and developmental approaches to self and identity have largely operated as parallel streams of research, although this has been more extreme in the social psychological literature. For example, in Leary and Tangney's (2012) review of the history of self and identity in psychology there is no reference at all to Erikson's theory or the wealth of empirical research that has followed it. Even when discussing the relevance of psychoanalytical theory for self and identity, Leary and Tangney do not invoke Erikson. The only developmental research that is discussed is Harter's (2015; Harter & Monsour, 1992) research on changes in evaluative traits across adolescence, an approach that is consistent with the social psychological study of the self.

To be sure, developmental research has been relatively insular as well, and there are subdivisions within the developmental approach to identity that have mostly failed to adequately interface with one another (i.e., the identity status and narrative approaches; see Syed, 2012; McLean & Syed, 2015). However, some developmental research, namely in the area of ethnic/racial identity, has explicitly sought to merge the social psychological and developmental perspectives (Phinney, 1990; Umaña-Taylor et al., 2014; Verkuyten, 2016; Yip & Douglass, 2013).

Despite these many different terms, and identical terms defined in different ways, all uses of self and identity reviewed previously conform to Leary and Tangney's (2012) definition of self as "the set of psychological mechanisms or processes that allows organisms to think consciously about themselves." Accordingly, our position follows the developmental psychologists' view that there is no meaningful distinction between self and identity, which may also be consistent with the social psychological view given the lack of discussion of the distinction. The questions we are now confronted with are: how are self and identity related to personality? What would it mean to use a "framework of self" instead of a " framework of personality"?

Self and Identity as Part of Personality

The major barrier to understanding how self and identity are part of personality is a limited understanding of what personality is. Personality has, unfortunately, come to be equated with personality *traits*. Personality traits are relatively stable descriptions of individuals' probabilistic tendencies in behavior, motivation, emotion, and cognition. Typically traits are constructs that could be applied to people in any culture at any point in history, rather than being culturally or personally specific (DeYoung, 2015). Traits are a central component of personality, but personality psychologists have never viewed traits as constituting the totality of personality. Rather, traits are viewed as one level of the broader personality structure.

In this section we outline this personality structure and locate self and identity, as used by social and developmental psychologists, within it. Using this framework helps resolve some of the confusion between social and developmental definitions of self and identity, and also helps facilitate an understanding of the cultural nature of self, identity, and personality.

Three Levels of Personality

Building upon McAdams' (1995) earlier work, McAdams and Pals (2006) outlined an integrative framework for understanding the complexities of the whole person. This framework highlighted five principles with which personality can be understood, with the middle three principles constituting three levels of personality:

> Personality is conceived as (a) an individual's unique variation on the general evolutionary design for human nature, expressed as a developing pattern of (b) dispositional traits, (c) characteristic adaptations, and (d) self-defining life narratives, complexly and differentially situated (e) in culture and social context.
>
> (p. 204)

Biology and culture are less distinct parts of personality than facts about the nature of human variation; that is, there is always a biological and a cultural foundation underlying any personality process. It is due to evolution that all human beings share a general biological plan for the body and brain, and personality stems from variations in this plan. Similarly, all human beings live within a cultural context that shapes their individual personalities. Thus, we focus on the three interior levels: traits, characteristic adaptations, and life stories.

Level 1: Traits

The term "personality traits" refers to relatively stable individual differences in behavior, motivation, emotion, and cognition that constitute the most basic, fundamental aspect of personality (Caspi, Roberts, & Shiner, 2005; Costa & McCrae, 1992; DeYoung, 2015). Although commonly equated with the "Big Five" of neuroticism, extraversion, conscientiousness, agreeableness, and openness, personality traits have been more broadly organized into a hierarchical model based on their patterns of covariation. Each of the Big Five traits subsumes two aspects, and each aspect consists of some unknown number of facets (DeYoung, Quilty, & Peterson, 2007). Moving up from the Big Five are the two meta-traits of *plasticity*, consisting of the shared variance between openness and extraversion, and *stability*, consisting of the shared variance of conscientiousness, agreeableness, and low neuroticism (i.e., emotional stability). Personality traits that cannot easily be fit into a hierarchy based on the Big Five are nonetheless personality traits, as long as they reflect differences in behavior and experience that can be meaningfully used to describe people across cultures. The Big Five are simply the major dimensions of covariation among the multitude of more specific personality traits. In this context, many of the characteristics that are seen as "virtues"—compassion, honesty, courage, etc.—are personality traits.

Level 2: Characteristic Adaptations

McAdams and Pals (2006) defined characteristic adaptations as "a wide range of motivational, social–cognitive, and developmental adaptations, contextualized in time, place, and/or social role" (p. 208). Fitting with this broad definition, they provided a long list of psychological constructs that are captured by this level, including goals, plans, self-images, and developmental tasks, all while noting that there is no agreed-upon taxonomy of characteristic adaptations akin to the hierarchical model of traits. DeYoung (2015) provided a simplified definition of characteristic adaptations, asserting that this aspect of personality can be decomposed into just three broad categories, *goals* that guide behavior, *interpretations* of self and world, and cognitive and behavioral *strategies* used to pursue goals, attempting to transform the state of existence as currently perceived into the one desired.

As communicated by the label *characteristic adaptations*, this level of personality is more squarely concerned with the persistent ways in which individuals have responded (i.e., adapted) to their specific life circumstances. Although characteristic adaptations are clearly more contextualized than traits, it would not be accurate to distinguish characteristic adaptations and traits as the contextualized vs. decontextualized aspects of personality, as a wealth of research has demonstrated the contextual nature of traits (Roberts & Caspi, 2003; Roberts et al., 2017; Thorne, 2000). Rather, traits are viewed as culturally universal dimensions of human variation whereas characteristic adaptations are responses to specific cultural, or even uniquely personal, demands. Moreover, the distinction between traits and characteristic adaptations is sometimes described as the "having" vs. the "doing" of personality (e.g., McAdams & Pals, 2006). This is also not accurate, as traits are also put into action for specific purposes.

Level 3: Integrative Life Narratives

Integrated life narratives consist of the stories that people tell about their personal past to make meaning and develop a sense of identity (McAdams & Pals, 2006). This level of personality evolved from a somewhat different tradition than traits and characteristic adaptations. Narrative psychology focuses on how individuals reason about their past experiences and how stories serve functional roles for self-understanding (McAdams, 2013). Narrating one's life allows for a sense of coherence across time and place to provide a sense of purpose and meaning. In contrast to traits and characteristic adaptations, the integrated life story emphasizes an individual life lived, extended through time. Personality at this level includes the complex and contextual ways in which traits and characteristic adaptations manifest in specific, yet potentially predictable, ways across lifetimes (Josselson & Flum, 2015). Moreover, integrative life narratives are necessarily situated within individuals' social, cultural, and historical contexts. Thus, this level of personality aims to understand what is truly unique about a person.

Self vs. Personality

Having laid out the three levels of personality, we now return to the question "What would it mean to use a 'framework of self' instead of a 'framework of personality'?" We believe that the personality structure outlined earlier provides two alternative solutions that simplify all of this a great deal. One solution is to define the self in the global sense and equate it with personality, as Leary and Tangney (2012) indicated is already done in some circles, and then recognize the distinct levels of the self within the complex structure of personality. Within this approach, self and personality constitute an instance of the *jangle fallacy* (two different terms that nevertheless refer to the same thing), and thus use of both terms should be avoided (in this case, the recommendation would be to cease using the vague term "self" in favor of "personality"). This solution fits well with the philosopher David Hume's conception of the self as a "bundle of perceptions." Hume did not have the benefit of research in contemporary personality psychology, but were he around today he likely would acknowledge the different components of personality discussed in the previous section and included them in his "bundle theory." This solution suggests there is no difference between a "framework of self" and personality.

An alternative solution would rely on the more narrow definition of self as referring to psychological mechanisms associated with conscious representation of who one is, which is consistent with developmental and most social psychological definitions of self. The self is one's conscious understanding of what one is as a person, including one's conscious beliefs about what one values, what one is capable of, what one's skills are, and how one orients toward the future. This definition makes the self a *part* of personality; reflective processes are a subset of the broader class of interpretations, which are themselves characteristic adaptations. Since even under the narrower conception of the self, most aspects of the self reflect levels 2 and 3 of personality (characteristic adaptations and integrative life narratives), it is not necessary to distinguish between a "framework of self" and a "framework of personality." The self (broadly or narrowly defined) is subsumed by the concept of personality.

Interlude: Defining Personality Levels as a Challenge to Deep Integration

Agreeing on the general structure of personality does not resolve all potential conflicts about how to conceptualize aspects of the personality system. Sorting complex constructs, such as self, identity, motivation, and virtue, into the different levels is certain to lead to disagreements among researchers coming from different traditions.

Identity is a case where we, the authors, do not completely agree. In the McAdams and Pals (2006) framework, identity is viewed as a level 3 construct whereas self-processes (in the reflexive sense of the term) are viewed as level 2. McAdams and Pals did not make an effort to distinguish between self and identity conceptually, and as we have already discussed, there is no meaningful distinction to be made. That said, from Moin's perspective identity *can* be defined at levels 2 and 3 not because of an artificial distinction between self and identity, but because each level provides a substantially different degree of information and insight into identity as part of personality (Syed, 2017). Identity clearly operates at level 2 with regard to how individuals engage with the specific domains of their identity (e.g., occupation, religion, family) over a relatively circumscribed period of time. Level 3, in contrast, focuses on the synthesis of the self across an extended period of time to create and maintain an overall sense of identity.

From Colin's perspective, interpretations of the self arise in response to specific cultural circumstances and are therefore characteristic adaptations. In this sense, integrative life narratives are certainly a key part of the self, but so are less elaborated forms of identity, including self-esteem and one's conscious beliefs about one's own traits. Thus, Colin rejects the ontological distinction between levels 2 and 3 and describes integrative life narratives as simply a special type of characteristic adaptation in the interpretation category (DeYoung, 2015).

Indeed, the source of this disagreement is rooted in a larger disagreement between Colin and Moin about whether levels 2 and 3 should be conceptualized as distinct levels of personality at all, even though they agree that the integrative life narrative is distinguishable from other types of characteristic adaptations. For Colin, the integrative life narrative is an interpretation of the self, and therefore a characteristic adaptation. For Moin, the integrated life narrative represents what is truly unique about a person and his or her life, and this degree of difference with respect to what we know about a person is sufficiently large so as to justify its status as a distinct level of personality. Colin asserts that there are truly unique aspects of a person's personality at both levels 2 and 3 in the McAdams and Pals framework and hence does not see the uniqueness of the life narrative as adequate justification for making it a separate ontological category.

Following prolonged discussion, we determined that the source of our disagreement is a difference in primary concerns: Moin's epistemological concerns (the importance of integrative narratives as a distinctive way for knowing the personality) and Colin's ontological concerns (what is the integrative narrative as a psychological entity that the individual produces?—it is an interpretation of self/world and hence a characteristic adaptation). This example is instructive because it highlights the differences that can exist within the discipline of psychology and how deep integration is needed not only between disciplines but within disciplines as well.

And what about motivation and virtue? How do we distribute these concepts in the broader personality system? As it turns out this was a rather straightforward issue for us that did not require deep integration. We are in agreement that all reasonably persistent psychological qualities are either traits or characteristic adaptations, and many qualities can be considered traits *or* characteristic adaptations, depending on their specific conceptualization and measurement (DeYoung, 2015).

With respect to virtue, we presume that both traits and characteristic adaptations can be virtues, and that every virtue is either a trait or a characteristic adaptation (although clearly not every trait or characteristic adaptation is a virtue). More specifically, virtue can be considered a quality that traits and characteristic adaptations may have, and a virtuous trait or characteristic adaptations can, therefore, be described as a "virtue." Many virtues—honesty, perseverance, kindness, courage, etc.—are obviously traits. Variation in them could be observed in any culture, and almost any virtuous trait can be classified within the hierarchical taxonomy provided by the Big Five (or as a blend of two or more traits from

Self, Motivation, and Virtue 19

the hierarchy). That said, not all virtues are traits; one may identify culturally specific virtues—for example, having the skill or motivation to carry out some particular social tradition, or to express a virtuous trait through some specific means—that are clearly characteristic adaptations. Importantly, this conceptualization of how virtues can be traits or characteristic adaptations is not unique to virtues and can easily be extended to motivation.

What defines a particular psychological quality as a trait or characteristic adaptation has little to do with its kind (e.g., motivational, emotional, or cognitive process) and more about its specific conceptualization and measurement. Again, contemporary followers of Hume will find this picture very sympathetic. Hume defined virtues as qualities that are useful or agreeable to the self or others. Reading the findings of personality psychology back into Hume, he could easily agree that virtues are traits or characteristic adaptations that are singled out as virtues because of their positive effects on the possessor of the virtue or on other people.

Deep Integration Continued: What Does All of This Mean for Well-Being?

As noted at the outset of this chapter, we approached our collaboration with a mutual interest in how personality is associated with well-being. Thus far we have focused on different conceptualizations of self, identity, and personality, but we also tend to work from slightly different conceptualization of well-being. As it turns out, however, our different conceptualizations were more similar than different.

One distinctive feature of well-being is that it is *good for* the creature who has it. In other words, it is a kind of value that is subject relative (Sumner, 1996). Psychological theories of well-being account for subject-relativity directly by holding that well-being is just a subjective state: it consists in feeling a certain way, or having certain attitudes toward one's life. Indeed, some psychologists (e.g., Diener, Lucas, & Oishi, 2002) restrict their attention to *subjective well-being* and do not claim to be studying well-being simpliciter.

Philosophers who aim to describe *well-being* (not merely "subjective well-being") have taken different approaches to accounting for the subject relativity of well-being. Some have defined well-being in terms of psychological states like pleasure (Feldman,

2004; Crisp, 2006) or life satisfaction (Sumner, 1996). Others have defended objective theories of well-being, according to which there are standards for what counts as good for a person that transcend the person him or herself (Bloomfield, 2014; Fletcher, 2013). Still others have defended theories of well-being according to which well-being consists in obtaining the objects of our desires, achieving our goals, or fulfilling our values (Heathwood, 2016; Keller, 2004; Tiberius, 2008).

The notion of subjective well-being favored by many psychologists has much in common with the hedonist's definition of well-being but does not offer much of obvious interest to other philosophical schools (Bedford-Petersen, DeYoung, Tiberius, & Syed, 2019; Tiberius, 2006). This is a serious obstacle to interdisciplinary research and one that we hoped to overcome. Happily, the philosopher on our team defends a value fulfilment theory of well-being, and the cybernetic theory of agency that informs DeYoung's personality research suggests a theory of well-being in the family of theories that includes value fulfillment and goal achievement theories. This view is also consistent with Syed's view of well-being rooted in developmental psychology, which often conceptualizes well-being as the successful resolution of normative developmental tasks (e.g., developing a sense of identity, forming and maintaining intimate relationships).

This, together with considerations about available measurement tools, led us to think of well-being in terms of success in personal projects (Bedford-Peterson et al., 2019). Personal projects are "extended sets of personally salient action in context" (Little, 2006). They are extended in that they take some time (days, weeks, even years) to carry out. They involve some goal that is personally salient—that is, reasonably important to the individual—along with its various subgoals, the strategies that are used to achieve those goals, and the interpretations of the relevant aspects of self and world that allow people both to define the context in which the goals are pursued and to judge when the goals have been met. Researchers who defend different theories of well-being will differ over whether success in personal projects is intrinsically good or good because it leads to something else (such as pleasure) and whether the relevant projects must be subjectively or objectively desirable, but few would deny that the fulfillment of at least some valued personal projects is a significant aspect of well-being.

This approach has the significant advantage that those who do not accept a goal fulfillment theory of the nature of well-being may nevertheless be interested in the results of the research. This is because personal projects include many things that philosophers who defend objective theories will consider to be objectively valuable (such as relationships, acquiring knowledge, and developing skills). Further, the personal projects approach clarifies the relationship between well-being and personality (and hence "the self"). Personal projects are, typically, characteristic adaptions; the values or goals that define well-being *are*, therefore, aspects of personality. Success in personal projects is also *facilitated* by certain traits and characteristic adaptions; for example, wanting to be a lawyer will be facilitated by the conscientiousness needed for Law School and the argumenativeness needed for the courtroom. Well-being is, at least in part, an aspect of personality that is affected by other aspects of personality, as well as by one's circumstances.

Conclusion

In this chapter we drew upon our interdisciplinary collaboration to provide a conceptual clarification of self, identity, and personality, and how they fit together. Our discussion was framed around the central focus of the Self, Motivation, and Virtue Project of using a "framework of self" instead of "personality" to understand motivation, virtue, and well-being. In clarifying these different concepts, we demonstrated that the concept of personality—when conceptualized as extending beyond personality traits—provides the broadest, most inclusive framework for understanding self, identity, motivation, and virtue, as well as all other traits and characteristic adaptations. Additionally, we have highlighted how bringing together scholars with diverse perspectives can lead to increased clarity of terms and concepts, which in turn can lead to greater scientific progress.

References

Ashmore, R. D., Deaux, K., & McLaughlin-Volpe, T. (2004). An organizing framework for collective identity: Articulation and significance of multidimensionality. *Psychological Bulletin*, 130(1), 80–114.

Bedford-Petersen, C., DeYoung, C. G., Tiberius, V., & Syed, M. (2019). Integrating philosophical and psychological approaches to well-being: The role of success in personal projects. *Journal of Moral Education*, 48, 84–97.

Bloomfield, P. (2014). *The virtues of happiness: A theory of the good life*. New York, NY: Oxford University Press.

Brewer, M. B. (1991). The social self: On being the same and different at the same time. *Personality and Social Psychology Bulletin*, 17(5), 475–482.

Caspi, A., Roberts, B. W., & Shiner, R. L. (2005). Personality development: Stability and change. *Annual Review of Psychology*, 56, 453–484.

Cooley, C. H. (1902). *Human nature and the social order*. New York, NY: Scribners.

Costa, P. T., & McCrae, R. R. (1992). Four ways five factors are basic. *Personality and Individual Differences*, 13(6), 653–665.

Crisp, R. (2006). Hedonism reconsidered. *Philosophy and Phenomenological Research*, 73(3), 619–645.

DeYoung, C. G. (2015). Cybernetic big five theory. *Journal of Research in Personality*, 56, 33–58.

DeYoung, C. G., Quilty, L. C., & Peterson, J. B. (2007). Between facets and domains: 10 aspects of the Big Five. *Journal of Personality and Social Psychology*, 93, 880–896.

Diener, E., Lucas, R. E., & Oishi, S. (2002). Subjective well-being: The science of happiness and life satisfaction. In C. R. Snyder & S. J. Lopez (Eds.), *Handbook of positive psychology*. New York, NY: Oxford University Press.

Erikson, E. (1950). *Childhood and society*. New York, NY: W W Norton & Co.

Erikson, E. (1968). *Identity: Youth and crisis*. New York, NY: W W Norton & Co.

Feldman, F. (2004). *Pleasure and the good life: Concerning the nature, varieties and plausibility of hedonism*. New York, NY: Oxford University Press.

Fletcher, G. (2013). A fresh start for the objective-list theory of well-being. *Utilitas*, 25(2), 206–220.

Habermas, T., & Köber, C. (2015). Autobiographical reasoning is constitutive for narrative identity: The role of the life story for personal continuity. In K. C. McLean & M. Syed (Eds.), *The Oxford handbook of identity development*. New York, NY: Oxford University Press.

Hammack, P. L. (2015). Theoretical foundation of identity. In K. C. McLean & M. Syed (Eds.), *The Oxford handbook of identity development*. New York, NY: Oxford University Press.

Harter, S. (2015). *The construction of the self: Developmental and sociocultural foundations*. New York: Guilford Publications.

Harter, S., & Monsour, A. (1992). Development analysis of conflict caused by opposing attributes in the adolescent self-portrait. *Developmental Psychology*, 28(2), 251–260.

Heathwood, C. (2016). Desire-fulfillment theory. In G. Fletcher (Ed.), *The Routledge handbook of philosophy of well-being* (pp. 135–147). Oxford and New York, NY: Routledge.

James, W. (1890). *The principles of psychology*. New York, NY: Holt.

Josselson, R., & Flum, H. (2015). Identity status: On refinding the people. In K. C. McLean & M. Syed (Eds.), *The Oxford handbook of identity development*. New York, NY: Oxford University Press.

Keller, S. (2004). Welfare and the achievement of goals. *Philosophical Studies*, 121(1), 27–41.

Leary, M. R., & Tangney, J. P. (2012). The self as an organizing construct in the behavioral and social sciences. In M. R. Leary & J. P. Tangney (Eds.), *Handbook of self and identity* (pp. 1–20). New York, NY: Guilford Press.

Little, B. R. (2006). Personality science and self-regulation: Personal projects as integrative units. *Applied Psychology: An International Review, 55,* 419–427.

McAdams, D. P. (1995). What do we know when we know a person? *Journal of Personality, 63*(3), 365–396.

McAdams, D. P. (2013). The psychological self as actor, agent, and author. *Perspectives on Psychological Science, 8*(3), 272–295.

McAdams, D. P., & Pals, J. L. (2006). A new Big Five: Fundamental principles for an integrative science of personality. *American Psychologist, 61,* 204–217.

McLean, K. C., & Syed, M. (2015). The field of identity development needs an identity: Introduction to the handbook of identity development. In K. C. McLean & M. Syed (Eds.), *The Oxford handbook of identity development.* New York, NY: Oxford University Press.

Mead, G. H. (1934). *Mind, self and society.* Chicago, IL: University of Chicago Press.

Meeus, W. (2011). The study of adolescent identity formation 2000–2010: A review of longitudinal research. *Journal of Research on Adolescence, 21,* 75–94.

Phinney, J. S. (1990). Ethnic identity in adolescents and adults: Review of research. *Psychological Bulletin, 108*(3), 499–514.

Roberts, B. W., & Caspi, A. (2003). The cumulative continuity model of personality development: Striking a balance between continuity and change in personality traits across the life course. In U. M. Staudinger & U. Lindenberger (Eds.), *Understanding human development* (pp. 183–214). Boston, MA: Springer.

Roberts, B. W., Luo, J., Briley, D. A., Chow, P. I., Su, R., & Hill, P. L. (2017). A systematic review of personality trait change through intervention. *Psychological Bulletin, 143*(2), 117–141.

Snow, N., & Narvaez, D. (2015). *SMV project detailed overview.* Retrieved from http://smvproject.com/about/overview/

Suddendorf, T., & Butler, D. L. (2013). The nature of visual self-recognition. *Trends in Cognitive Sciences, 17*(3), 121–127.

Sumner, L. (1996). *Welfare, happiness, and ethics.* Oxford: Clarendon Press.

Syed, M. (2012). The past, present, and future of Eriksonian identity research: Introduction to the Special Issue. *Identity: An International Journal of Theory and Research, 12*(1), 1–7.

Syed, M. (2017). Advancing the cultural study of personality and identity: Models, methods, and outcomes. *Current Issues in Personality Psychology, 5*(1), 65–72.

Syed, M., Azmitia, M., & Cooper, C. R. (2011). Identity and academic success among under-represented ethnic minorities: An interdisciplinary review and integration. *Journal of Social Issues, 67*(3), 442–468.

Tajfel, H. (1981). *Human groups and social categories: Studies in social psychology.* Cambridge: Cambridge University Press.

Thorne, A. (2000). Personal memory telling and personality development. *Personality and Social Psychology Review, 4*(1), 45–56.

Tiberius, V. (2006). Well-being: Psychological research for philosophers. *Philosophy Compass, 1,* 493–505.

Tiberius, V. (2008). *The reflective life: living wisely with our limits.* New York, NY: Oxford University Press.

Umaña-Taylor, A. J., Quintana, S. M., Lee, R. M., Cross, W. E., Rivas-Drake, D., Schwartz, S. J., . . . Ethnic/Racial Identity Study Group. (2014). Ethnic and racial identity revisited: An integrated conceptualization. *Child Development*, 85(1), 21–39.

Verkuyten, M. (2016). Further conceptualizing ethnic and racial identity research: The social identity approach and its dynamic model. *Child Development*, 87(6), 1796–1812.

Way, N., & Rogers, O. (2015). "[T]hey say Black men won't make it, but I know I'm gonna make it": Ethnic and racial identity development in the context of cultural stereotypes. In K. C. McLean & M. Syed (Eds.), *The Oxford handbook of identity development*. New York, NY: Oxford University Press.

Yip, T., & Douglass, S. (2013). The application of experience sampling approaches to the study of ethnic identity: New developmental insights and directions. *Child Development Perspectives*, 7(4), 211–214.

2 Expansive Interdisciplinarity and the Moral Self

Javier Gomez-Lavin, Jesse Prinz, Nina Strohminger, and Shaun Nichols

Introduction

Our investigation of the moral self has been a long journey, with various twists and turns. We knew from the start that the questions we wanted to answer—those at the center of our understanding of personhood, identity, and their interrelations with morality—would require a multi-pronged interdisciplinary approach, but we anticipated neither the range of methods that we would want to deploy, nor the lessons of those efforts. It is still a journey in progress, and we've been learning every step of the way. We've faced challenges that have required the acquisition of new skills and new research collaborators and conversation partners. Our vision of where we would go has not aligned perfectly with where we ended up, but each change in course was directed by something encountered along the way, and each re-routing has deepened our understanding of the phenomenon we are investigating. We still have a long way to go, but there is also much to share in this progress report. Here, we take a moment to share a bit of what we've learned.

Central to this story is the process of doing interdisciplinary work, and frequent realizations that required us to expand our skill set. We've come, through this process, to think that the study of morality and the self is indeed one of the most demanding domains we know in the human sciences, one that requires moves beyond our primary fields of training: philosophy, cognitive neuroscience, and psychology. This recapitulation of our journey is also a plea for a more expansive interdisciplinary framework. We have come to think that "cognitive science"—a phrase that once labeled our conception of what it means to combine methods—is too restrictive.

Theoretical and Empirical Background and Team Formation

Our journey began with a simple hypothesis: moral values are one of the facets of human psychology that people consider important to personal identity. Indeed, we thought moral values are more important than many other facets that have been the focus of philosophical work on personal identity, including memory, narrative, agency, cognitive faculties, and personality, among others. We call the conjunction of these two claims the "moral self hypothesis": morals matter for identity, and they matter more than many other things. All members of our team had been exploring this hypothesis when we decided to join forces.

One of us (Jesse Prinz) had been exploring the moral self hypothesis in theoretical work for some time. He gave a theoretical paper on these ideas on March 14, 2007, in Delmenhorst, Germany, and wrote an (unpublished) article at the time. Another team member (Shaun Nichols) had begun working on the self around the same time, and was using experimental philosophy to investigate intuitions about personal identity, including an investigation of ideas stemming from the philosopher Bernard Williams. On March 21, 2010, Prinz presented his theoretical work on the moral self at a meeting of the Moral Psychology Research Group in Princeton. During this meeting, Prinz and Nichols joined forces and began to design experiments, which were eventually published in the *Routledge Handbook of Philosophy and the Social Mind* (Prinz & Nichols, 2016). Over the next few years, those experiments were refined and conducted by Nichols at the University of Arizona. Around this time, Nichols began a collaboration with psychologist Nina Strohminger, which resulted in a 2014 paper entitled, "The Essential Moral Self." In 2015, Prinz began collaborating with Javier Gomez-Lavin, a doctoral student in philosophy who had been trained in cognitive neuroscience. The four of us decided to form a research team, and this project is the result of those efforts.

We already had an overlapping history of collaboration and were unified by three things: shared faith in our hypothesis—this idea that morality and identity are deeply interconnected—a conviction that there were more questions to be answered, and confidence that a mix of philosophy and experimental psychology were the ideal tools for answering those questions. It was one of those rare and exciting moments of convergence, and we were eager and excited to embark on the next steps together. Along the way, some of this has changed. The hypothesis has undergone some transformations—some subtle, some more significant, and some unresolved. Our sense of the most pressing questions has also evolved, and we have followed leads that we didn't anticipate. We have also come to see that philosophy and psychology are only two tools in telling a story that actually requires many more.

Philosophical Feedback and Conceptual Clarification

While working on our collaboration, we've had many opportunities to reflect on our original hypothesis. We have been led to revise and rethink various things, and some questions have opened up that remain unresolved. Some of this revision process has been conceptually driven and prompted by feedback on article submissions and from audiences at talks. We want to mention two examples here, because they underscore one key aspect of the interdisciplinary project. Though three of us are philosophers, we have tried to provide empirical evidence for the claims we are making. This requires operationalizing philosophical theories. But, once operationalized, some of our interpretations of our findings have met with philosophical resistance both from within the team and from those who learn about our work. That back and forth from philosophy to experiment, and then back to philosophy has been one of the most rewarding aspects of this endeavor.

Here we illustrate with two examples. The first example is the seminal discussion of personal identity in Western philosophy that occurs in John Locke's *Essay Concerning Human Understanding* (Locke, 1690/1975). Locke is interested in diachronic identity: what makes a person count as the same as she or he undergoes changes over time. He offers the somewhat cryptic suggestion that temporal stages of a person are united by having the same consciousness, and, more helpfully, this gets worked out in his examples in terms of memory connections. I am linked to my past life stages through my capacity to call up past experiences in my mind. Our earlier research, before our participation in the Self, Motivation, and Virtue (SMV) grant project, had looked extensively at this memory idea and contrasted it with the idea that continuity of values might be even more important for survival over time. But, in pursuing that work, we'd left out a second major contribution of Locke's influential discussion. He suggests there that personal identity is a "forensic" concept, meaning we need it to assign praise and blame for past events. This suggestion, which has been widely endorsed, links personal identity to responsibility: I can be held responsible for the actions of a past self, if that self can be shown to be me, according to some criterion of diachronic identity. If intuitions about responsibility do not relate in some way to an alleged criterion of identity, that would be a reason to doubt the criterion of identity. In one of our first studies for this grant project, we tried to explore the relationship between moral continuity and responsibility.

We came up with a study design that used vignettes about parole hearings. In brief, we asked participants to imagine an incarcerated individual who had either changed moral values while in prison, or, in contrast, who had merely decided that he would refrain from future crimes because he wanted to avoid another prison term. That is, incarceration can lead to moral transformation or simply exert a deterrent effect. We then operationalized responsibility as participants' support for parole. We reasoned that changes in identity would result in a situation where the person who was coming up for parole wasn't exactly the same as the person who has committed the crime and should therefore be let out early. That is, if moral change is more related to identity than mere behavioral change (i.e., the deterrence vignette), then participants should favor parole in the former case more than the latter case even when controlling for expectations about recidivism. This is what we found. We also found that people are more likely to say the morally changed person is a different person, and this answer significantly mediates their parole decision.

In presenting this study in writing and lectures, we've met with some resistance. Some people think the finding is simply too weak to support the strong conclusion that we need: that a morally changed person is really a different individual and therefore shouldn't be held responsible for past deeds. At the same time, we have obtained survey responses that are strong and explicit. Strictly speaking we didn't predict that, since we recognize that morality is multi-faceted, and the contribution of moral continuity, though significant, does not encompass all aspects of identity. The prisoner is somewhat different as a person after a moral transformation, but not an entirely new person. Still, there is a deflationary interpretation on which he is not really a new person at all. Perhaps he is just a *better* person and should be rewarded for his progress. This response suggests that participants are answering the "new person" probe somewhat metaphorically—an interpretation that we have tried to rule out in other work. We are not persuaded by the objection, but we do see that the study is really just the start of what must ultimately be a more thoroughgoing exploration of responsibility and the moral self. We want to pursue experimental designs that do not rely on such an indirect measure of responsibility, and we want to devise other scenarios to measure this mitigation effect. We also want to come up with additional ways to tease apart the idea that blame is reduced because of a change in identity as opposed to the competing hypothesis that it is just a reward for moral improvement. We continue to think our parole studies are suggestive, but feedback has helped us see that they can only be a first step toward answering the questions about responsibility presented in the philosophical literature.

The second example illustrating the "back and forth" between theory and experiment concerns another nagging worry that comes up when we present this material. We have conducted many vignette studies showing that moral change is interpreted as impacting identity, and that people think that a person who undergoes moral change is literally, to some degree, not the same person. But these findings can be interpreted in terms of two notions of identity: qualitative and numerical. Qualitative identity refers to attributes that affect the classification of an object (Geach, 1973). When a caterpillar becomes a butterfly, it is a different kind of animal, qualitatively speaking. Numerical identity refers to being the exact same individual. So, a butterfly may be numerically identical to the caterpillar from whence it came. The philosophical topic of personal identity is usually framed as a question about numerical identity. What makes a person the same exact individual over time? In principle, two numerically distinct people (perfect duplicates) could be qualitatively identical, and one qualitatively changing individual could be numerically the same across those changes (like the butterfly case). As of yet, our moral self-effect does not settle between these options. If moral transformations are merely qualitative, questions will arise about whether the moral self hypothesis really competes with philosophical theories of personal identity.

This is a tricky question from a methods perspective, but it has put our group into dialogue with Vilius Dranseika, a researcher who is conducting experimental philosophy studies in Lithuanian, a language that contains different adjectives for qualitative and numerical identity. This provides a way to ask questions about the different kinds of identity in a way that is very natural. Preliminary evidence suggests that moral changes may be merely qualitative (Berniūnas & Dranseika, 2016)! This may require a revision of our hypothesis. But the jury is still out. For one thing, we are not sure about the premise that other philosophical theories really concern numerical identity. There are famous puzzles (explored by Derek Parfit in *Reasons and Persons*, 1984) about applying concepts of numerical identity to selves. Moreover, philosophical theories of personal identity, such as the Lockean memory approach, may be best interpreted as qualitative. It would be useful to obtain cross-linguistic evidence about what kind of identity is impacted by memory loss. We predict that these changes would most greatly impact qualitative identity. If so, such findings may require a clarification not just of our view, but of personal identity theories more generally. That is work in progress.

Empirical Revisions of Hypothesis

Revision of our hypothesis has also been prompted by experimental findings. This too illustrates the value of interdisciplinary work, since the changes in question would not have been noticed without attending to empirical findings. Here we illustrate with an example that required mastery of methods that were new to some members of our team.

In our original formulation, we had proposed that moral values are important to identity. But what about other kinds of values? And what about moral norms promoted by a society that aren't valued by a given participant in our studies? We hadn't set out to answer this question, but we did sometimes include questions that used the word "moral" and others that used variants of "value." For instance, a prompt may require that a participant answer, "How morally bad would lacking x trait make you?" or, conversely, "How much do you value x trait?" where x would be substituted with one of many differentially valenced traits (e.g., honesty, curiosity, ebullience). In one study where we used both "moral" and "value" prompts, we noticed that responses were not identical. This ultimately required that we learn some statistical techniques and software that allow us to qualify which of these two constructs has a bigger impact on identity, including the use of advanced causal modeling methods, mediation and moderation analyses, and multidimensional scaling techniques (Hayes, 2013;

Hout, Papesh, & Goldinger, 2012). To our surprise, valuing a given trait seems to be more important than participants' ratings of how moralized a given trait is. This initial finding led us to do follow-up work, which seems to confirm that valuing drives our effects, not morality as such. We are still doing follow-up work to tease apart some inconsistencies in our findings. Here, the data will ultimately settle the hypothesis.

We came across the same issue in other ways as well. We were trying to run a cross-cultural test on one of our moral self-effects in Germany. With U.S. participants we had found that political party affiliation could serve as a proxy for moral values. When asked about a hypothetical individual who changed political parties, Americans tended to say that this was a change in identity. This pattern of responses contrasted with other kinds of changes that we had coded as non-moral, such as changes in musical taste. We wondered whether the effect would hold up in Germany because their partisanship—at least before the most recent parliamentary elections in 2017—was less fixed and polarized than in the U.S. We predicted (and obtained) a substantial weakening of the effect. Party changes are not seen as identity changes in Germany to the same degree. But we also obtained a surprising result: changes in musical taste were regarded as having a sizable impact on identity! This has led to some follow-up work, replicating and extending the finding. Some individuals seem to have "aesthetic selves," such that they see matters of taste as contributing to identity. This adds support to the idea that values outside of morality may matter to our sense of self. Once again, an unexpected empirical finding has led to new or revised hypotheses.

We first considered the very real possibility that this unexpected effect of musical taste on identity in our German sample was a fluke, or a product of an error in our experimental design. Our original study had provided the following prompt to make explicit the sense of transformation amongst our study questions; for a change in music we asked participants to "imagine that you had only liked listening to classical music, but now you find yourself enjoying pop music," and then asking them to rate how much of an impact on identity—both perceived from their own, first-person perspective and from a third-person perspective—this change would have. Of course, once we found this effect in our German sample, we immediately thought that this may have been driven by the intuitive association between classical music and a kind of

German national pride; after all, many of the "greats" of classical music share a German or Austrian heritage. Thus, perhaps our choice of example implicated political or other strongly valenced values—maybe even moralized values associated implicitly with German nationalism, and this in fact drove our effect. However, to ascertain whether this was the case, we needed to get a sense as to how musical genres were related to one another and whether this overall network of relations differed between German and American populations.

This led us to a technique, popular in psychology, known as *multidimensional scaling* or "MDS" (Hout et al., 2012). In its most simple guise, MDS requires that participants rank the similarity of a class of stimuli against one another—so for instance, if you wanted to rank the similarity of bird species, you would pick your species to be studied, and for each one, say "cardinal," you would ask participants to give a rating, "How similar is a cardinal to x?" where x would be serially filled-in by the other species you were interested in (e.g., ostriches and blue jays). MDS has also recently been used successfully in other experimental philosophy paradigms, particularly in understanding folk perceptions of collective action (Tollefsen, Kreuz, & Dale, 2014). Using a few algorithms—including PROXSCAL[1]—allows us to then transform these responses into a map-like space of similarity, where similar stimuli—as rated by the participants—are grouped together. Thus, using MDS we were able to create maps of the similarity space of ten common musical genres that had been previously examined in the context of personality psychology (e.g., which Big Five personality traits correlate with common musical genres—see Rentfrow & Gosling, 2003). One example map of "common space" from our German sample is reproduced in Figure 2.1.

As you can see from the map of similarity scores, pop music is centrally located, and as would be expected, classical and jazz music are grouped in one quadrant, while folk and country are closely grouped in another. Importantly, the absolute location of genres on the map is not informative; only their relative distances from one another are. Just as we can produce a "common map" that averages across all the participants in a given sample, we can also produce maps of group differences, for instance, taking the similarity judgments only of participants who scored highly on another measure, such as an authoritarianism scale, and then comparing these maps against one another.

Expansive Interdisciplinarity, Moral Self 33

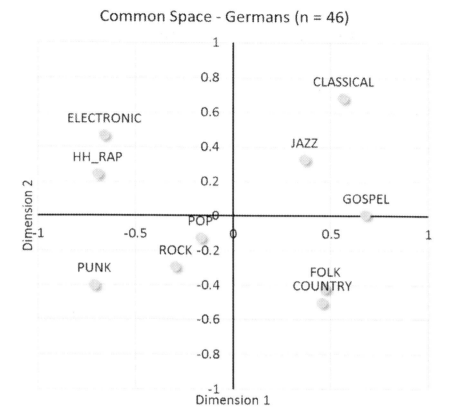

Figure 2.1 Averaged Similarity Map of Musical Genres Generated From Ratings of Our 46 German Participants Produced With the PROXSCAL Algorithm

Currently we are still sifting through the large amount of data collected, but we can state that—in general—the maps of common space between our American and German samples are similar (with the only significant difference being in the relative location of "hip-hop/rap," coded as "HH_RAP" in Figure 2.1). Crucially for our original question, the relative locations of pop and classical genres in both our American and German sample are very similar—hence, the relative perception of musical genres is not driving our effect in Germany. Further exploratory work conducted in conjunction with Joerg Fingerhut and others in the Berlin School of Mind and Brain has revealed that this effect—the impact of aesthetics on identity—generalizes. We are in the process of developing more measures to isolate this effect of "aesthetic selves" and its unique mechanisms.

Cross-Cultural Psychology

Our studies in Germany—along with later work in a similar vein in Taipei—have required acquisition of new methodological competencies and new partnerships. Some team members had never done cross-cultural studies, and we needed to learn some basic things: how to work with an internal, university ethics review board abroad; how to recruit participants; how to create and test a translation; and so on. We also needed to learn about other cultures to generate hypotheses, and we needed to reflect on the pros and cons of cross-cultural work.

Beginning with the last of these issues, we had come to think that cross-cultural work tended to be vulnerable to two opposing risks: a kind of Scylla and Charybdis for cross-cultural psychology. Some of this work is too universalizing, brushing over significant cultural differences in order to establish that a phenomenon is pan-cultural. In testing the moral self hypothesis overseas, we didn't want to assume its truth or construct designs that would overlook differences. We wanted test instruments that were sufficiently sensitive to pick up on subtle cultural differences in the phenomenon. A related risk is that some cross-cultural research is too simplistic in its analyses of difference. A surprising volume of work in this area uses the East/West contrast and distinguishes these using a single coarse dimension, such as collectivism versus individualism. Such work can be informative, but it blurs over differences that exist between Eastern populations and Western populations, and it tends to promote harmful, essentializing stereotypes such as "the Asian mind" (Markus & Kitayama, 1991; Nisbett, 2003).

To overcome these risks and hurdles, our challenge was to formulate hypotheses that did not rely on coarse stereotypes and distinctions that blur important differences. Our aforementioned choice to investigate partisanship and identity in Germany was part of this effort. We want to show that not all Western nations respond in the same way. Likewise, when testing our vignettes and prompts in Taipei, we focused on perceived differences amongst major religions and their affiliated practices and cultures in Taiwanese society. Morality may be important to identity in both cultures, but it gets grounded in different social-group affiliations. We needed to find informants who could tell us about political attitudes in Germany, subtle religious differences in Taiwan, and their relations to morality. We learned many things. For example, Germans tend to think it is wrong to publicly discuss who they voted for, and class structure is often interwoven with religious background in Taiwan.

We conducted studies in Taiwan, a far Eastern setting, for two principle reasons. We were curious whether moral self-effects could be found outside of the West, and we also wanted to exemplify an East/West comparison that did not rely on the usual reductive assumptions about individualism and collectivism. Having looked at political party affiliations as a proxy for morality in the United States and Germany, we wanted to do the same in Asia. We considered Japan, but its biggest parties are very closely related, and China, but it is really a one-party system. We chose Taiwan, which has significant, popular religious and political divisions, and we set to work trying to understand these. This required a lot of research. We read about the history of Taiwan, its religions, its political parties, and its elections. We also identified collaborators at Taipei Medical University and asked them about local politics and values. This was a very new way to do research for us, and it was both challenging and exciting. We made many discoveries. The most interesting, perhaps, is that the liberal/conservative distinction, which is so divisive in the United States, is not viewed as the major political fault line there. Instead, parties and people divide on attitudes toward China: are the Han people of Taiwan the true Chinese who will eventually reunite with the mainland, or are they Taiwanese—a truly separate cultural and political entity? We also learned much about religion in Taiwan, for example, that Buddhism is considered more refined than Taoism, and that Mandarin has no word for Taoism. We worked closely with psychologists, philosophers, and neuroscientists in Taipei to develop a survey instrument. We confirmed the moral self effect but in a way that reflected social identities specific to Taiwan.

Our cross-cultural work has been a steep learning curve, and our international collaborations will continue. We wanted to explore both universality and difference—a pan-cultural tendency to link values and identity, but in culturally specific ways. This is what we have found, and we are excited to be doing East/West comparisons that move beyond familiar stereotypes.

Shifting Priorities: Real-World Cases

Along the way, there has also been a shift in our priorities, and that shift has played a guiding role in our interdisciplinary collaboration and even in our idea of what interdisciplinary work should look like.

With backgrounds in philosophy, psychology, and neuroscience, we began with an interest in a psychological effect—namely, our robust, repeatable moral self-effect—and the mechanisms that underlie it. The effect had already been established in our earlier work, and we thought we'd spend a lot of time looking at mechanisms in our collaboration. In thinking about mechanisms, we were really focused on internal mechanisms—more specifically on psychological constructs such as emotion and executive function. In our prior work, we had also mostly explored the moral self using vignettes that describe morality in a very generic way: "imagine a person whose moral values change . . .".

As our work began, these priorities guided our efforts. We developed an elaborate reaction time study to look at the role of executive function, and team members also carried out a study looking at the impact of personality variables, such as psychopathy. These efforts were worthwhile, but we were increasingly convinced that the most interesting thing about the moral self hypothesis lies elsewhere. We began to think that our vignettes were, like many thought experiments in philosophy, too hypothetical. We wondered, do moral transformations happen in the real world? Two team members (Nichols and Stohminger) had published a study that used both hypothetical vignettes (e.g., a brain transplant—Strohminger & Nichols, 2014) and scenarios that could occur in real life (e.g., cases of dementia; see in particular, Strohminger & Nichols, 2015). We began to think more broadly about real-world cases, and we came up with many examples. This, we now think, is the most interesting, important, and pressing direction for our research—that is, to look back on the plethora of examples of moral transformation and identity change provided by history itself.

Our study of parole intuitions was a move in that direction. Prison reform is one real context where values can change. We plan to continue that work in a more applied way, looking at actual parole decisions and other archival work. Our studies of partisanship also fall into this category, and we have conducted several studies looking at attitudes toward religious conversion (as well as some theoretical work on "cults" or new religious movements).

To take another example, we became interested in the European immigration crisis. We conducted a series of studies in Germany asking people about their attitudes toward immigrants. We found that when Germans consider immigrants who come from an Islamic country, they regard it as positive when they assimilate in their values, not just their behavior. They also consider value assimilation to involve a change in identity. In effect, they want immigrants to become new people.

An additional example concerns something called "moral injury." The term refers to a kind of post-traumatic stress experienced by soldiers who are deployed in combat zones. Witnessing or participating in acts of war can make people feel like they have confronted behavior that violates their moral norms. This can make reimmersion in civilian society difficult. In some exploratory studies we showed that people regard such changes as moral in nature and as changes in personal identity. We hope to follow up on this work with military populations with collaborators from other SMV project teams. In particular, we want to examine military personnel before and after engaging in recruit, or "boot camp" training, to measure whether moral values are significantly affected by this process. Additionally, partnering with medical professionals who work primarily with veterans may allow us to empirically test whether moral injury plays an important role in veterans' mental health, including in pathological cases such as post-traumatic stress disorders.

All these studies have come with their own challenges. We have had to learn about parole practices, international politics, and military psychiatry, among other areas. This has required a lot of reading in fields outside our areas of training. We have also opened dialogue and collaborations with people in other fields and other countries. One team member, Jesse Prinz has also been teaching a graduate seminar in political psychology with a number of political science students, to get up to date on studies of political attitudes. Learning these things has been one of our biggest challenges, and one of the more rewarding aspects of this collaboration.

We've also come to see that real-world cases require something beyond knowledge of current events; they require knowledge of history. We realize now that it would have been valuable to have a historian on the team (and perhaps a political scientist and a sociologist). We have been looking at historical events that involve moral change. Examples include: the emergence of liberal democracies, the rise of the Third Reich and subsequent de-Nazification programs, and the Cultural Revolution in China. We want to understand how these changes occurred, and how they impacted identity. For example, supporters of Mao frequently talked about the construction of a "New Man," and re-education initiatives were described as transformative. We have been reading cultural and political history, and also scouring qualitative research for evidence of a link between values and identity. For example, Theodore Newcomb's classic study of political indoctrination in college (*Personality and Social Change: Attitude Formation in a Student Community*, 1943) contains many interviews with students. Reading these, we've been struck by the use of language that makes explicit references to identity transformations.

All of these efforts have required the pursuit of new skill sets. Reading history, looking through databases for primary sources (e.g., articles on de-Nazification efforts published just after the war), and scrutinizing qualitative research were not part of our standard repertoire before we started. We've opened up dialogues with new conversation partners, too, and we are seeing new avenues for research. The move to real-world cases has made it vividly clear to us that our previous fields of training—philosophy, cognitive neuroscience, and psychology—work at a level of abstraction that tends to block off many dimensions of human variation. These fields tend to treat all people as alike and ignore the impact of life experiences and history. There are exceptions of course, but efforts to include such dimensions of variation are often done without the hard toil of studying social and historical conditions in detail. We have realized how important this is, how hard it is, how much we have to learn, and how much we can benefit from the expertise of others.

Conclusion: Toward an Expansive Moral Psychology of the Self

In conclusion, ours has been a journey of changing paths and discoveries. Our thinking has evolved, our priorities have changed, and our skill sets are slowly expanding.

Some of the challenges we met were expected. Combining philosophy and psychology has been a central goal for each of us individually, and, in collaboration, we have found a constant need to move back and forth between theory and experimental design. This has involved spelling out theoretical statements, operationalizing, looking at results, getting feedback, and revising theories accordingly. A constant, mutually informative dialogue exists between theory and data.

There have also been some challenges that required new skills within this framework of psychologically informed philosophizing. Though our initial studies began with the research tools of experimental philosophy, with a focus on vignette paradigms and rather simpler statistical analyses, we quickly found ourselves learning and using more sophisticated statistical methods to model the relationship among our variables of interest. For instance, modeling the interactions of our dependent variables—that is, changes in the measures that we're interested in closely examining, such as changes to perceived identity—required that we use both structural equation and causal mediation models to help us determine the directionality of our findings.[2] This was particularly relevant when we were examining participants' judgments about responsibility in our parole case; after all, we wanted to determine that it was participants' perceptions of identity change that determined their parole decisions. These models allowed us to test our hypothesis that participants' attitudes about whether a character's identity has changed were the driving force for their judgments about the dependent variables of interest; for example, responsibility in our parole studies, and assimilation in our immigration studies. Importantly, use of these models allowed us to probe the possible causal relationship among the various independent and dependent variables of interest—for instance, seeing whether perceived changes in identity are a direct result of a moral change or if there is some mediating factor, such as the perceived value of the trait in question, that also influences participants' judgments of identity. In our research on the aesthetic self, one philosopher in our team (Gomez-Lavin) also learned multi-dimensional scaling; this technique allowed us to visualize how individual differences—say, participants' scores on a third-party scale of authoritarianism—affected how they conceptualized the similarity among aesthetic genres. For instance, we've found that high-scorers on authoritarianism scales tend to view hip-hop and rap music as the least similar to other genres, yielding significantly different similarity spaces than other groups. These similarity spaces are constructed by taking into account hundreds of participant ratings of the similarity of various, traditional musical genres (e.g., we would ask participants to rate how similar hip-hop is to punk music and so forth). These new skills will allow us to do things that go beyond what is found in most experimental philosophy.

More surprising was the realization that our hypothesis would benefit from methods that go beyond philosophy and experimental psychology. We have had to learn some political science, some psychiatry, some criminology, and some history. We have pursued these efforts with passion, though much work lies ahead. Some of us remember those early days when philosophers first started running psychological studies. The early studies were primitive and flawed, but also empowering. If we compare the skills of those of us in that first wave (Nichols and Prinz) with those in the new generation (Gomez-Lavin), it is very gratifying. Some philosophers are now doing work that meets the standards of psychology. These advances have been possible in part because of psychologists (e.g., Strohminger) who are interested in philosophical ideas and are willing to work with philosophers. Both philosophy and psychology have benefitted by those ongoing alliances.

We are now, perhaps, in a similar position with respect to fields such as history. Cognitive science has left such fields out, even though they have much to teach us about human behavior. We are in the foothills of a daunting learning curve but united in the recognition that we would benefit from moving beyond the form of interdisciplinarity that has been institutionalized as cognitive science. When dealing with constructs as rich as morality and identity, mental processes and mechanisms can only take us so far. The micro-level of analysis might be combined with the macro-level. Our journey has, in many ways, been a journey to that point of discovery. We've made progress on our original hypothesis, but that may be less important, ultimately, than the methodological lessons. More than anything, we emerge with a deep and humbling appreciation of the limitations of our training, the narrowness of our conversations, and the need for a more expansive approach to the study of the human mind.

Note

1. PROXSCAL stands for PROXimity SCALing and enables the scaling of relative similarity, or dissimilarity, distance-like data from a higher dimensional to a lower dimensional space that can easily be visualized. For more information, please consult Commandeur and Heiser (1993).
2. These variables contrast with what psychologists term "independent variables," or the manipulations that we, as the experimenters, introduce into our experiment; for instance, by providing two conditions in our parole study, one in which our character undergoes a moral transformation, while in the other the character only undergoes a behavioral shift.

Bibliography

Berniūnas, R., & Dranseika, V. (2016). Folk concepts of person *and* identity: A response to Nichols and Bruno. *Philosophical Psychology*, 29(1), 96–122.

Commandeur, J. J. F., & Heiser, W. J. (1993). *Mathematical derivations in the proximity scaling (PROXSCAL) of symmetric data matrices* (Tech. Rep. No. RR-93-04). Leiden, The Netherlands: Leiden University, Department of Data Theory.

Geach, P. (1973). Ontological relativity and relative identity. In M. K. Munitz (Ed.), *Logic and Ontology*. New York, NY: New York University Press.

Hayes, A. F. (2013). *Introduction to mediation, moderation, and conditional process analysis: A regression-based approach*. New York, NY: Guilford Press.

Hout, M. C., Papesh, M. H., & Goldinger, S. D. (2012). Multidimensional scaling. *Wiley Interdisciplinary Reviews: Cognitive Science*, 4(1), 93–103.

Locke, J. (1690/1975). An essay concerning human understanding. In P. H. Nidditch (Ed.), *The clarendon edition of the works of John Locke*. Oxford: Clarendon Press.

Markus, H. R., & Kitayama, S. (1991). Culture and the self: Implications for cognition, emotion, and motivation. *Psychological Review*, 98(2), 224–253.

Newcomb, T. M. (1943). *Personality and social change: Attitude formation in a student community*. Fort Worth, TX: Dryden Press.

Nisbett, R. E. (2003). *The geography of thought: How Asians and westerners think differently—and why*. New York, NY: Free Press.

Parfit, D. (1984). *Reasons and persons*. Oxford: Oxford University Press.

Prinz, J., & Nichols, S. (2016). Diachronic identity and the moral self. In J. Kiverstein (Ed.), *The Routledge handbook of philosophy and the social mind*. Abingdon: Routledge.

Rentfrow, P. J., & Gosling, S. D. (2003). The do re mi's of everyday life: The structure and personality correlates of music preferences. *The Journal of Personality and Social Psychology*, 84(6), 1236–1256.

Strohminger, N., & Nichols, S. (2014). The essential moral self. *Cognition*, 131(1), 158–171.

Strohminger, N., & Nichols, S. (2015). Neurodegeneration and identity. *Psychological Science*, 26(9), 1469–1479.

Tollefsen, D., Kreuz, R., & Dale, R. (2014). Flavors of "togetherness". In J. Knobe, T. Lombrozo, & S. Nichols (Eds.), *Oxford studies in experimental philosophy* (Vol. 1). Oxford: Oxford University Press.

3 The Virtues of Interdisciplinary Research
Psychological and Philosophical Inquiry Into Self, Motivation, and Virtue

Blaine J. Fowers and Bradford Cokelet

Each interdisciplinary collaboration is its own puzzle, needing to be solved in the particulars of the disciplines involved, the specific collaborators, and the topic of interest. Fortunately for us, our collaboration significantly predated the onset of the Self, Motivation, and Virtue (SMV) Project. We began collaborating in 2010 in planning an interdisciplinary conference entitled, "Eudaimonia and Virtue: Rethinking the Good Life." We invited philosophers and psychologists to share their work in these domains. The conference was a great success for its time, but the meshing of these two disciplines was far from smooth. In general, philosophers and psychologists found it difficult to talk with one another despite our common interests and the presence of significant good will (and the latter is not to be taken for granted). We believe that this interdisciplinary conversation improved over the course of the conference we convened in 2011, but we could see that it is not easy to establish.

Following this conference, we met regularly to discuss eudaimonia and virtue from psychological and philosophical perspectives. These discussions were enlivened by our mutual interest in one another's discipline, not just a common interest in virtue. As a psychologist, Fowers had a long and deep interest in moral philosophy, and, as a philosopher, Cokelet had a strong interest in psychological methods and results. This history provided an important baseline of respect and common interest that positioned us very well for our SMV collaboration.

As psychologists have become increasingly interested in virtue and eudaimonia, the possibility of collaborating with moral philosophers, who had already forged a rich theoretical pathway (e.g., Anscombe, 1958; Hursthouse, 1999; MacIntyre, 1999, 2007; Snow, 2010), became a live possibility. Two "facts on the ground" promoted this kind of collaboration. First, the two disciplines have the potential for a good deal of common ground in this topic domain. It has been possible to study virtue and eudaimonia independently as either a philosopher or a psychologist. In addition, both disciplines must rely on some version of a moral psychology. This potential common ground is illustrated in Figure 3.1.

Although the potential for common ground exists, the methods and approaches of the two disciplines have been disparate. There is a recognizable psychological sub-discipline of moral psychology that is composed of a loose amalgam of developmental, personality, social, and cognitive psychologists. There is relatively little consensus on the domain, theoretical framework, or purpose of this sub-field. In addition, moral psychology as a sub-discipline of psychology bears virtually no resemblance to the various moral psychologies found among moral philosophers. Moral philosophers have debated moral psychology for millennia, but these debates have centered on questions about the role of emotion, reason, and knowledge in *ideal* moral motivation and about how answers to those questions bear on more general philosophic

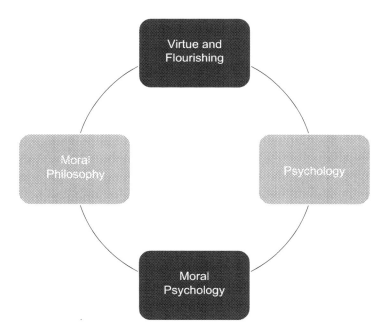

Figure 3.1 Common Content for Interdisciplinary Research on Virtue and Eudaimonia

issues, for example, about the objectivity or rational authority of moral considerations. These topics are no doubt important, but in focusing on them, philosophers have generally ignored questions about moral development and the contingent psychological factors that lead ordinary people to be more or less moral. Generally, philosophers have tended to set aside such empirical questions for psychologists; perhaps, as a consequence, psychologists have seldom recruited philosophers to help them study the virtues and vices that ordinary people tend to have.

Against this backdrop, Flanagan's (1991) call for psychological realism can be recognized as a vital spur for change and collaboration in moral psychology. He insisted that any moral psychology worth having must identify defensible but practicable ideals and norms—ones that ordinary humans can sensibly aspire to emulate or live up to. Philosophers and psychologists who embrace the imperative of psychological realism will debate the rational defensibility of various *normative* ideals but they will also work to understand human psychology and formulate ideals that are within psychological reach. Our budding collaboration was inspired by discussion of this inter-disciplinary, methodological imperative and recent work that resonates with it (e.g., Morgan, Gulliford, & Kristjánsson, 2017; Woodard & Pury, 2007).

As we moved from discussion to substantive collaboration, we realized that we had to bracket discipline-specific assumptions about what was worth studying and why in order to pursue our interdisciplinary aim: to help develop a psychologically realistic moral psychology. In pursuit of this aim, we were forced to recognize and purposefully combine our complementary strengths and weaknesses—strengths and weaknesses that we take to be typical of philosophers and psychologists. Philosophic training typically yields skills in conceptual analysis that allow philosophers to theorize in much greater depth, scope, and exactingness than psychologists, but philosophers are not trained to theorize in ways that can fruitfully and efficaciously advance empirical inquiry about human psychology and how it develops. To heed the call for psychological realism, philosophers need to harness, and sensibly rein in, their powers of conceptual analysis; they need to work with psychologists to figure out how to best contribute to psychological theorizing and empirical inquiry. Psychologists, on the other hand, are typically skilled at designing fruitful empirical investigations—they are trained to design studies that can assess specific empirical hypotheses about actual human subjects. To collaborate profitably, the psychologist must take an interest in, or at least tolerate, the philosopher's sometime speculative flights of analysis, wade into thorny debates about which ideals are normatively justified and why, and take a lead in judging whether further conceptual refinement in moral psychological research will be empirically profitable or not. As this suggests, collaboration requires both philosophers and psychologists to leave their comfort zones and to defer to and learn from one another. Inevitably, this will lead to tension or conflict, but that need not impede us from pursuing the ideal of psychologically realistic moral psychology. The tension arises because philosophers and psychologists have different strengths and weaknesses, but with patient effort those differences can be brought into alignment; the differences can fruitfully complement one another and generate creative interdisciplinary results.

Interdisciplinary Research

A primary shared goal of our project team was to have both represented disciplines contribute substantively to the overall quality of the project. We believe that philosophy and psychology have complementary strengths that can help us to more fully address the complexity of virtue, overcome artificial disciplinary boundaries, and productively use conceptual analyses and innovative empirical methods. In this section, we discuss this collaboration in terms of the challenges inherent in interdisciplinary research (IDR), the external resources necessary for its success, and the character strengths that we believe are necessary to flourish as an interdisciplinary scholar.

Challenges

It is little wonder that IDR is relatively uncommon because there are many daunting challenges. Foremost among them are career-threatening promotion and reward structures. If a potential collaborator works in a setting that places a high premium on success within a sole discipline, then this will be reflected in strict expectations for a high degree of specialization within the discipline. In this context, IDR will not be supported, and it may be actively discouraged or even punished. Successful IDR requires institutional support that goes beyond lip service to recognize the value of this work in tenure, promotion, and reward processes. For better or for worse, the prestige of a department or school may hinge largely on the researchers' prominence within a specific discipline, which can influence the unit to insist on within-discipline specialization. During the short period of the SMV Project, we, the authors, have been members of three departments, two of which overtly support IDR and one that was distinctly unsupportive. This issue is particularly salient for untenured professors, and an aspiring interdisciplinary researcher must attend to the intellectual climate of his or her environment. It would be wise for new professionals who have a strong interest in IDR to seek out workplaces that overtly value IDR and for senior faculty to take steps to move their academic and disciplinary structures toward greater support for it.

At the same time, one of the most important supports for scholarly work in general is found in the frameworks of theory, practices, methods, and standards that each discipline provides to guide researchers' efforts. Although there are some sources of general information about how to structure IDR efforts (e.g., National Research Council, 2015) and there are some examples to follow, each team must work out its own framework for how to collaborate. Each set of disciplines requires distinct forms of integration and each set of specific researchers needs an understanding of how their joint work will be structured. Collaborators must set aside time to establish a framework for their research so that each knows how they fit in and what role they will play. Disciplinary knowledge and methods typically do not integrate themselves, and the potential complementarities of the disciplines only become actual through intentional and concerted effort. The grant-writing process is a good place to set out an initial framework. The grant-writing and -reporting process of the SMV Project built this framework-setting task into its expectations and processes, which encouraged our planning and reflection.

IDR can be seen as a form of cross-cultural experience. Every discipline (and many sub-disciplines) has its own language, customs, expectations, and social practices. Successful IDR requires a curiosity about and an openness to the other discipline's culture. Clarifications are often needed to inform one another of how topics are discussed, what criteria the discipline has for quality scholarship, why certain methods are preferred, and so forth. When important disciplinary standards remain as unquestioned assumptions, miscommunications and unproductive conflict will almost certainly ensue.

As we have mentioned, many academic units and disciplines place a very high premium on intense specialization within a specific discipline. Individuals who have been trained in such environments and especially those who have succeeded in this specialization tend to take a good deal of pride in their disciplinary knowledge and skill. This is natural and can be, in many ways, positive. In IDR, however, this pride can all too easily result in disciplinary snobbery. This natural discipline-centricity can be counteracted through a healthy modesty about the limits of one's discipline, an open-mindedness about the value of the other discipline(s), and an awareness of this natural tendency. Disciplinary snobbery is toxic to IDR because it can lead to contempt and superiority competition that are destructive to collaboration.

The converse of disciplinary snobbery is that when one collaborates with people from other disciplines, one's ignorance of the other discipline's knowledge and methods will be exposed. This can be uncomfortable and it may even encourage a retreat to the security and supposed superiority of one's own discipline. Although ignorance exposure can be discomfiting, it also provides an excellent opportunity for learning and expanding one's knowledge. This sort of reframing is important in taking advantage of the complementarities of the disciplines.

Clearly, the effective management of these challenges takes time, which is often a resource in short supply for strongly engaged scholars. Setting aside the required time to deal with the challenges of high-quality IDR can be difficult, but it is unlikely that good collaboration will emerge without a significant time commitment. Time is also necessary to assemble the resources for IDR, some of which we describe in the next paragraph.

Resources

As already noted, we drew on multiple resources to improve our chances for success in this interdisciplinary endeavor. First, we had a previously established relationship with common interests and mutual respect. Second, the SMV Project provided what can be called "glue money" to fund the time to interact intensively and ensure regular face-to-face meetings in which we could expand and deepen the common ground in the research. Third, the SMV

Project, with its annual meetings and planned publications provided outlets for our work and an encouraging and informative audience for that work. Fourth, the SMV Project was very structured, which created a kind of institutional leadership to facilitate our collaboration. Finally, one of us has been housed in a very IDR-friendly academic unit, and the other moved from an unfavorable environment to a more favorable one.

Character Strengths for IDR

To meet the challenges of IDR and fruitfully employ available resources, we view the researchers' character strengths as central to success. We have identified a non-exhaustive set of virtues and roughly corresponding vices that seem to be particularly germane to this form of scholarship. Table 3.1 summarizes these qualities. As we noted, no set of personal strengths is likely to be sufficient for IDR success without an IDR-supportive environment. Of course, we want to qualify our comments here by explicitly stating that we do not see ourselves as paragons of any of these virtues. At times, we have found ourselves enacting each of these vices, and, at other times, struggling to embody the virtues to which we aspire. We have found that, to the extent that we have been able to act in line with these virtues, our collaboration and our project have benefitted.

The most basic requirement for any research, but for IDR especially, is commitment to the project and to one's collaborators. We see the tendency to opportunism, whether that is an effort to obtain a quick or easy return on invested time or an exploitive approach to collaborators as inimical to IDR. Given the arduous nature of IDR, a lack of commitment to the process will quickly undermine collaboration. The time required for IDR also places

Table 3.1 Virtues and Vices of Interdisciplinary Research

Virtues	Vices
Commitment	Opportunism
Patience	Results insistence
Mutual valuing	Discipline-centrism
Trust	Self-protection
Good communicator	Territoriality
Courage	Risk-aversiveness
Open-mindedness	Knowledge demonstrativeness

the virtue of patience at a premium. Most scholars have developed patience because it is required for virtually any form of research. With IDR, a particular focus of patience is the tolerance for the process of developing a framework for collaboration and nurturing the project. Successful scholars tend to have a strong focus on obtaining results, but if an insistence on results is not balanced by patience with the process, IDR will become frustrating.

Successful collaborators must mutually value one another. This regard is basic to any relationship, but it is particularly salient in IDR, given the many challenges collaborators face. The consistent pull of discipline-centrism opposes mutual valuing. When collaborators value one another, trust and trustworthiness can be developed. A characteristic tendency toward self-protection is the opposite of trust. This can take many forms, but disciplinary snobbery and other forms of demonstrating superiority are very common ones. A trusting relationship is necessary to support the communication necessary to developing a shared framework for the project. A tendency toward withholding information or territoriality impedes the communication necessary for collaboration. As we noted, ignorance exposure is inevitable in IDR because each of the participants knows things the other(s) does not. Trust allows the collaborators to expose their ignorance with less fear of negative consequences.

Clearly, IDR involves risk. Courage is the virtue of taking reasonable risks to pursue worthwhile ends. The enhanced knowledge that IDR makes possible is the primary end that justifies taking these risks. A characteristic risk aversiveness is a disposition that will seriously undermine a scholar's ability to participate well in IDR.

We would be remiss if we did not stress the virtue of open-mindedness. Like the other virtues, open-mindedness is a virtue trait for scholars in general, but it is even more important in IDR. The primary scholarly end of obtaining and sharing knowledge can encourage a scholar to become excessively focused on demonstrating his or her knowledge. This posture of demonstrating knowledge can undermine the ability to value one's collaborator(s), to allow one's ignorance to be exposed, and to recognize the ways in which other disciplines can contribute to the common project.

Putting Philosophy and Psychology to Work in Tandem

We had the good fortune to begin this project with a positive collaborative history and with mutual regard for the value of one another's discipline. The project was defined, from the beginning, as a set of empirical investigations into self, motivation, and virtue. The practical resources and systematicity of investigation available in psychological research was appealing from a philosophical point of view. Many philosophers have come to appreciate the possibilities for gathering evidence as another way to examine philosophical claims. The clarity and depth of the conceptual analyses provided by philosophy were welcome from a psychological point of view because theory in psychology tends to be rather shallow and lacking in the rigor so standard in philosophy. Psychological virtue theory, in particular, has been characterized more by common-sense notions, ambiguous formulations, and superficial relationships among variables. Our common interest in the content of the study and the mutual valuing of alternative disciplinary approaches strongly facilitated the inclusion of both disciplines.

Philosophical Contributions and the STRIVE-4 Model

From the beginning, a primary goal of our collaboration was to examine a philosophically rigorous theory of virtue empirically. This meant taking philosophical investigations into virtue seriously and moving beyond simplistic one-time survey studies of global virtue dispositions. In the process of our discussions, data gathering, and data interpretation, a conceptual model of virtue emerged that we came to call the STRIVE-4 Model (see Cokelet & Fowers, 2019; Fowers, Carroll, Leonhardt, & Cokelet, 2019 for more complete descriptions). This acronym integrates multiple elements of virtues. We see virtues as *scalar traits*, meaning that individuals can have more or less of a virtue trait. This is an integration of the psychological realism emerging in moral philosophy (Flanagan, 1991) and the quantitative measurement methods of psychology, which facilitate studying constructs with assessments that have a quantitative range. We conceive of virtues as *role-sensitive*, which means that the enactment of virtue will vary depending on the particular role in which one finds oneself. For example, parents have more responsibility for the education and welfare of their own children than they do as members of the community for other children in the community. Consistent with contemporary trait concepts in psychology (e.g., Fleeson, 2001), it is important to recognize that virtue expression *interacts* with features of the environment. We hypothesize that individuals with strong virtue traits will be mildly affected by features of situations, whereas those with weaker virtue traits will be more heavily influenced by situational factors. This addresses the philosophical doubts about virtue traits that arose based on the abundant evidence for situational influence on prosocial behavior (e.g., Doris, 2002; Miller, 2013). Incorporating a trait-situation interaction in our model is consistent with the predominant perspective in psychology (Webster, 2009) and is a more moderate approach to situational influence than outright skepticism. Virtues are also related to *valued* states of affairs, which include personal and communal goals and goods. People enact virtues to bring about desirable ends. These ends should conduce to a *eudaimonic* life. Virtue is not an end-in-itself because virtues are the characteristics that make it possible to live well as a human being. Unfortunately, much psychological theory and research entirely neglects the relationship between virtues and eudaimonia (Fowers, 2016).

Moral philosophers since Aristotle (1999) have conceptualized virtues as multi-component traits, including knowledge, behavior, motivation, and disposition. It was important to us to incorporate these *four* components in our model of virtue and in our investigation of the virtues of fairness and kindness. Individuals must enact virtues behaviorally. The behavioral aspect of virtue was particularly important to us because moral philosophers stress the importance of right or virtuous action. In contrast, behavioral measurement of virtue is very limited in psychology, where a single time point, global self-report assessment is the most common approach (Fowers, 2014).

A virtuous person must also enact the virtue knowingly, meaning that he or she knows what constitutes the virtue and enacts it based on that knowledge. When acting virtuously, one's emotions are concordant with the actions because one is genuinely motivated to act in a kind, fair, or courageous manner. Finally, virtues must be habitual and reliable responses in daily life. In other words, virtues are dispositional. Each of these four components plays an irreplaceable role in virtue enactment.

The STRIVE-4 Model is our primary theoretical innovation in this project. It provides a way to organize the aspects of specific virtues and to encourage well-informed empirical research. There is, of course, much more to virtue theory. The features of role sensitivity and trait-situation interaction can be elaborated to incorporate the fact that virtue enactment is guided by *phronesis*, which clarifies which virtues are called for in a particular circumstance and helps to define what constitutes virtue in that situation. There are also important issues regarding the cultivation of virtues and about the unity of virtues that have not yet been fully incorporated into the model. More development of the STRIVE-4 Model is necessary to satisfactorily address these and other questions. At present, it is a model that provides much needed philosophically informed guidance for empirical investigations of virtues.

Psychological Contributions to the Study of Virtue

Psychologists have excelled at developing sophisticated methods to investigate phenomena of interest. These methods often outstrip the theoretical resources psychologists can bring to bear, but strength in empirical methods makes psychology a good complement to philosophy. We sought psychological methods that would allow us to investigate the virtues of fairness and kindness as multi-component traits. The density distribution approach (Fleeson, 2001) is a cutting-edge method of trait investigation in which multiple occurrences of stronger or weaker virtue enactment over time can indicate the degree to which a virtue trait is evident. Experience sampling research is a method for collecting data multiple times per day for one to three weeks, which provides many samples of the degree of individuals' virtue enactment, and these occurrences allow a reasonable estimate of an individual's overall virtue trait. The density distribution model predicts that, if a trait exists, there will be (1) significant within-person variance in the trait occurrences as a result of the person's responsiveness to varying situations, (2) substantial within-person consistency in trait occurrence stability, and (3) clear individual differences in average trait levels. This method has been fruitful for assessing personality traits (Fleeson & Gallagher, 2009) and virtue traits (Bleidorn & Denissen, 2015; Meindl, Jayawickreme, Furr, & Fleeson, 2013). The primary study in the project used this approach to study fairness and kindness. Our results were entirely consistent with these hypotheses for three of the four virtue components included in the STRIVE-4 Model: behavior, motivation, and self-consistency (Fowers, Lange, et al., 2017).

The chief advantage of the density distribution approach is that it allows investigators to identify traits within individuals. This is vital because traits are features of individuals, not of groups, which is an obvious, but nonetheless frequently ignored distinction in psychological research. Most psychological research focuses on group-level results. Although finding differences among experimental groups or correlations within a sample can be informative about the probabilities and distributions of variables and relationships in groups, these approaches cannot tell us anything about individuals or their traits. Making inferences from group-level results to individuals is known as the "ecological fallacy" (Robinson, 1950), and discussions of individuals' virtue traits based on group-level data are subject to this fallacy. The density distribution approach allows us to examine within-person results and address the presence of virtue traits more directly, making this approach congenial to philosophical accounts of virtue.

Another advantage of experience sampling is that the participants are asked about their actions in the past two hours. In contrast, the items in global self-report scales ask individuals to judge their overall behavior, motivation, and disposition and share this self-assessment by giving a single response to each item. Such self-ratings are prone to a good deal of error because of the complexity of the mental calculations required to provide a single summary report of lifelong patterns of action. Moreover, these reports, like self-reports in general, are subject to doubts about veracity, particularly because subject reports can be distorted by social desirability.

Similar to other experience-sampling studies of virtue (Bleidorn & Denissen, 2015; Meindl et al., 2013), all behavior items in our measures were very specifically targeted only to participants' actions four times each day for 14 days. This provides up to 56 assessment points per participant *in situ*. We asked them to report about what they had done within the previous two hours. This method dramatically reduces the mental calculations required for responses, and it has been found to be minimally influenced by social desirability (Meindl et al., 2013).

We built on previous density distribution work with seven innovations in methods. First, in contrast with previous density distribution research on virtues, we assessed the participants' motivations for their behavior. Motivational concordance with behavior is an essential feature in all accounts of virtue. We drew on Fowers, Mollica, and Procacci (2010) in developing our measures of motivation. Second, we assessed the degree to which the participants saw their behavior as consistent with their self-perception. Self-consistency is a way to assess the dispositional component of virtue, which is also a key element in virtue accounts. We drew on the research on self-concordance (e.g., Sheldon & Houser-Marko, 2001) and self-expressiveness (Waterman, 1993) to construct our measure of self-consistency. Previous studies did not assess these components separately. We found that these three components were strongly related, but distinct constructs (Fowers, Lange, et al., 2017).

A third innovation in methods was to ask participants to identify the specific persons and settings in which they had an opportunity for fairness or kindness. This made the measurement of the virtues very specific and allowed us to examine whether the type of relationship (e.g., family, friend, or acquaintance) and the setting (home, work, or commercial) influenced the degree to which virtues were expressed. Bleidorn and Denissen (2015) did inquire about two social roles (work and parenting) and about the number of people present during the reporting time. We wanted to significantly expand this assessment to examine whether MacIntyre's (1999, 2007) worries about the fragmentation of modern life is undermining the opportunities for virtue enactment. Therefore, we also asked our participants to identify a specific person and setting in which they enacted more or less fairness or kindness, which was prompted by MacIntyre's (1999, 2007) worries that the fragmentation and instrumentalization of the modern world would undermine the cultivation of virtuous character.

For these reasons, we engaged in a lengthy and rigorous process of measurement development. We could not use previously designed measures because they did not match the aims of our study. The construction of the items also exemplifies the integration of philosophy and psychology. Our research team (consisting of the authors and a group of doctoral and undergraduate students) devoted considerable time to clarifying the concepts we wished to study. Psychologists typically begin self-report measurement design with an intuition about a construct they wish to study and move directly to creating items consistent with that intuition. Instead, we took a more philosophical line and recognized the importance of reflecting more on our initial concepts, which were initially rather vague ideas of fairness and kindness in personal relationships. As we developed the measures of fairness, we recognized that there are many ways to conceive of it (e.g., utilitarian, deontic, virtue, libertarian), each of which picks out different behaviors and motivations. Philosophical analysis was extremely helpful in sorting out the various conceptions. Because we were interested in fairness and kindness as virtues and we wanted relatively frequent instances to assess, we decided that the best approach was to assess fairness and kindness in terms of how they manifested in interpersonal relations, most commonly dyadic relations. We reasoned that there would be sufficient opportunities for acting fairly and kindly in interpersonal relationships to be able to evaluate whether interpersonal fairness could be described as a trait. From there, we created items for behavior, motivation, and self-consistency. We also conducted cognitive interviews with a subsample of participants to ascertain how they understood the items. This information led to another round of item culling and revision. We followed a similar procedure for kindness.

A fourth innovative method is that we followed up the quantitative data collection by selecting ten participants who had strong virtue enactment and ten who reported lower virtue enactment, and we conducted narrative interviews with them. This was one of the ways that we went beyond relying on survey instruments. We are interested in a broader understanding of how participants do or do not experience these virtues in their lives. We inquired about the virtues' development course and narrative themes, and how they fit into the participants' lives overall. We have just completed the analyses of these interviews.

A fifth innovation in methods was that we conducted a six-month follow-up to assess the participants' hedonic and eudaimonic well-being. Although all philosophical accounts of virtue tie it to eudaimonia, psychological research generally neglects this central theoretical connection (Fowers, 2016). This follow-up is based on a self-report survey, which allowed us to measure perceptions of well-being, but is, of course, inadequate to assess eudaimonia proper.

We believe that this in-depth examination of fairness and kindness adds importantly to the empirical literature on virtue, but we also understand that the ESM data are self-report. For this reason, we included a sixth innovative method in our project, an experimental study of fairness. We had already conducted an experimental study of kindness, which suggested that trait kindness predicts helping behavior better than Big Five traits or a potent situational condition (Lefevor & Fowers, 2016). We employed an economic game so that we could obtain a measurable behavioral indicator of fairness behavior. When we reviewed the literature, conceptual analysis of the most commonly used games (dictator, ultimatum, and trust games) suggested that their results were ambiguous with respect to fairness, and the researchers seemed largely oblivious to these ambiguities. (See Fowers, Lane, et al. (2019) for a more detailed account of this analysis.) Participants' behavior in these games could have indicated their commitment to fairness, but the behaviors could also have been expressions of envy, pity, generosity, or punitiveness.

We selected a resource game because we believed that it provides a more direct assessment of fairness behavior. In this game, participants could withdraw resources from a replenishable source for six iterations. Participants could withdraw a replenishable amount of the resource or take more of the resource. If they took more of the resource, it could be entirely depleted. Thus, we deemed taking more than a replenishable amount as unfair because it amounted to taking more than one's fair share. In a seventh innovation, we attempted to measure the four components of fairness (knowledge, behavior, emotion/motivation, and disposition) by creating knowledge, behavioral, and dispositional self-report scales of fairness to accompany the Justice Sensitivity scale (Schmitt, Baumert, Gollwitzer, & Maes, 2010), a well-established measure of affective reactions to injustice. We failed to support the construct validity of the fairness knowledge scale, and the fairness behavioral and dispositional scales were too strongly correlated to be treated as independent scales. Thus, we failed in our aim to create self-report virtue component scales for fairness. Nevertheless, our primary aim was to assess the STRIVE-4 prediction that participants lower in trait fairness would be strongly influenced by situational factors to behave more unfairly, whereas individuals higher in trait fairness would not be influenced by the situation (Fowers, Lane, et al., 2019). This prediction was confirmed in our experiment. Justice sensitivity was unrelated to fairness behavior in the study. The important element of this study is that it provides behavioral evidence for trait fairness.

An interesting example of interdisciplinary disagreement arose with the use of the Justice Sensitivity scale. On a philosophical analysis, the items in the scale did not seem to track justice very closely, with items suggesting punitiveness, envy, and grudge-holding. This seemed to require changing the items to ensure that they track justice more closely. This interest ran counter to the way that construct validity is assessed by psychologists. This assessment is a kind of bootstrap operation in which new scales (fairness knowledge, behavior, and disposition) are assessed partly in terms of whether they relate in predicted ways to established scales (e.g., Justice Sensitivity). Because we were relying on the validity of the Justice Sensitivity scale to give us confidence that our new scales were assessing a fairness concept (and this was the case, at least for behavioral and dispositional fairness), we could not alter the existing scale and still claim that it provided a construct validity check. In this case, the requirements of construct validity were more compelling than the desirability of revising the items based on conceptual clarity about fairness.

This relatively small issue proved to be the most contentious issue in pursuing our project. We attribute that interdisciplinary harmony to building on an already established, productive, and collaborative relationship, to the mutual value we see in one another's discipline, and to the modesty we have about the claims of our own disciplines.

Conclusions

We believe that this interdisciplinary collaboration has been successful on five counts. First, we developed a much richer theoretical basis for our research than has been previously available in psychology. By bringing philosophical resources into our conceptualization of psychological research, we created the STRIVE-4 Model to guide our own and possibly others' empirical research on virtue. It is important to note that the criterion of psychological realism was a constant influence on our theorizing. This was particularly evident in the incorporation of the ideas that virtue traits (1) come in degrees (i.e., they are scalar), (2) are role-sensitive, and (3) interact with situational factors.

Second, we have incorporated significant conceptual analysis of the topics of fairness and kindness, which strengthened and clarified these concepts, our measures, and our study procedures in ways that are uncommon in psychological research. This philosophical enrichment of psychological research methods was a primary goal of the project.

Third, our pursuit of tangible evidence in the investigation of our model and of the virtue traits of fairness and kindness represents an important strength of psychological research. This search for evidence provides a way to keep scholars honest in making their theories psychologically realistic and in moving beyond speculation.

Fourth, we selected the cutting-edge psychological method for trait investigation (the density distribution approach) precisely because it provides the best approach to assessing the evidence for the virtue traits conceived by philosophers. The most important way that a density distribution method mirrors virtue theory is that it focuses on variation and stability of actions within the individual. This is essential because evidence for the existence of virtue traits must be obtained at the individual level.

Finally, consistent with a rigorous research program in psychology, we also conducted a study to evaluate whether fairness behavior could be observed. Psychologists tend to doubt the value of purely self-report findings and appreciate the value of multimodal investigations of a theory or construct. When corroborative results are obtained through diverse methods, it is possible to have greater confidence in the findings and the theory that generated the hypotheses.

In sum, we believe that this IDR approach to virtue research has been fruitful in ways that are not possible when working with the resources of either philosophy or psychology independently. Our conceptual and empirical results have added depth and nuance to the field that builds on decades of scholarship in both disciplines. There is much more to learn, and we hope our contributions have helped pave the way to greater knowledge about virtue.

References

Anscombe, G. E. M. (1958). Modern moral philosophy. *Philosophy*, *33*, 1–19.
Aristotle. (1999). *Nicomachean ethics* (M. Ostwald, Trans.). Upper Saddle River, NJ: Prentice Hall.
Bleidorn, W., & Denissen, J. J. A. (2015). Virtues in action: The new look of character traits. *British Journal of Psychology*, *104*, 700–723.
Cokelet, B., & Fowers, B. J. (2019). Realistic virtues and how to study them: Introducing the STRIVE-4 Model. *Journal of Moral Education*, *48*(1), 7–26.
Doris, J. M. (2002). *Lack of character: Personality and moral behavior*. Cambridge: Cambridge University Press.
Flanagan, O. (1991). *Varieties of moral personality: Ethics and psychological realism*. Cambridge, MA: Harvard University Press.
Fleeson, W. (2001). Toward a structure- and process-integrated view of personality: Traits as density distributions of states. *Journal of Personality and Social Psychology*, *80*, 1011–1027.
Fleeson, W., & Gallagher, P. (2009). The implications of Big Five standing for the distribution of trait manifestation in behavior: Fifteen experience-sampling studies and a meta- analysis. *Journal of Personality and Social Psychology*, *97*, 1097–1114.

Fowers, B. J. (2014). Toward programmatic research on virtue assessment: Challenges and prospects. *Theory and Research in Education*, *12*, 309–328.

Fowers, B. J. (2016). Aristotle on eudaimonia: On the virtue of returning to the source. In J. Vittersø (Ed.), *The handbook of eudaimonic well-being* (pp. 67–83). New York, NY: Springer.

Fowers, B. J., Carroll, J. S., Leonhardt, N., & Cokelet, B. (2019). *The emerging science of virtue*. Manuscript in review.

Fowers, B. J., Lane, A. A., Lange, S. F., Abbomante, J. M., Cokelet, B., & Anderson, A. R. (2019). Does trait interpersonal fairness moderate a situational influence on fairness behavior? Manuscript in review.

Fowers, B. J., Lange, S. F., Lane, A. A., Cokelet, B., Laurenceau, J-P., & Anderson, A. R. (2017). Justice as interpersonal fairness: An experience sampling study. Manuscript in preparation.

Fowers, B. J., Mollica, C. O., & Procacci, E. N. (2010). Constitutive and instrumental goal orientations and their relations with eudaimonic and hedonic well-being. *Journal of Positive Psychology*, *5*, 139–153.

Hursthouse, R. (1999). *On virtue ethics*. Oxford: Oxford University Press.

Lefevor, G. T., & Fowers, B. J. (2016). Traits, situational factors, and their interactions as explanations of helping behavior. *Journal of Personality and Individual Differences*, *92*, 159–163.

MacIntyre, A. C. (1999). *Dependent rational animals: Why human beings need the virtues*. Chicago, IL: Open Court.

MacIntyre, A. C. (2007). *After virtue: A study in moral theory* (3rd ed.). Notre Dame, IN: University of Notre Dame Press.

Meindl, P., Jayawickreme, E., Furr, R. M., & Fleeson, W. (2013). A foundation beam for studying morality from a personological point of view: Are individual differences in moral behaviors and thoughts consistent? *Journal of Research in Personality*, *59*, 81–92.

Miller, C. B. (2013). *Moral character: An empirical theory*. New York, NY: Oxford Press.

Morgan, B., Gulliford, L., & Kristjánsson, K. (2017). A new approach to measuring moral virtues: The multi-component gratitude measure. *Personality and Individual Differences*, *107*, 179–189.

National Research Council. (2015). *Enhancing the effectiveness of team science*. Washington, DC: The National Academies Press.

Robinson, W. S. (1950). Ecological correlations and the behavior of individuals. *American Sociological Review*, *15*, 351–357.

Schmitt, M., Baumert, A., Gollwitzer, M., & Maes, J. (2010). The Justice Sensitivity Inventory: Factorial validity, location in the personality facet space, demographic pattern, and normative data. *Social Justice Research*, *23*, 211–238.

Sheldon, K. M., & Houser-Marko, L. (2001). Self-concordance, goal attainment, and the pursuit of happiness: Can there be an upward spiral? *Journal of Personality and Social Psychology*, *80*, 152–165.

Snow, N. E. (2010). *Virtue as social intelligence: An empirically grounded theory*. New York, NY: Routledge.

Waterman, A. S. (1993). Two conceptions of happiness: Contrasts of personal expressiveness (eudaimonia) and hedonic enjoyment. *Journal of Personality and Social Psychology*, *64*, 678–691.

Webster, G. D. (2009). The person-situation interaction is increasingly outpacing the person-situation debate in the scientific literature: A 30-year analysis of publication trends, 1978–2007. *Journal of Research in Personality, 43,* 278–279.

Woodard, C. R., & Pury, C. L. S. (2007). The construct of courage: Categorization and measurement. *Consulting Psychology Journal: Practice and Research, 59,* 135–147.

4 Virtue and Self-Distancing

Warren Herold, Walter Sowden, and Ethan Kross

Introduction

In *The Theory of Moral Sentiments* (TMS), Adam Smith develops an account of critical self-evaluation that depends crucially on our social nature and capacity to take a distant perspective on our own circumstances and conduct. Smith believes that, without society, self-evaluation would be impossible, that a person raised in social isolation, without any opportunity to interact with other people, would be incapable of any kind of self-reflective thought. "Were it possible," Smith writes,

> that a human creature could grow up to manhood in some solitary place, without any communication with his own species, he could no more think of his own character, of the propriety or demerit of his own sentiments and conduct, of the beauty or deformity of his own mind, than of the beauty or deformity of his own face. All these are objects which he cannot easily see, which naturally he does not look at, and with regard to which he is provided with no mirror which can present them to his view.
>
> (TMS III.1.3)[1]

Fixated on "the objects of his passions," Smith argues that such a person's passions themselves would "scarce ever be the objects of his thoughts." The consideration of his own joy would "excite no new joy, nor that of his sorrow any new sorrow." Using Harry Frankfurt's terminology, we could say that such a person would have first-order desires, but no second-order desires—that is, no desires about his own desires (Frankfurt, 1971). He would have thoughts and feelings, but he would have no thoughts or feelings *about his thoughts or feelings*. Indeed, he would not be able to conceive of his thoughts or feelings as *his*. Lacking the ability to self-reflect, he would have no conception of himself *as a thinking or feeling self*.

Charles Griswold writes that, for Smith, we are not born with "individual selves" that are "just 'there,' pre-given and waiting to be discovered" (1999, p. 106). On the contrary, we create our "individual selves," in Smith's view, by engaging with other people, observing their conduct, and examining ourselves as we so naturally examine the feelings and behavior of others—and as they examine us. We create our individual selves, according to Smith, not by viewing the world from our own first-person perspective but by interacting with other people and examining our feelings and behavior from an informed but distant point of view (TMS III.1.5). Put simply, we create our "*selves*" by thinking about ourselves as if we were an "*other*". We self-evaluate by examining our conduct from a *self-distant* point of view—"as we imagine any other fair and impartial spectator would examine it" (TMS III.1.2).

For Smith, distance is essential. He writes that we "can never survey our own sentiments and motives" unless we "remove ourselves" from "our own natural station" and imaginatively view ourselves "as at a certain distance" (TMS III.1.2). It is this process of *self-distancing*, in his view, that enables individuals to acquire the perspective that they need to engage in the process of critical self-reflection on which the development of the self depends. Without it, the development of the self would be impossible. And, if Smith is right, then it is a process with profound significance. For, as we shall see, Smith believes that examining ourselves from a distant point of view can change the way we think and feel: that it can alter the way we interpret and respond to our own circumstances and experiences, enhance our capacity for self-control, and even change the way we view our relations to other people and our place in society. And if Smith is right, then the process by which we learn to develop a sense of ourselves *as selves* can lead us to acquire a new set of desires: to want to be a particular type of person—one characterized by a specific set of virtues that Smith thinks the process of self-distancing promotes.

This chapter has two primary aims. The first aim is to explore and introduce the reader to Smith's claims regarding the effects of self-distancing and the connection between self-distancing and a particular conception of virtuous motivation and conduct. The second aim is to scrutinize the empirical claims on which Smith's theory depends. Along the way, we also say a few words about the collaborative process—among two social psychologists and a philosopher—that produced this work. The chapter proceeds as follows. We review Smith's claims regarding the effects of self-distancing in the next section. We examine Smith's account of virtue in the section after that. Next, we scrutinize Smith's empirical claims—explaining which are supported by empirical evidence, which are not, and which require additional study—and conclude in the last section.

Smith on the Effects of Self-Distancing

What happens when we think about our own circumstances, feelings, and behavior from a distant point of view? What are the effects of self-distancing? Smith makes two general claims.

First, Smith claims that thinking about our circumstances from a distant point of view tends to moderate our emotional reactivity. Smith believes that people naturally tend to overreact to things. Caught up in the moment, he writes that the "eagerness" of our passions often prevents us from examining our circumstances with "the candour of an indifferent person" (TMS III.4.3). Trapped in our own first-person point of view, our "magnified" feelings prevent us from thinking past our immediate circumstances and concerns—or even thinking about them in a reasonable manner. This tendency is particularly pronounced when we are alone. It is then, Smith observers, that we are most "apt to feel too strongly whatever relates to ourselves"—to be "too much elated by our own good and too much dejected by our own bad fortune" (TMS III.3.38). The presence of one or more spectators can help:

> The mind [. . .] is rarely so disturbed, but that the company of a friend will restore it to some degree of tranquility and sedateness. The breast is, in some measure, calmed and composed the moment we come into his presence. We are immediately put in mind of the light in which he will view our situation, and we begin to view it ourselves in the same light.
>
> (TMS I.i.4.9)

By "placing" ourselves in our spectators' shoes, Smith argues that we naturally begin to conceive "some degree" of that "coolness about [our] fortune" with which they so naturally view it (TMS I.i.4.8). The more distant the spectator, the greater the effect. He writes that the presence of a "common acquaintance" will lead us to view our own circumstances from a greater distance than will the presence of a friend, and that of an "assembly of strangers" from a greater distance still. As a result, Smith claims that the presence of an acquaintance will compose us "more than that of a friend; and that of an assembly of strangers still more than that of an acquaintance." By forcing us outside of ourselves, their presence enables us to do precisely that which we were unable to do when we were alone: view our situation in a "candid and impartial light."

Smith believes that the moderating effect of distance is both real and beneficial. His claim is not merely that we act *as if* we feel with less intensity when we self-distance—that is, that we fake it whenever other people are around. He believes that the presence of other people can *actually* compose us (TMS I.i.4.9; see also III.3.25). When we think about our situation from a distant point of view, our good fortune will often begin to look less significant and our bad fortune less catastrophic; our good deeds less heroic and our injuries less horrific; the ups and downs of life less dramatic and thus more tolerable. And this, Smith thinks, is as it should be. For he believes that the ordinary ups and downs of life really are less substantial than we often take them to be. Despite what we may think about the desirability of altering our circumstances in one way or another (e.g., by acquiring more wealth, more fame, more power, more prestige), Smith writes that such changes typically make "no essential difference" to our lives (TMS III.3.30).[2] For, what, he asks,

> can be added to the happiness of the man who is in health, who is out of debt, and has a clear conscience? To one in this situation, all accessions of fortune may properly be said to be superfluous; and if he is much elevated upon account of them, it must be the effect of the most frivolous levity.
>
> (TMS I.iii.1.7)

Even the most humble life can provide those "pleasures from which we [...] derive our real happiness" (TMS III.3.31). Distance is beneficial, in Smith's view, in part because it helps us to see this. By moderating our emotional reactivity, distance enables us to "see what relates to ourselves in its proper shape and dimensions" (TMS III.3.1).

The tendency of people to overestimate the significance of superficial changes in their lives is not a harmless error, in Smith's view. On the contrary, he describes it as one of the principal impediments to human happiness:

> The great source of both the misery and disorders of human life, seems to arise from over-rating the difference between one permanent situation and another. Avarice over-rates the difference between poverty and riches: ambition, that between a private and a public station: vain-glory, that between obscurity and extensive reputation. The person under the influence of any of those extravagant passions, is not only miserable in his actual situation, but is often disposed to disturb the peace of society, in order to arrive at that which he so foolishly admires.
>
> (TMS III.3.31)

As Smith sees it, there is little that a healthy and financially secure person whose conscience is clear can do to improve their situation. Such a person has everything they need. To risk what they have, then, in a misguided effort to obtain more wealth, fame, or power, is, in Smith's view, the height of imprudence. It is, as he puts it, to stake "everything against scarce a thing."[3]

For Smith, happiness consists not in the accumulation of ever greater wealth, fame, or power, but in "tranquility and enjoyment" (TMS III.3.30). And this, he thinks, can be obtained in nearly any "permanent situation." As long as one has enough resources to meet their basic needs, Smith denies that shifts in wealth, fame, or power do anything to affect an individual's well-being—at least, in the long-term (see TMS III.3.30). Instead, he argues that the primary "source of that inward tranquility and self-satisfaction" in which our happiness consists is not any material possession, but rather our "consciousness" of the fact that our character is the object of favorable regard (TMS III.1.7). In short, once our basic needs have been met, Smith claims that happiness depends primarily on the extent to which we are conscious of "being beloved"— or, more precisely, on the extent to which we feel that our conduct has been such as to render us the proper object of approbation and love (TMS I.ii.5.1). More than anything else, Smith thinks, we are happy when we are confident that we *deserve* to be beloved:

> What so great happiness as to be beloved, and to know that we deserve to be beloved? What so great misery as to be hated, and to know that we deserve to be hated?
>
> (TMS III.1.7)

Even when everything else goes wrong, the "virtuous man" can at least still enjoy the "complete approbation of his own breast," as well as the assurance that he has the "love and esteem of every intelligent and impartial spectator, who could not fail both to admire his conduct and to regret his misfortune" (TMS VII.ii.1.28). Our self-approbation can sustain us even when other aspects of our lives are imperfect.

This brings us to Smith's second claim. In addition to reducing our tendency to overestimate the importance of relatively superficial changes to our lives (and in enhancing our sensitivity to what matters), Smith believes that self-distancing can at least partly mitigate our tendency to exaggerate the value and importance of our own lives and experiences, relative to those of others. In Smith's view, humans are naturally self-centered:

> To the selfish and original passions of human nature, the loss or gain of a very small interest of our own, appears to be of vastly more importance, excites a much more passionate joy or sorrow, a much more ardent desire or aversion, than the greatest concern of another with whom we have no particular connection.
>
> (TMS III.3.3)

And as long as we view the world from our own first-person point of view, Smith believes that we will continue to think in this way. We will pursue our (apparent) interests without regard to "how ruinous" our actions are to others (TMS III.3.3). Even the "most frivolous" personal injuries will cause us more distress than the "ruin" of a 100 million people to whom we are in no way connected (TMS III.3.4). We will think almost exclusively of ourselves.

How, then, when our "passive feelings" are so "sordid and so selfish," do we learn to make "proper" comparisons between our own interests and those of other people (TMS III.3.4 & III.3.1)? Smith's answer is that we change our position: we weigh our rights and interests against those of other people by viewing the world neither from our own first-person perspective nor from theirs, but "from the place and with the eyes of a third person" (TMS III.3.3). And this, he thinks, has a profound effect. He writes that viewing our own circumstances and interests from a distant point of view teaches us "the real littleness of ourselves, and of whatever relates to ourselves (TMS III.3.4). It shows us that we typically "value ourselves too much and other people too little" (TMS III.3.5). It enables us to see the "propriety of generosity and the deformity of justice"—that is, the propriety of "resigning the greatest interests of our own, for the yet greater interests of others, and the deformity of doing the smallest injury to another, in order to obtain the greatest benefit to ourselves" (TMS III.3.4). In short, Smith claims that self-distancing causes us to rethink our role in society: to see ourselves not as more important or valuable than anyone else, but as *an equal* among many—as "one of the multitude, in no respect better than any other."

If Smith is right, then self-distancing should mitigate our natural tendency to be *selfish*. He does not suggest, though, that self-distancing will lead individuals to be *selfless*. This is not his view. On the contrary, Smith clearly believes that it is entirely proper for individuals to pursue their own interests. He writes, for example, that in "the race for wealth, and honours, it is permissible for a person to "run as hard as he can, and strain every nerve and every muscle, in order to outstrip all his competitors" (TMS II.ii.2.1). What is impermissible is not to attempt to further one's own interests, but to attempt to do so in a way that violates the rights of others:

> But if he should justle, or thrown down any of them, the indulgence of the spectators is entirely at an end. It is a violation of fair play, which they cannot admit of. This man is to them, in every respect, as good as he: they do not enter into that self-love by which he prefers himself so much to this other, and cannot go along with the motive from which he hurt him.
> (TMS II.ii.2.1)

Taking up a distant and impartial perspective does not show us that it is necessarily wrong to prefer ourselves to others, or to pursue our own interests with more "earnest assiduity" than we exhibit when we work on behalf of others. All that it shows is that we must never "prefer ourselves so much" as to "injure" other people in the pursuit of our own good (TMS III.3.6; see also II.ii.2.1).

If Smith is right, then thinking about our circumstances, feelings, and behavior from a distant point of view can simultaneously enhance our capacity to pursue our own interests and increase our tendency to respect the rights and interests of others. The process of self-distancing enhances our capacity to pursue our own interests, according to Smith, by regulating our emotions, enhancing our self-control, reducing our tendency to make imprudent choices (i.e., risking what we have for a chance to acquire what we do not need), and making possible the type of positive self-evaluative judgment on which Smith believes so much of our real happiness depends. At the same time, the process increases our tendency to respect the rights and interests of others, in Smith's view, by leading us to view ourselves as we are: merely one among equals, neither more nor less important than any other. If Smith is right, then the overall effect of self-distancing will be to lead us to more effectively pursue our own interests, subject to the constraint that we only do so in a way that respects the rights and interests of others.

Smith on Virtue

Let's turn now to Smith's account of virtue. How does he describe the perfectly virtuous moral agent? What sorts of characteristics does the virtuous agent exhibit? Smith's early discussions of virtue tend to emphasize two categories of virtue: the "amiable" virtues of empathy and humanity, and the "respectable" virtues of self-denial and self-government (see TMS I.i.5.1–4). He writes in the first edition of TMS, for example, that the:

> Man of the most perfect virtue, the man whom we naturally love and revere the most, is he who joins, to the most perfect command of his own original and selfish feelings, the most exquisite sensibility both to the original and sympathetic feelings of others. The man who, to all the soft, the amiable, and the gentle virtues, joins all the great, the awful, and the respectable, must surely be the natural and proper object of our highest love and admiration.
>
> (TMS III.3.35)

Some passages appear to identify selflessness as a type of virtue. For example, Smith argues that we exhibit a virtuous character when we "feel much for others and little for ourselves" (TMS I.i.5.5). We act virtuously, according to this account, when we "restrain our selfish" and "indulge our benevolent affections." Just as "to love our neighbour as we love ourselves is the great law of Christianity," Smith concludes that "to love ourselves only as we love our neighbour" is the "great precept of nature."

In his later work, Smith defends a slightly different account of virtue. Rather than focusing exclusively on the virtues of humanity and self-command, Smith's discussion in the sixth and final edition of TMS (published shortly before his death) emphasizes four distinct virtues: prudence, justice, benevolence, and self-command. He defines prudence as the virtue which aims to protect one's own health, fortune, rank, and reputation—or, as he puts it, the "objects" upon which the "comfort and happiness in this life are supposed principally to depend" (TMS VI.i.5). Undeceived by the false promises of greater wealth, fame, and power, Smith believes that genuinely prudent individuals are more concerned about losing what they have than in acquiring what they lack (TMS VI.i.6). Their principal objectives are to preserve a "healthful state of the body," to "keep out of harm's way," to secure the respect of their equals, and to protect their rank and status in society (TMS VI.i.1–3). Of course, a person's health depends in part on their wealth, as do their "rank and credit" in society. The prudent individual therefore has at least some reason to seek material wealth (TMS VI.i.3–4). But Smith argues that our rank and status are also—perhaps primarily—determined by "our character and conduct, or upon the confidence, esteem, and good-will, which these naturally excite in the people we live with" (TMS VI.i.4). In addition to pursuing wealth and security, then, Smith concludes that prudent individuals will be motivated to secure the esteem and good-will of others. Prudent people will do what it takes to ensure that they are the proper object of approval and esteem, not disapproval or resentment.

Prudence aims to secure one's own present and future happiness. In contrast, the business of justice and beneficence is to secure the present and future happiness of others. Each aims at this in its own way. We satisfy the requirements of justice by refraining from harming people—or, more generally, by avoiding actions that could be properly resented. In many cases, this will not require very much. We may "often fulfil all the rules of justice," Smith observes, "by sitting still and doing nothing" (TMS II.ii.1.9). Benevolence is more demanding. In contrast to the "negative virtue" of justice, benevolence is active. When we act with benevolence, our aim is not merely to avoid harming other people; it is to actively "promote" their happiness (TMS VI.concl.1). We act with benevolence when we go out of our way to benefit other people.

For Smith, the rules of justice are both "accurate in the highest degree, and admit of no exceptions or modifications" (TMS III.6.10). If I owe someone a certain sum of money, Smith claims that justice requires that I pay them exactly what I owe. The observance of the rules of justice "is not left to the freedom of our own wills"; it may be "extorted by force" (TMS II.ii.1.5). In contrast, Smith claims that benevolence is "always free" and can never be "extorted by force" (TMS II.ii.1.3). The state cannot force anyone to be benevolent. This is so, in part, because, unlike violations of the rules of justice, which cause "real and positive" harm, and are therefore the proper object of regulation and enforcement, violations of the rules of proper benevolence "do no real positive evil" (TMS II.ii.1.5 & II.ii.1.3). But it is also because the rules of proper benevolence cannot, in Smith's view, be articulated with the level of clarity and precision that would be required for them to be enforced. Indeed, Smith believes that this is true not only of benevolence, but of all the virtues save justice:

> The general rules of almost all the virtues [the exception being justice], the general rules which determine what are the offices of prudence, of charity, of generosity, of gratitude, of friendship, are in many respects loose and inaccurate, admit of many exceptions, and require so many modifications, that it is scarce possible to regulate our conduct entirely by a regard to them.
> (TMS III.6.9)

How, then, do we figure out what these virtues require? How does the virtuous moral agent determine what is required of them? How do they decide how to act? Smith writes that we regulate our conduct not "by any regard to a precise maxim or rule" (TMS III.6.10), but "by a certain idea of propriety" (TMS III.6.10). We determine what prudence and benevolence require, in other words, and resolve all conflicts between them, by referring not to some predetermined set of rules (as in the case of justice), but to "the decision of the man within the breast, the supposed impartial spectator, the great judge and arbiter of our conduct" (TMS VI.ii.1.22):

> If we place ourselves completely in his situation, if we really view ourselves with his eyes, and as he views us, and listen with diligent and reverential attention to what he suggests to us, his voice will never deceive us. We shall stand in need of no casuistic rules to direct our conduct.
>
> (TMS VI.ii.1.22).

We identify the duties of prudence and benevolence, and weigh them against each other, in Smith's view, by engaging in a process of self-distancing: by imaginatively viewing our own circumstances and conduct from a third-person point of view.

Of course, it is one thing to know what the rules of prudence, justice, and benevolence require, and to know how they ought to be balanced; it is another thing to act in accordance with them. For Smith, virtue requires something closer to the latter than the former: it requires proper conduct, not just knowledge of what is proper (see TMS VI.iii.1). But even that is not quite right. For Smith notes that it is possible to act in accordance with the rules of prudence, justice, and benevolence without exhibiting any virtue, or to act virtuously while nonetheless violating one or more of these rules. Following the rules is often easy. It is prudent to eat when one is hungry (TMS I.i.5.7); and, as already noted, it is often possible to fulfill the rules of justice by simply "sitting still and doing nothing" (TMS II.ii.1.9). But Smith writes that it would be "absurd" to call such conduct virtuous (TMS I.i.5.7). And he argues that there are other cases in which an action may be called "virtuous" even if it falls short of "the most perfect propriety"— provided that it comes closer to "perfection" than can reasonably be expected, given the difficulty of adhering perfectly to the relevant standards of conduct (TMS I.i.5.8).

Virtue, for Smith, is more than just adhering to the rules of perfect prudence, strict justice, and proper benevolence. He describes virtue as "excellence" (TMS I.i.5.6). It is "something uncommonly great and beautiful, which rises far above what is vulgar and ordinary." We act with virtue when we manage to act in a way that approximates adherence to the rules of prudence, justice, and benevolence *despite the substantial difficulty of doing so*:

> To act according to the dictates of prudence, of justice, and proper beneficence, seems to have no great merit where there

is no temptation to do otherwise. But to act with cool deliberation in the midst of the greatest dangers and difficulties; to observe religiously the sacred rules of justice in spite both of the greatest interests which might tempt, and the greatest injuries which might provoke us to violate them; never to suffer the benevolence of our temper to be damped or discouraged by the malignity and ingratitude of the individuals toward whom it may have been exercised; is the character of the most exalted wisdom and virtue.

(TMS VI.iii.11)

No action can be called virtuous, according to Smith, unless it is "accompanied with the sentiment of self-approbation" (TMS III.6.13). And, in Smith's view, the extent of our own self-approbation will necessarily vary "exactly in proportion to the degree of self-command which is necessary in order to obtain" it (TMS III.3.26). It thus follows that, for Smith, no action can be called virtuous unless it requires a considerable degree of self-command. Self-command is not only a virtue in itself; it is the virtue from which all the other virtues "derive their principle lustre" (TMS VI.iii.11). It is the virtue that makes all other virtues possible. We act virtuously when we employ our capacity for self-command to act in a way that more closely adheres to the proper balance of prudence, justice, and benevolence than can be reasonably expected of us.

From Self-Distancing to Virtue: Empirical Evidence

Smith's theory provides a complete—and plausible—account of the relationships among self-evaluation, the self, and virtuous motivation. We are motivated to self-evaluate, according to this account, by feelings of accountability to others, which lead us to examine our circumstances, feelings, and conduct from a distant point of view. Smith claims that the process in turn moderates our emotional reactivity, enhances our self-control, and changes the way we view ourselves and our relations to others. If Smith is right, then the process by which we learn to self-evaluate and develop our "individual selves" also leads us to more effectively pursue our own interests, subject to the constraint that we only do so in a way that respects the rights and interests of others. In short, if Smith is right, then self-distancing should enhance virtuous motivation by leading individuals to act in a way that properly balances the demands of prudence, justice, and benevolence.

Are Smith's empirical claims correct? Does self-distancing have the effects that he suggests? Begin with the first claim. Is there evidence that self-distancing moderates emotional reactivity and enhances self-control? Is there reason to think that self-distancing can enable people to gain valuable perspective on their lives? There is. A growing body of research on self-distancing over the past decade largely supports Smith's claim (for a review, see Kross & Ayduk, 2017). In an early paper, Kross, Ayduk, and Mischel (2005) examined how people can reflect on painful negative experiences without becoming overwhelmed with distress. They suggested that people often fail to work through their negative experiences in a healthy way because they tend to analyze them from a *self-immersed* (first-person) perspective, which leads them to narrowly focus on *recounting* the details of their actual experience (i.e., how they felt at the time). To facilitate adaptive self-reflection, they suggested that people ought instead to adopt a *self-distanced* or "fly on the wall" perspective. Their hypothesis was that analyzing negative experiences from a self-distanced perspective would lead people to *reconstrue* their experiences, rather than *recount* them, and thus enable them to think about the events in ways that provide insight and closure, and that reduce distress.

These predictions have since been borne out in multiple experiments.[4] The results indicate that prompting subjects to self-distance (either by asking them visualize their experiences from the perspective of an observer or "fly on the wall" or by instructing them to refer to themselves in the second or third person or by focusing on how they will feel in the distant future) transforms the way they think and feel about their own feelings and experiences. Individuals who self-distance tend to recount less and reconstrue more. That is, they focus less on how they felt at a particular time, and more on abstract representations of the situations that they were in at that time. And they experience less distress as a result (Kross & Ayduk, 2008; Kross et al., 2005). More specifically, self-distancing has been found to moderate negative emotions, including anger, depression, and anxiety (Ayduk & Kross, 2008; Gruber, Harvey, & Johnson, 2009; Kross et al., 2005; Wisco & Nolen-Hoeksema, 2011). It has also been found to moderate positive emotions, such as gratitude and joy (Park et al., 2014; Verduyn, Van Mechelen, Kross, Chezzi, & Van Bever, 2012). Self-distancing also has buffering effects. One study (Kross & Ayduk, 2008) found that people who analyzed a negative experience from a self-distanced perspective underwent less distress not only initially, but also when they thought about the same experience again one week later. They also ruminated less over time compared with individuals who either analyzed their experience from a self-immersed perspective or were distracted (for additional longitudinal results, see Ayduk & Kross, 2010b; Verduyn et al., 2012).

Subsequent research has uncovered additional (related) effects. For example, numerous cross-sectional, physiological, and longitudinal studies have shown that individuals vary in their natural tendencies to spontaneously self-distance while analyzing their own feelings, and activating this process spontaneously leads to similar short- and long-term consequences that are mediated by the same mechanisms as when this process is manipulated (Ayduk & Kross, 2010b; Verduyn et al., 2012). Self-distancing has also been found to mitigate a number of harmful behavioral patterns associated with rumination. For example, at least two studies have found that self-distancing reduces aggressive behavior when people are provoked (Ayduk & Kross, 2010b; Mischkowski, Kross, & Bushman, 2012). Another study found that cueing participants to reflect on their anxious feelings about giving a public speech from different perspectives can affect their subsequent performance. Individuals who reflected from a self-distanced perspective were found to deliver better speeches (according to expert judges) than individuals who reflected from a self-immersed perspective (Streamer, Seerly, Kondrak, Lamarche, & Thomas, 2017).

The beneficial effects of self-distancing have been observed not only in healthy adults (Ayduk & Kross, 2010a; Kross & Ayduk, 2011), but also in a variety of vulnerable populations. For example, preliminary findings suggest that the short-term benefits of self-distancing can be observed in people with dysphoria (Kross & Ayduk, 2009; Wisco & Nolen-Hoeksema, 2011), people with major depressive disorder (Kross, Gard, Deldin, Clifton, & Ayduk, 2012), people with bipolar disorder (Gruber et al., 2009), children (Kross, Duckworth, Ayduk, Tsukayama, & Mischel, 2011; White, Kross, & Duckworth, 2015), and the parents of pediatric cancer patients who suffer from high levels of post-traumatic stress symptomatology (Penner et al., 2016). Indeed, some of these studies suggest that the benefits associated with self-distancing are more pronounced for vulnerable populations than for healthy people

(Kross & Ayduk, 2009; Kross et al., 2012; Penner et al., 2016). Overall, these findings suggest that self-distanced reflection may be particularly useful for those who stand to gain the most from this technique.

These empirical results provide strong support for Smith's claim that examining ourselves from a distant point of view can help to moderate our emotional reactivity and provide us with a valuable perspective on our own circumstances and experiences. In particular, the data suggest that self-distancing supports emotional and behavioral patterns that fit nicely with Smith's conception of the perfectly prudent individual—an individual who can successfully navigate the ups and downs of life. A recent line of research adds additional support to this view by suggesting that, in addition to moderating emotional reactivity, self-distancing can also enable people to reason more wisely about their circumstances and feelings in the face of personal dilemmas. For example, one study examined the way that college students and recent college graduates (who were unsuccessful in their initial attempt to secure a job after graduation) reason about how the economic recession (at the time of the study) would affect their career prospects (Kross & Grossmann, 2012, study 1). The results indicated that participants who self-distanced displayed higher levels of two common characteristics of wise reasoning (*dialecticism* and *intellectual humility*) than participants who thought about themselves from a self-immersed point of view. That is, individuals who self-distanced were more likely to recognize that the future is uncertain or likely to change (dialecticism; see Basseches, 1984; Kramer [Woodruff, D. S.], 1986) and to acknowledge the limits of their own knowledge (intellectual humility; see Baltes & Smith, 2008; Ryan, 2012).

A follow-up study (Kross & Grossmann, 2012, study 2) replicated these findings in a different context (see also Grossmann & Kross, 2014). Specifically, the study examined how individuals think about how various foreign and domestic policy issues would play out if their preferred candidate were to lose the 2008 US presidential election. Once again, the data indicate that participants who self-distanced displayed higher levels of dialecticism and intellectual humility than participants who thought about the issues from a self-immersed point of view. Interestingly, the study found that the participants who self-distanced also exhibited more cooperative or prosocial tendencies: they endorsed their own political views less vehemently, and they signed up to join bipartisan discussion groups at a higher rate than participants who deliberated from a self-immersed perspective.

These effects of self-distancing are significant. People are often better at thinking about *other people's* problems, and offering *them* advice, than they are at thinking about their own personal dilemmas (Kross & Grossmann, 2012). The aforementioned results suggest that, by leading individuals to think about themselves not as *themselves*, but as if they were an "*other*," the process of self-distancing can enable individuals to do for themselves what they naturally do for others. Indeed, a subsequent study (Grossmann & Kross, 2014, study 2) has confirmed that this is the case. This study found that participants who think about their own personal problem from a self-distanced perspective reason as wisely as participants who think about another person's problem, and more wisely than participants who think about their own personal problem from a self-immersed perspective. The data suggest that self-distancing eliminates the self-other asymmetry that normally characterizes the way that people reason about personally meaningful problems. Thinking about ourselves as an "*other*" can help us to reason as well about our own problems as we reason about problems encountered by actual others.

Taken together, these empirical findings provide strong support for Smith's claim that self-distancing enhances prudential reasoning. But what about his other claims? Is there evidence that self-distancing reduces our natural tendency to exaggerate the value and importance of our own lives and experiences, relative to those of others? Is there evidence that it increases our altruistic motivations, or that it enhances our sensitivity to the rights and interests of other people? Can examining ourselves from a distant point of view increase our benevolent motivation? Can it increase our adherence to moral principles?

Evidence of a connection between self-distancing and prosocial motivation is mixed. There is evidence that self-distancing can support prosocial behavior in at least certain types of situations. A recent study by Grossmann, Brienza, and Bobocel (2017) found that self-distancing eliminates the negative effect of deliberation time on cooperation in a (one-shot) *public goods game*. A public goods game is an experiment in which subjects are allocated a sum of money and then asked to decide how much of it to keep for themselves and how much to contribute to the "public good." Contributions to the latter are multiplied by some factor (greater than 1, but less than the number of participants) and then divided evenly among all of the participants. The study found that whereas participants who deliberated from a first-person perspective tended to contribute less money to the group when they were allowed more time to think about their decision, deliberation time had no effect on the contributions of those who deliberated from a third-person point of view. Moreover, the study found significant differences between the way subjects in the first- and third-person groups thought about the game. Subjects who reflected on the public goods game from a first-person perspective tended to focus primarily on self-serving concerns (i.e., maximizing their own payoff), whereas subjects who reflected from a third-person perspective emphasized the participants' interdependent interests (i.e., the fact that each participant's payoff depends not only on their own behavior, but on the behavior of every other participant). The results support the hypothesis that, at least in certain situations, self-distancing will lead individuals to think less about promoting their own interests, and more about acting in accordance with principles of justice, fairness, reciprocity, and so forth.

When we began working on this project, we suspected that this result would generalize in a fairly straightforward way. That is, we predicted that self-distancing would both reduce people's tendency to exaggerate the value and importance of their own lives and experiences, relative to others, and increase their tendency to promote the interests of others, and that we would observe this pattern in a variety of circumstances. One of the most striking effects of our interdisciplinary collaboration was that it convinced us that we were wrong. The relationship between self-distancing and altruistic motivation is not as simple as we had initially thought. Indeed, our work suggests that the effects of self-distancing on an individual's tendency to act altruistically are anything but simple: they depend on features of the individual's circumstances, as well as aspects of their relationships with other people, that we had not originally considered. This has been the primary benefit of our close interdisciplinary collaboration: it has forced us to consider variables that we had initially ignored.

To see this, consider again the results of the Grossman, Brienza, and Bobocell study just discussed. The study suggests that, at least in the context of a public goods game, self-distancing can enhance prosocial behavior by causing people to think about the interdependence of everyone's interests, rather than focusing exclusively on their own interests. These results are consistent with the claim that self-distancing increases altruistic motivation in general. But, importantly, the results do not entail the general claim. It is possible that when people face a decision in a context in which their interests are not interdependent, self-distancing may not support prosocial behavior—or that it may even have the opposite effect. As it turns out, our own (ongoing) research on the effects of self-distancing on prosocial behavior suggests that this is in fact what happens. Consider, for example, the case of a (one-shot) *dictator game*. A dictator game has two participants: a *dictator* and a *recipient*. The dictator is allocated a fixed sum of money and asked to decide how much to keep and how much to give to the recipient. The recipient has no choice but to accept whatever money they are given. In contrast to the participants in a public goods game, whose interests are interdependent, the participants in a dictator game have neither interdependent interests nor any opportunity for mutually beneficial cooperation. The dictator is playing a zero-sum game. And our data suggest that in the context of such a game, self-distancing does not support prosocial behavior. On the contrary, self-distancing may lead some individuals to be less altruistic than if they deliberated from a first-person point of view. That is, at least in the context of a zero-sum game, self-distancing may actually increase self-interested behavior in some segments of the population.

All of this is consistent with Smith's account. Smith's central claim is not that examining one's situation from a spectator's point of view will necessarily increase altruistic motivation in all cases, but rather that doing so will help individuals balance self-interested and other-interested considerations. The suggestion is that self-distancing will support prudential reasoning *and* increase adherence to moral principles. These effects play out differently in different contexts. In a public goods game, the best way to maximize one's own payoff is to contribute nothing to the public good, and hope that others contribute a great deal. If one were to pursue such a strategy, however, and if other people were to contribute to the public good, then one would be free-riding on the good-will of others. The strategy violates a basic principle of reciprocity. It should not be surprising, then, that self-distancing has been found to support prosocial behavior in the context of a public goods game. The situation is different, however, in a dictator game. In a dictator game, reciprocity plays no role. If an individual playing the role of the dictator were to keep all or most of the money for themselves, the recipient would likely feel disappointed; but they would have no ground for resentment, as they had no claim to the money in the first place. It should therefore not be surprising that self-distancing supports self-interested behavior in the context of a dictator game.

Moreover, there is other research—with nothing to do with economic games—that provides additional support for the claim that self-distancing supports adherence to at least certain moral principles. A recent study by Weidman, Sowden, Berg, and Kross (in press) examines how people's reasoning about moral transgressions is influenced by the closeness of their relationships to the people who committed them. Their results show that, in general, the tendency of people to lie to police officers about whether they witnessed a crime is positively related to the closeness of their relationship to the perpetrator of that crime. That is, their data show that individuals are more likely to lie about whether they witnessed a crime if the perpetrator of the crime is someone to whom they are closely related than if the perpetrator is someone to whom they are only distantly related. Thus, people's reasoning tends not to be impartial. And the more severe the crime, the stronger the tendency. However, self-distancing partly eliminates this effect. More precisely, the authors found that self-distancing reduces people's tendency to lie about severe transgressions that have been committed by close relations. The results provide additional evidence that self-distancing can, at least in certain conditions, increase our tendency to adhere to moral principle. Self-distancing can increase our adherence to a principle of impartiality when reasoning about severe moral transgressions that have been committed by close friends or family members.

Concluding Comments

When we first began to think about the effects of self-distancing on prosocial motivation and conduct, we suspected that the relationship would be relatively simple. Specifically, we predicted that self-distancing would tend to reduce people's natural tendency to exaggerate the value and importance of their own lives and experiences, relative to the lives and experiences of others, and that it would increase their altruistic motivation. And when we first began to think about the relationship between self-distancing and virtue, we had in mind a correspondingly simple conception of virtue. We thought of virtuous motivation as something like altruistic motivation, and we predicted that self-distancing would enhance virtuous motivation, so defined.

Our interdisciplinary collaboration forced us to rethink many of our initial assumptions, definitions, and empirical predictions. It convinced us that the effects of self-distancing are anything but simple—indeed, that they are exceedingly complex and far-reaching. Some effects are, by this point, well documented and relatively well understood. There is clear evidence that self-distancing moderates both positive and negative emotions in a wide range of populations, including healthy and clinical populations, children and adults. It has been found to moderate both positive and negative emotional experiences, as well as to reduce rumination and other maladaptive behavioral patterns. And there is evidence that individuals who self-distance are more likely to recognize the fluidity of their circumstances, to acknowledge the limits of their understanding, and to listen to opposing points of view. All of these findings provide support for the claim that self-distancing enhances prudential reasoning, as Smith understands it.

Recent empirical work has also shown that self-distancing can enhance prosocial conduct in at least some social contexts. These findings lend at least some credibility to our initial prediction that self-distancing can enhance virtuous motivation, understood as altruistic motivation. But our own (ongoing) work suggests that there are at least some social contexts in which self-distancing may actually reduce prosocial conduct and lead individuals to focus more on their own interests, rather than the interests of others. This suggests that the relationship between self-distancing and altruistic motivation is more complex than expected—and thus that the relationship between self-distancing and virtue is more complex and nuanced than we had originally believed. This realization has, in turn, forced us to expand our conception of virtue—that is, to think of virtuous motivation not in terms of altruistic motivation alone, but as a balance of altruistic and prudential considerations. More work is needed to determine when and why self-distancing has the effects that it has, and whether there is sufficient evidence to support Smith's claim that self-distancing can lead individuals to act in a way that properly balances the demands of prudence, justice, and benevolence.

Notes

1. References to *The Theory of Moral Sentiments* are generally by part, section, chapter, and paragraph (e.g., "TMS I.ii.3.4"). For parts that have no section, references are by part, chapter, and paragraph (e.g., "TMS III.1.3).

2. Smith is most likely right about this. There is evidence to support his claim (see Kahneman, Krueger, Schkade, Schwarz, & Stone, 2006).
3. In one of his more memorable passages, Smith writes: "The inscription upon the tomb-stone of the man who had endeavored to mend a tolerable constitution by taking physic; *I was well, I wished to be better; here I am*; may generally be applied with great justness to the distress of disappointed avarice and ambition" (TMS III.3.31).
4. For reviews, see Ayduk and Kross (2010a) and Kross and Ayduk (2011).

References

Ayduk, O., & Kross, E. (2008). Enhancing the pace of recovery: Self-distanced analysis of negative experiences reduces blood pressure reactivity. *Psychological Science, 19*, 229–231.

Ayduk, O., & Kross, E. (2010a). Analyzing negative experiences without ruminating: The role of self-distancing in enabling adaptive self-reflection. *Social and Personality Psychology Compass, 4*, 841–854.

Ayduk, O., & Kross, E. (2010b). From a distance: Implications of spontaneous self-distancing for adaptive self-regulation. *Journal of Personality and Social Psychology, 98*(5), 809–829.

Baltes, P. B., & Smith, J. (2008). The fascination of wisdom: Its nature, ontogeny, and function. *Perspectives on Psychological Science, 3*(1), 56–64.

Basseches, M. (1984). *Dialectical thinking and adult development*. Norwood, NJ: Ablex.

Frankfurt, H. (1971). Freedom of the will and the concept of a person. *The Journal of Philosophy, 68*(1), 5–20.

Griswold, C. L. (1999). *Adam Smith and the virtues of enlightenment*. Cambridge: Cambridge University Press.

Grossmann, I., Brienza, J. P., & Bobocel, D. R. (2017). Wise deliberation sustains cooperation. *Nature Human Behaviour, 1*, 61.

Grossmann, I., & Kross, E. (2014). Exploring Solomon's paradox: Self-distancing eliminates the self-other asymmetry in wise reasoning about close relationships in younger and older adults. *Psychological Science, 25*(8), 1571–1580.

Gruber, H., Harvey, A. G., & Johnson, S. L. (2009). Reflective and ruminative processing of positive emotional memories in bipolar disorder and healthy controls. *Behaviour Research and Therapy, 47*, 697–704.

Kahneman, D., Krueger, A. B., Schkade, D., Schwarz, N., & Stone, A. A. (2006). Would you be happier if you were richer? A focusing illusion. *Science, 312*, 1908–1910.

Kramer, D. (Woodruff, D. S.). (1986). Relativistic and dialectical thought in three adult age-groups. *Human Development, 29*(5), 280–290.

Kross, E., & Ayduk, O. (2008). Facilitating adaptive emotional analysis: Distinguishing distanced-analysis of depressive experiences from immersed-analysis and distraction. *Personality and Social Psychology Bulletin, 34*(7), 924–938.

Kross, E., & Ayduk, O. (2009). Boundary conditions and buffering effects: Does depressive symptomology moderate the effectiveness of distanced-analysis for facilitating adaptive self-reflection? *Journal of Research in Personality, 43*(5), 923–927.

Kross, E., & Ayduk, O. (2011). Making meaning out of negative experiences by self-distancing. *Current Directions in Psychological Science, 20*(3), 187–191.

Kross, E., & Ayduk, O. (2017). Self-distancing: Theory, research, and current directions. *Advances in Experimental Social Psychology*, 55, 81–136.

Kross, E., Ayduk, O., & Mischel, W. (2005). When asking "why" does not hurt distinguishing rumination from reflective processing of negative emotions. *Psychological Science*, 16(9), 709–715.

Kross, E., Duckworth, A. L., Ayduk, O., Tsukayama, E., & Mischel, W. (2011). The effect of self-distancing on adaptive versus maladaptive self-reflection in children. *Emotion*, 11(5), 1032–1039.

Kross, E., Gard, D., Deldin, P., Clifton, J., & Ayduk, O. (2012). "Asking why" from a distance: Its cognitive and emotional consequences for people with major depressive disorder. *Journal of Abnormal Psychology*, 121(3), 559–569.

Kross, E., & Grossmann, I. (2012). Boosting wisdom: Distance from the self enhances wise reasoning, attitudes, and behavior. *Journal of Experimental Social Psychology: General*, 141(1), 43–48.

Mischkowski, D., Kross, E., & Bushman, B. J. (2012). Flies on the wall are less aggressive: Self-distancing "in the heat of the moment" reduces aggressive thoughts, angry feelings and aggressive behavior. *Journal of Experimental Social Psychology*, 48, 1187–1191.

Park, J., Ayduk, O., O'Dennell, L., Chun, J., Gruber, J., Kamali, M., . . . Kross, E. (2014). Regulating the high: Cognitive and neural processes underlying positive emotion regulation in bipolar I disorder. *Clinical Psychological Science*, 2(6), 661–674. https://doi.org/10.1177/2167702614527580

Penner, L. A., Guevarra, D. A., Harper, F. W., Taub, J., Phipps, S., Albrecht, T. L., & Kross, E. (2016). Self-distancing buffers high trait anxious pediatric cancer caregivers against short- and longer-term distress. *Clinical Psychological Science*, 4, 629–640.

Ryan, S. (2012). Wisdom, knowledge, and rationality. *Acta Analytica*, 27(2), 99–112.

Smith, A. (1976 [1790]). *The theory of moral sentiments* (6th ed.). Oxford: Oxford University Press.

Streamer, L., Seerly, M. D., Kondrak, C. L., Lamarche, V. M., & Thomas, S. L. (2017). Not I, but she: The beneficial effects of self-distancing on challenge/threat cardiovascular responses. *Journal of Experimental Social Psychology*, 70, 235–241.

Verduyn, P., Van Mechelen, I., Kross, E., Chezzi, C., & Van Bever, F. (2012). The relationship between self-distancing and the duration of negative and positive emotional experiences in daily life. *Emotion*, 12(6), 1248–1263. https://doi.org/10.1037/a0028289

Weidman, A. C., Sowden, W., Berg, M., & Kross, E. (in press). "Punish or protect? How close relationships shape responses to moral violations. *Personality and Social Psychology Bulletin*.

White, R. E., Kross, E., & Duckworth, A. L. (2015). Spontaneous self-distancing and adaptive self-regulation across adolescence. *Child Development*, 86(4), 1272–1281.

Wisco, B. E., & Nolen-Hoeksema, S. (2011). Effect of visual perspective on memory and interpretation in dysphoria. *Behaviour Research and Therapy*, 49, 406–412.

5 Admiring Moral Exemplars
Sketch of an Ethical Sub-Discipline[1]

Robert Roberts and Michael Spezio

Introduction: The Grammar of Moral Exemplar

We consult exemplars in many contexts: grammar, science, arts, crafts, and professions (see the practice of apprenticeship), among other possibilities. We propose some reflections on the nature of a moral exemplar and the currently rather new sub-discipline of ethics, exemplarism or exemplar studies. Because one of the significant issues in exemplarism is the nature of admiration and its function in the ethical exemplarity relation, we devote a good portion of this chapter to these topics. Then we provide a couple of illustrative anecdotes with commentary, and end by reflecting on community practices that foster the exemplarity relation. The anecdotes, and the inspiration for our particular understanding of the exemplarity relation, come from two communities of reconciliation, l'Arche founded by Jean Vanier and Homeboy Industries founded by Father Gregory Boyle. We want this chapter to be an overview, of sorts, of exemplarism and to propose a few rather particular preliminary points within the new discipline.

Jean Vanier founded the l'Arche communities in 1970 when he invited two men with mental disabilities to live in friendship with him. From that small beginning, l'Arche (French for ark, as in Noah's ark of rescue) has grown to more than 145 communities across the world, in which persons with intellectual disabilities ("Core Members") live in fellowship with neurotypical persons ("Assistants"). Homeboy Industries grew out of Father Gregory Boyle's ministry in the 1980s at Dolores Mission Church in Los Angeles. Its focus is present and former gang members who work side by side with their former enemies in a variety of "industries"— a bakery, a tattoo removal service, a silk screening factory, and various restaurants, as well as educational enterprises—all staffed by the "homies" and spiritually nourished by the engaging words of Father Greg and other leaders in the community. A tee shirt often seen around Homeboy Industries reads, "Nothing stops a bullet like a job." In both l'Arche and Homeboy Industries, the governing image for relationships is that of solidarity in accompaniment involving welcome, celebration, forgiveness, compassion, and the formation of active love, all over an extended period of time.

In the context of ethics, the concept of an exemplar or paradigm has the following grammar:

E is an exemplar of Q for R by way of M.

E is a person or perhaps a community of persons. Q is a (broadly) moral quality or set of qualities of E. R, the recipient of E's moral influence, is the person or community of persons for whom E functions as exemplary. And M is the mode of influence that E's Q has on R in making E an exemplar for R. The concept of exemplarity is thus a fundamentally relational concept (being a relationship between an exemplar and a recipient), but our general grammar of *moral exemplar* leaves unspecified many normative particulars of the relationship.

To explain this grammar in its broadest application—to get a perspicuous representation of the varieties of exemplarity—we must answer the following interconnected and overlapping questions. What kinds of persons function as exemplars? What kinds of persons function as recipients of the influence of an exemplar? In what qualities do exemplars have their influence? And, what are the modes of influence of exemplars on their recipients?

Exemplars

What kinds of persons function as exemplars? The idea of a moral exemplar or paradigm individual brings to mind persons of outstanding moral virtue and wide influence such as Moses, Socrates, Jesus of Nazareth, the Buddha, Mahatma Gandhi, Dorothy Day, Rachel Carson, Mother Teresa, Mairead Mcguire, Wangari Maathai, Nelson Mandela, and Tawakkol Karman. We might call such people canonical paradigm individuals. But they are by no means the only kind of persons who actually function as moral exemplars. More "ordinary" people, the ones we daily rub shoulders with, often function more powerfully as moral exemplars than the canonical ones. This fact would seem to explain, in part, the enormous power of communities (including the family) to form and maintain the moral character of their members. Our present discussion focuses especially on this "ordinary" kind of exemplar, the kind who are present in person to the recipient.

Recipients

What kinds of persons function as recipients of the influence of an exemplar? Apparently, to be susceptible to the moral influence of an exemplar, a recipient needs to be sensitive to the qualities that he or she picks up in (from) the exemplar. The recipient must not only notice (in some sense) the qualities but must also be ready to respond affectively to them—say, to find them attractive or repellant. Susan Wolf (1982) sees moral saints as repellant in certain ways. She can see them this way because she thinks they represent a distortion of the good life. For her, moral saints are negative, or inverse, exemplars—they represent a way of being human *to be avoided*. Her repugnance for them signals them as incongruent with the good as she sees it.

Attraction tends to facilitate a change in the recipient that is congruent with the quality of the exemplar (e.g., imitation of or inspiration by the exemplar), while repulsion facilitates an incongruent change (say, an effort to be unlike the exemplar in a relevant way). This preparation of susceptibility to the exemplar seems to be a matter of the recipient's character: it takes some degree of virtue to be attracted to persons on account of their virtues (say, their readiness to forgive) or repelled by persons on account of their vices (say, vindictiveness), and some vice to be attracted to a person on account of his vices, or repelled on account of virtues. Because most people's character is a mixture of virtuous and vicious traits, most have some attraction to both virtuous and vicious exemplars. These dispositions may be buried or hidden so that the recipient is unaware of them and becomes aware only in the response to the exemplar (say, in feeling admiration for her or him).

The preparation to be susceptible to the virtuous exemplar may also be more or less "subtractive" in the sense that what is needed is an elimination of *obstacles* to moral perception, an absence of moral blinders. Because such openness facilitates moral insight and positive change, we can think of it too as a positive character trait or disposition. Humility in the recipient seems to be a virtue that facilitates the exemplarity relation in this way. On humility as "subtractive" of moral blinders, see Roberts and West (2017), and Roberts and Spezio (2019).

Qualities

In what qualities do broadly moral exemplars have their influence? As our notes on the exemplar and the recipient of the exemplar's influence already suggest, the quality of the exemplar by which she or he influences the recipient will often be a morally significant character trait. This is true of our examples later in this chapter. But morally valenced character traits are not the only morally relevant features of the exemplar to influence a recipient. In our examples, an important feature of the exemplar is his *basic humanity*—what he shares with every other human being. This quality of *being fully human* or *being a person* may shine through something like a virtue, but it is not the same as a virtue. In both of our examples the basic humanity of the exemplar becomes visible through a virtue. The basic "glory" that is partially realized in virtues becomes visible.

Not all people who function as exemplars exemplify the good. We readily pick up bad moral habits of thought, emotion, and action from others who exemplify such conduct, especially if we are "close" to them. And in the class of evil exemplars, there is also a canonical group—such people as Caligula, Nero, Hitler, and Osama bin Laden. On some people, the power of their exemplary influence for evil can be as great as that of Socrates or Jesus on others for good.

But exemplars of vice can serve growth in the good through what we might call "inverse" exemplarity: A friend recently explained why he had lavished time on his two daughters, when they were growing up, by saying that his father had always been unavailable to him. He thus treats his father as in this one respect an inverse exemplar, a warning guidepost in his pursuit of the virtues of fatherhood. But our stress in this paper is on positive exemplars and their influence.

Modes

What are the modes of influence of exemplars on their recipients? Exemplarity in our context is not merely *being an example of* but rather being an example *with a moral effect*. Virtues and vices both may either attract or repel. When virtues attract or vices repel, the moral effect is good; when virtues repel or vices attract, the moral effect is bad. However, we want to make plenty of room for ambivalence about virtue and vice; that may indeed be the default attitudinal position for human beings.

What is the nature of the attraction or repulsion? We follow Linda Zagzebski (2017, Chapter 2) in affirming that a chief form of attraction to an exemplar is admiration, though we think that admiration, where it is an attitude toward a moral exemplar, mediates the exemplarity relationship most effectively when it is "affectionate" and "personal." Optimally, it is the kind of admiration that one has for a friend, a brother, a sister, a father, a mother, a beloved professor. It involves a certain "identification" of the recipient with the exemplar, a sense of kinship. It is the kind of admiration that was on display in the common people of the world at the death of Abraham Lincoln (Miller, 2008, pp. 417–423); they saw and felt him to be "theirs" in a way that members of elites were less inclined to do. Again, the humility of the recipient in recognizing qualities of shared humanity seems to be an important factor.

As to repulsion, Zagzebski writes, though with some hesitation, of contempt as the negative counterpart of admiration (2017, pp. 31, 38–40). Contempt is indeed symmetrical with admiration, but it seems too harsh for many cases, and probably not optimal for moral growth through inverse emulation. Consider the friend who lavished time on his daughters in response to his father's neglect of him. Which negative emotion toward the negative exemplar is most conducive to virtue? Some options other than contempt are anger, resentment, disgust, disappointment, regret, and sorrow. We think that the most promising candidate is an emotion that is only half "negative"—compassion. In compassion, we do feel averse to the condition of the other—something like sorrow or regret. But at the same time compassion is strongly *for and inviting movement toward* the other as a person. So the friend who sought to be unlike his father might have sorrowed for his father and himself for what they missed in his childhood, while adopting an empathic attitude to the father and maybe, in this attitude, even straining to find something to admire in the man. Such an attitude may also sensitize one, by sympathy, to the moral liabilities that the exemplar succumbed to, and thus enhance one's agency vis-à-vis the defect.

Thus, even inverse emulation can involve "identification" with the exemplar. By contrast, contempt, especially if it is of the dismissive variety (Roberts, 2003, pp. 255–256; see also West, 2015), might place the object so low that he can't even function as a warning guidepost. As our examples later in this chapter illustrate, when basic (universal) human nature makes an impression of its glory, the moral effect is of the recipient's kinship with the exemplar, and so plants a seed of affectionate admiration, compassion, forgiveness, or at least indulgence, in the recipient.

Another mode of the influence of an exemplar is that of imparting to a community a pervading spirit or ethos that envelops other members of the community. Such a spirit, ethos, or "culture" builds up a community through its effect on the minds and hearts, and thus on the interactions, of individual members. This kind of influence is perhaps most evident in leaders of communities. One might even say that to be a person whose exemplary influence in a community pervades some sizable part of the community *is* to be de facto a leader, whether or not the exemplar officially occupies a leadership role. Notable contemporary examples of such leader-exemplars are Father Greg Boyle and Jean Vanier, who infuse their communities with a spirit of accompaniment, solidarity, humility, truthfulness, self-giving, celebration, and reconciliation, and by doing so support each of the members to function as exemplar for others. On the low end, it seems that Donald Trump infused his White House (and indeed, the nation he "led") with an ethos of invidious competition, distrust, selfish ambition, egoism, mendacity, and small-minded vindictiveness.

Exemplarism as We Understand It

So far, we've given a very brief sketch of some kinds of topics that belong to a discussion of moral exemplarity. We base our sketch on a proposed grammar of exemplarity. Our chapter belongs to a practice not very much pursued today, a branch of ethical inquiry that might be called exemplarism[2] or, perhaps better, exemplar studies. In our conception of it, this is not a comprehensive ethical theory (compare Zagzebski, 2017, Chapter 1) after the style of utilitarianism, Kantian deontology, or, more recently, the "virtue ethics" of Michael Slote (2001) and Gary Watson (1997). That is, we are not proposing that the idea of an exemplar, or exemplars themselves, provide the unique ultimate foundation for such other features of ethical life as motives for ethical action, evaluation of ethical actions, ethical institutions, ethical judgments, ethical duties, the evaluation of ethical outcomes, and so forth.[3] However, exemplars and exemplarity are interestingly *related to* these other topics, which might well be treated in exemplarism as we conceive it. We think that the mono-foundationalist aspiration that marks modern ethical theories is likely to lead "exemplarist moral theory," as it has led the other foundationalist theories, into the paralytic dead-end of interminable academic debate and distortions of the concepts it examines (see Roberts, 2013, Chapter 1).

We propose instead that exemplar studies be an investigation of an aspect of the moral life, including such topics as the following:

- The nature of the role of exemplars and of the people who play that role
- Whether communities, as well as individuals, can function as moral exemplars, and if they can, whether they are exemplars for individuals or for communities
- The psychology of the person(s) who respond to the exemplar, the "recipient(s)"
- The disciplines and communal contexts that are most conducive to the effects of exemplars on others
- The recipients' mental states and attitudes toward exemplars
- Recipients' relationships with the person(s) who function as exemplars for them
- The moral psychological pre-conditions (character) required for such attitudes
- How such attitudes lead to long-term character change
- How practices involving exemplars are carried on in moral communities like l'Arche and Homeboy Industries
- More generally, the practices involved in intentionally treating persons as exemplars and in resisting the influence of negative exemplars
- Whether there can be mutual exemplarity, in which people function as exemplars for each other
- Other topics involving the concept of an exemplar

Exemplarism in this sense is an essential part of the discipline of moral psychology, both empirical and conceptual, and of philosophical ethics. This chapter sketches provisional comments about such topics.

We'll present cases of admiration and its moral influence from the communities of l'Arche and of Homeboy Industries in which "ordinary" people function as exemplars and objects of admiration.

Admiration's Nature and Functions

Here is a first attempt at characterizing admiration. *Admiration is an appreciative perception of something as remarkably important and good.* In saying *appreciative*, we intend to say that the perceiver takes *pleasure* in what she perceives, and (usually) approves it. The approval may not be all-things-considered; we may admire a person selectively—say, admire her courage and steadfastness without admiring her choice of goals. Thus, admiration is *discriminating*, distinguishing admirable things or aspects of things from ones that are not so admirable. It can therefore be *wise* or *foolish*, or a mixture of the two (wise about some things, foolish about others). Nor need our admiration enjoy *reflective endorsement*. A case of this would be a child's admiration of a parent of whom the child reflectively disapproves (while nevertheless emulating him, perhaps). Children's position as *children* makes for ambivalence if they disapprove of their parents.

Admiration is a type of emotion (Zagzebski, 2017, p. 32). On a plausible understanding of emotions (Roberts, 2003, pp. 141–151), they are based on the specific cares and personal values of the person experiencing the emotion. To care about something is to have *some* understanding of it, and to have a virtuous care about it, that understanding must be of a good quality. Your admiration of woodworking won't be worth much if you have a poor (undiscriminating, inaccurate) understanding of woodworking. Thus, a person who loves woodworking and has a good understanding of what excellence in woodworking is will be more likely to admire fine woodworking than someone who lacks this care (love, interest) and understanding. Similarly, a person's "taste" in human characters and refinement of understanding of excellence in human character will affect which exemplars he or she admires. Thus, some people are better admirers than others, and people may be good admirers of fine woodworking while being only mediocre admirers of fine character (or vice versa).

Since caring about and understanding moral objects is a necessary aspect of virtues such as justice and compassion, the psychological conditions necessary for admiration of exemplars would seem to be similar to the conditions necessary for having these virtues. Some compassion and justice seem to be required for properly admiring exemplars of compassion and justice. A person who utterly lacked the dispositional concerns and understanding basic to compassion and justice would also be incapable of admiring exemplars of these virtues, though she needn't care about and understand them with the same intensity and depth as the exemplar.

The admirer need not have prior awareness of his concern for and understanding of what he admires in an exemplar. Often we are not fully aware of our dispositional concerns or of our understanding of their objects, and discover these only by way of the emotions that indicate them. For example, a person might not realize how much he loves someone or what she "means" to him, but discover his love by the intensity of his "missing" her, or the joy he feels in seeing her again. In the same way, a person might discover, by the admiration with which he perceives an exemplar of compassion, that he values compassion and understands its value. In this way, a person can be surprised by his own admiration, and it may be an avenue of self-discovery.[4]

In saying that the admirer finds the quality *remarkably* important and good, we mean that it impresses him with its supposed importance and goodness. Adam Smith speaks of surprise or astonishment: "For approbation heightened by wonder and surprise, constitutes the sentiment which is properly called admiration, and of which applause is the natural expression" (1976/1783 Part I, Section 1, Chapter 4, 64; see also Descartes, 2015, p. §53). Wonder may be what we are calling the sense of the remarkable, but surprise seems to require that the quality is unexpected. The essential idea here is that the impression is lively, impressive; but we don't think it necessary to admiration that it involve surprise or the unexpected. It need only be to a certain degree striking.

We think, too, that the admirer's sense that what she admires is remarkable doesn't imply a comparison with herself—say, that in admiring someone's wisdom, she sees herself as less wise than the admired one. The human predilection for narcissistic self-preoccupation may make such comparison typical, but admiration itself doesn't require it. Two equally courageous persons may admire each other's courage without underestimating their own, or even thinking about their own. Each appreciates the other's courage as strikingly excellent.

We agree with Zagzebski (2017, pp. 20, 33) that admiration motivates emulation in the sense of imitation without necessarily motivating emulation of any particular aspect of the exemplar's conduct. We can admire an athlete's feat of skill and daring without having any inclination to train for similar feats. Can we admire a *moral* exemplar without wanting to be like her? Common sense might suggest that something like this is possible: we admire her ability and willingness to put herself at social risk for the sake of the community, but don't really want to be like that ourselves. But here we might naturally ask about the nature of this "appreciation" of the exemplar: If we *really* appreciated her, wouldn't we want to be like her? After all, the moral is an arena to which we are *all* called and, as we pointed out previously, the capacity to admire or appreciate a moral exemplar *as* a moral exemplar requires an interest in moral objects similar to that of the admired exemplar. The question *whether* a specifically moral appreciation of an exemplar implies a motive to be like her in the admired respect raises the question how *deep* the recipient's understanding of the admired one and her trait has to be, to count as appreciation. Understanding admits of degrees beyond a threshold, and the question is where the threshold is for appreciation in this context. The fact that common sense might regard the threshold as met while a more critical moral stance would not suggests that the location of the threshold is not very definite, and may vary with interest and context.

We think that explicit efforts to imitate are less important as mediating the moral influence of an admired individual on the admirer than what we call *inspiration*, which has links to the concept of *imitatio*, especially in the Abrahamic traditions (Spezio, 2016) of which l'Arche and Homeboy Industries are representative. Inspiration suggests a breathing-in of the "spirit" of the admired one, an internalization of a kind of paradigm of vision and possibility, even a sort of incorporation of the mind of the admired one into the mind of the admirer. If "incorporation" is too strong, we might say that the mind of the admired one leaves an impression on the mind of the admirer. Note the ambiguity of "impression": we use the word for perception-like mental states—he impressed me as arrogant—but also to speak of a shaping influence: the ancient leaf has left an impression in the shale. In this second sense, the moral exemplar leaves an impression on the moral mind of the recipient. It shapes or forms the recipient, but does so by making an impression in the first sense; it shapes via perception, and that perception is admiration. People we admire tend to influence us; they "flow into" our minds by the conduit of our aroused admiration and love.

This incorporation is at its most beneficial and powerful when the admirer feels loved and accepted by the admired one. That may lead to "imitative" conduct, but the fundamental thing is the "spirit." The apostle Paul speaks of having the mind of Christ. I Corinthians 2.16: "'For who has known the mind of the Lord so as to instruct him?' But we have the mind of Christ." Philippians 2.4: "Let the same mind be in you that was in Christ Jesus.'" Also, historically (and perhaps faintly even today?) "emulate" suggests rivalry (*aemulāri* L. to rival—OED); and this is opposite from admiration as we wish to understand it. Instead, we associate the kind of admiration that mediates moral improvement with *imitatio*, friendship, affection, and the pride of kinship.

We sometimes breathe in the spirit of people we *don't* admire— or do we admire them covertly? If they are our parents, however bad they may be, we look "up" to them, perhaps without realizing it. It can be hard *not* to look up to certain persons, because of their seniority, their appearance, their power, their apparent authority. Also, for better or worse, parents are our caretakers if we are small; we are comprehensively dependent on them. Might our breathing in their spirit be simply a matter of habituation? Their way becomes, in a sense, the only way we "know," without our evaluating them and their way at all? But it seems compelling that *some* evaluation is involved. We may look up to them against our better judgment. If this isn't admiration, it is something similar.

A related emotion type is *respect*. We can respect people without exactly admiring them, but like admiration, respect is a perception that attributes worthiness. So even if the mode of emulation is respect, rather than admiration, and even if the respect is misplaced or misguided, it is a kind of approval through which the spirit of the respected may make and leave an impression in the mental dispositions of the respecter. Because both respect and admiration can go badly wrong, taking objects that are neither admirable nor respectable, proper response to exemplars requires a minimum of prior good character. This is one reason why a good upbringing is important for moral formation; without it we are likely to adopt bad exemplars, or not to adopt the best ones. A similar function is served by intentional communities like l'Arche and Homeboy Industries; they can provide a kind of therapeutic and corrective substitute for a good upbringing. It is also a reason for endorsing explicit moral teaching that will guide away from bad, and toward good, exemplars.

So far, we've talked about admiration from the admirer's side, so to speak. But often, when Jean Vanier speaks of admiration, he is concerned about human beings' interest in *being* admired. What he says about admiration is nevertheless relevant to our topic of admiration as a mode of the exemplar's influence on the recipient, because he marks two very different rationales for desiring to be admired, and the difference between them is crucial to the moral formation that is mediated by admiration. People may have either of two very different interests in being admired, and these correspond to different kinds of admiration. The desire for one of these puts a person at risk of losing his consciousness of being a person:

> Young children are perhaps the only people who are loved for their weakness and vulnerability. Because the baby is loved, he isn't afraid; he doesn't need to hide himself, but is exposed, completely naked in all his vulnerability, and is happy. The mother's love, her tenderness, her sweet words, show the baby who he is: he's precious, he has worth, he is somebody. At the same time, his trust touches the mother's heart, and she learns from him who she is. Then, little by little, the child grows, and he enters the world of the Normal (*la normalité*). He needs to succeed, to get good grades, become an achiever admired in other people's eyes, and so conform to his parents' "wishes." Thus he risks losing his consciousness of being a person, formed in communion and freedom.
> (Vanier, 2011, pp. 76–77)

In this passage, Vanier contrasts the desire to be admired with the desire to be loved. The mother's love for the child involves admiration: to her, he is special and glorious. The desire to be loved, Vanier thinks, is universal in human beings, and is healthy. By contrast, the desire to be admired for achievements arises by way of a certain cultural formation and a certain deprivation, and risks smothering our sense of being a person, accepted and cherished as such, in communion with other persons:

> If that thirst to belong and to be in communion with another is not satisfied, the pain of anguish rises up and with it feelings

of guilt, anger, and hate. . . . All that dirt is hidden away. But with the dirt, the heart itself, the wounded heart craving for communion, is also hidden away. The child can now get on with living, achieving, obtaining success, being admired, seeking independence. Instead of love, the child wants admiration.
(Vanier, 1989, p. 14)

In a similar vein, Adam Smith comments that:

This disposition to admire, and almost to worship, the rich and the powerful, and to despise, or, at least, to neglect persons of poor and mean condition, though necessary both to establish and to maintain the distinction of ranks and the order of society, is, at the same time, the great and most universal cause of the corruption of our moral sentiments. That wealth and greatness are often regarded with the respect and admiration which are due only to wisdom and virtue; and that the contempt, of which vice and folly are the only proper objects, is often most unjustly bestowed upon poverty and weakness, has been the complaint of moralists in all ages.
(Smith, 1976/1783, pp. I.3.3.1, 126)

The person whose inspiration is mediated by this morally truncated admiration, this admiration abstracted from love and communion, undergoes formation, to that extent, in a character belonging to the Normal, that ethos in which nearly all of us are immersed and infected, the "culture" that makes personal value contingent on strength, talent, accomplishments, prominence, and the relative inferiority, in these regards, of many of the others in our social ambience. This is a character to which personal love and communion are alien. Someone immersed in this ethos will conceive his desire to be admired in the way that he admires the successful, the strong, the vengeful, the competitive. He will have become hypersensitive to this kind of admirability and correspondingly blind (see Vanier's "hidden away") to the contrasting kind that we will expound in a moment.

In another work, Vanier cites Aristotle as making the same distinction and suggesting that admiration is sometimes substituted for love:

Aristotle says that when a person does not feel loved, he or she seeks to be admired. To be neither loved nor admired is like

> death. Human beings need the attention of others who appreciate, love, admire, and affirm them. If they do not get this, or if people around them despise them, reject them, fear them, or treat them as though they do not exist, then emptiness, anguish, and depression engulf them. People will do anything to find someone who will affirm them and make them feel valued.
>
> (Vanier, 1997, p. 21)

Vanier goes on to tell about a prisoner who got his sense of worth from being the best car thief in Cleveland. No doubt some of his fellow crooks admired him for this (they may even have treated him as an exemplar of car-thieving excellence, given their affective conception of excellence), and he had a sense that he was admirable. Both the admiration of the fellow crooks and the prisoner's satisfaction in feeling that their admiration affirmed him as a person of worth were misguided, showing that admiration, and the desire to be an object of it, can be false and unworthy. This admiration, and the desire to be an object of it, expresses the valuation characteristic of the tyrannical Normal: the crucial relevance of success, skill, intelligence, productivity, etc., to the worth of persons.

But notice that in the foregoing quotation Vanier mentions admiration, not only in *contrast* to love, but also in a list of the attitudes we need to be made the object of if we are to be whole: "appreciate, love, admire, and affirm." The fact that we *all* need to be admired corresponds to the admiration that we can have for any human being whomsoever. While Vanier most frequently attributes admiration, and the desire for it, to the defective ethos of the Normal that glorifies only strength, success, and power, he does occasionally use "admiration" for an attitude toward what is genuinely good:

> I have met many people in slum areas and in broken situations all over the world who seem wonderfully free, uncluttered by the need for power and human glory. I am in awe of such people, and I love and admire them. There is a presence of God in them, a gentleness, a compassion, a wholeness, and a humility.
>
> (Vanier, 1998, p. 120)

Clearly, in admiring such people, Vanier treats them as exemplars of a truer humanity from which he draws moral inspiration. Both in their virtue and in the basic humanity that shines through it, Vanier perceives with appreciation something that is remarkably important and good. This phrase, from our earlier more abstract discussion of admiration, seems perfectly apt for describing an aspect of love—at least of a kind of love. Perhaps we are not in awe of everyone we love, though maybe we should be, and would be if we properly appreciated what Søren Kierkegaard (1995, pp. 86–89) calls their inner glory.

Kierkegaard uses a couple of analogies to make a point about the epistemic/emotional character of love of neighbor. He likens the actual world to a stage play in which all the characters are dressed in costumes and are playing parts that distinguish them from one another, but these are, of course, only an outer appearance. Underneath, all the actors are just human beings. Similarly, in our life in this world each of us has qualities and roles that differentiate us and give us a relative status vis-à-vis one another. But in eternal truth, this is but an outward appearance. We are all the same before God, and so the person who loves the neighbor in God (God is the "middle term") is able to penetrate the disguise with his spiritual vision. But what he sees is not of neutral value, but "glorious" (89); the eyes of faith are eyes for the "inner glory" (87–88) of the neighbor. Seen in his human glory and without the gradations of value imposed by the ethos of the Normal and expressed in the hollow concept of admiration that is emblematic of the Normal, the ordinary human being—the neighbor—is remarkable in her or his worth and importance. She is worthy of admiration. Here, admiration is not to be contrasted with love, but is an aspect of it.

So we have seen three kinds of admiration, all with a broadly moral import: the admiration that is a part of love and penetrates to the inner glory of the human being, the conditional admiration that belongs to the distorting ethos of "the Normal," and the admiration of outright evil. According to the anthropology that is taught and expressed in the l'Arche and Homeboy communities, only the first of these kinds of admiration achieves truth and genuine humanity. The two examples that follow display epistemic penetration of the cultural "disguise" that hides the glory of the ordinary other's self and so reveals the kinship between self and initially alien other.

Taking Ordinary People as Moral Exemplars: Two Anecdotes

The first example is from a l'Arche community, and is fairly typical for l'Arche. It has seven features that may mark the influence of exemplars: 1) The exemplar in question is not canonical, but a "lowly" person. 2) He clearly evokes admiration. 3) He exemplifies virtues. 4) He exemplifies fundamental humanity, which the recipient "sees" through the experience of admiration. 5) The admiration is of a special kind, infused with personal affection (attachment, love, feeling of friendship or kinship, connection, identification) in response to affection on the part of the exemplar. 6) The recipient responds to the exemplar with self-comparing self-criticism. 7) The recipient's response is prepared by a certain development of virtue and would not have been possible without this preparation that is due in large part to the accompaniment, celebration, and forgiveness at the heart of l'Arche community.

A long-term l'Arche caregiver named Katherine tells of how the person she accompanies models true human life for her and fosters a transformed understanding of herself:

> One of the core members was named Trent. He is blind and emotionally troubled. He was in an institution all his life, since a year old. I had this real love for Trent—a connection with him. I could calm him down, I enjoyed him. One night I was giving him his bath and I was drying off his back. He says, 'You're my friend, right?' I stopped for a minute. What occurred to me is how many people had bathed this man; complete strangers. How many people didn't see this sacred life in front of them, just wanted to get the job done. How many times he had to put up with that. What he's really saying is, 'Can I trust you? Are you safe? Are you my friend?' It occurred to me that this man probably lived through hell. Abuse. People being incredibly insensitive to him. Yet he can love. He can still trust. I could never ask somebody to be my friend. I realized that I was in a transforming moment, knowing that I'm more broken than Trent.
>
> (Reimer, 2009, pp. 53–54)

Compare this with Father Gregory Boyle's comment: "Here is what we seek: a compassion that can stand in awe at what the poor have to carry rather than stand in judgment at how they carry it" (Boyle, 2010, p. 67). What the poor achieve in light of the systemic conditions of economic injustice arrayed against them is admirable. "Awe" here might as well be "admiration" because the object of the emotion is a kind of heroism of the poor, and the attitude in which it is felt is a self-referential humility that says, "I'm sure I could not carry such a load as well as they do."

In this transformative moment of admiration, Katherine is impressed with the excellence of two things: First, Trent's basic humanity, the "sacredness" of his life, his personhood, his full humanity. It seems that many who have "cared" for Trent in the past, including perhaps even Katherine, have not entered into accompaniment with Trent and welcomed Trent to accompany them, and so have not much noticed his full humanity. And second, she sees Trent's virtue: his humility, honesty, authenticity, and openness; his frank and trusting interest in friendship. She turns this reckoning on herself, informing her moral self-assessment. It's a moment of self-criticism, of penitence, of felt "brokenness," of insight into being human, of deep personal encounter and communication.

She acknowledges her shortfall of humility ("I could never ask somebody to be my friend"); yet in doing so she expresses some, or even much, humility. Contrition presupposes humility: Her insight is not likely to come to someone who is thoroughly arrogant, vain, or conceited. Trent's virtue speaks to virtue in Katherine that allows her to scaffold a bit higher, by way of her virtuous admiration of him. Another virtue behind Katherine's admiration is compassion: "It occurred to me that this man probably lived through hell." "Here is what we seek: a compassion that can stand in awe at what the poor have to carry rather than stand in judgment at how they carry it." We can guess that her compassion too grows through this experience with Trent, becoming more empathically insightful into human suffering, and the humanity of this sufferer. And, speaking of preparation for this experience, not to be overlooked is that she's there in the l'Arche community, that she saw fit to undertake, and to persevere in, fellowship with and service to Trent and others, and to welcome others into fellowship and service with and of her. Core Members accompany Assistants as surely as Assistants accompany Core Members.

A second story of epiphany in admiration comes from Father Gregory Boyle's work with gang members in Los Angeles. As in Katherine's epiphany, the perception of remarkableness, the wonder in this admiration of humanity, seems to be enhanced by the apparent prior improbability of seeing the glory, given the outward costume in which the sacred life is clothed. The integration of these aspects evokes something like surprise (see Adam Smith), making the impression lively. But we might suspect that the apparent prior improbability is a function of the deceptive ethos of the Normal.

Boyle tells us that in 2005, First Lady Laura Bush chose Homeboy Industries as the gang intervention program to visit during her Helping America's Youth campaign. Her visit led to an invitation to Father Greg to speak to a conference at Howard University, and to bring three homies with him, after which they were invited to dinner at the White House. Alex, who gives tours to visitors at Homeboy Industries, was one of the three. "Alex is thickly built, in his midtwenties, a handsome guy with tattoos stretching across his neck" (Boyle, 2010, 200). After 37 laser treatments to remove the ones on his chin and forehead, they are fainter than the others. Alex is by no stretch of the imagination a whiz kid, but he has an excellent heart. At the White House dinner:

> The Gold Room holds the buffet. Never in my life have I seen or tasted more exquisite food. I go back three times. Rack of lamb—perfection. A salmon the size of a duffle bag. Pastas, salads. They have these small, white potatoes, cut lengthwise, with a hole carefully bored and filled with caviar garnished with a sprig of chive. I'm standing with Alex as he pops one of those suckers into his mouth. And almost as quickly, with his discretion valve turned off, he spits the potato mess into a napkin and says, "THIS SHIT TASTES NASTY." His volume turns heads, and perhaps it was my imagination, but it sure seems that the Secret Service lunges, ever so slightly, in our direction.
> (Boyle, 2010, p. 204, all caps original)

On the return to L.A., Alex departs for the restroom at the back of the plane and is gone for 45 minutes. Greg asks for an explanation:

> 'Oh,' Alex says, with his signature innocence. 'I was just talkin'' to that lady over there.' I turn around and see a lone flight attendant standing in the back. Alex winces a bit. 'I made her cry. I hope that's okay.' 'Well, Alex,' I brace myself, 'that might depend on what you actually said to her.' 'Weellll,' Alex begins, 'She saw my Homeboy Industries shirt and tattoos and, weellll, she started to ask me a gaaaannng a'questions, so . . .' He pauses with a whiff of embarrassment. 'So, I gave her a tour of the office.' At 34,000 feet, Alex walks this woman through our office. He introduces her to our job developers, explains

our release program, and hands her goggles to watch tattoos being removed. 'And I told her that last night we made history,' he says, with brimming excitement. 'For the first time in the history of this country, three gang members walked into the White House. We had dinner there. . . . I told her the food tasted nasty.' He pauses and gets still. 'And she cried.' I get still myself. 'Well, *mijo*, whaddya 'spect? She just caught a glimpse of ya. She saw that you are somebody. She recognized you . . . as the shape of God's heart. Sometimes people cry when they see that.'

(Boyle, 2010, pp. 204–205)

We're told neither about the flight attendant's preparation for perceiving Alex's humanity nor about the effect the experience had on her going forward. But we think both past and future must have harbored moral vitality and dynamism. Not everyone has the receptivity to initiate a conversation inquiring into the personal life of a large male stranger sporting gang tattoos. For many, that outward appearance would have a blinding effect. The apostle Paul prays that members of the church at Ephesus might have the "eyes of [their] heart illuminated," that God might give them a "spirit of wisdom and revelation, in the knowledge of him" (Ephesians 1.17 & 18). Father Greg's interpretation of what had happened to the flight attendant as Alex gave her that heartfelt tour seems to fit Paul's idea. In that epiphanic moment she sees Alex, and he's the shape of God's heart. The evident gentleness and love of goodness and enthusiasm about the work at Homeboy that Alex displays in his guided tour lights up the eyes of the flight attendant's heart and acquaints her with his deeper identity—in Greg's interpretation, Alex's likeness to God. It is plausible that experiences of admiration like hers have an incremental effect on one's character. They lodge in the memory, making it just a little more likely that the next time she encounters a human being garbed in blinding tokens of alienness, she'll see through them, too.

Does the flight attendant's admiration prompt her to emulation? Does she feel an urge to take Alex as a model for her living? Well, maybe, perhaps in rededicating her own relationships and life to overcoming some long-imagined insurmountable fault, incapability, or despair. The flight attendant need not have seen the detailed content of Alex's very personal, transformative experiences as inviting *imitatio*. It would be enough for her to perceive the possibility for renewal of life and spirit that Alex so clearly communicated to her. Here is Father Greg's comment on the story: "Suddenly, *kinship*—two souls feeling their worth, flight attendant, gang member, 34,000 feet—no daylight separating them." Inspiring her by his humanity, Alex draws her into his fellowship, while she, by her interested listening, draws him into hers; and both feel their humanity in each other's attention. Does she emulate Alex? We can imagine the flight attendant feeling encouraged to be openly enthusiastic in the manner of Alex, but primarily, the transaction is not so much one individual admiring another individual and so imitating him, as of two persons experiencing their common human value through each other's attentive presence.

Practicing Admiration

Like other virtuous activities, the practice of admiration both presupposes and fosters virtuous formation (compare Roberts & Wood, 2007, Chapter 5). For example, the capacity to admire extraordinary truthfulness depends on a capacity to appreciate truthfulness, which in turn depends on a virtuous concern for truth, and thus a fundamental element of truthfulness; but as an appreciative impression of the excellence of a truthful person, admiration also reinforces or even deepens the admirer's truthfulness. Admiration that correctly identifies the admirable also presupposes practical wisdom. Put in Aristotelian terms, the virtue of admiration would consist in the disposition to admire the right persons, in the right respect, for the right reason, to the right degree, contrary to significant obstacles, and so forth (see Aristotle, 1980, pp. 1106b 21–23, 38). Such discrimination requires a degree of wisdom. In both Homeboy and l'Arche and beyond, certain practices *are* practices of admiration because they involve and foster the feeling of admiration. Let us illustrate with a couple of examples.

In l'Arche, people without profound intellectual disabilities live in full human communion (friendship, adopted kinship—common activities like eating together, cleaning together, enjoying entertainments together) with persons who have such disabilities. By virtue of sustained living in a community that intentionally values the core humanity of persons who are typically marginalized by "Normal" social systems, the Assistants often come to appreciate and admire those with disabilities *as persons* and *as virtuous*. This intentional living together, along with a bit of conceptual guidance originating in the thought of Jean Vanier, fosters such appreciation: "So-and-so [Core Member] is a spiritual giant," reported one of the Assistants whom we interviewed. Noting the tone of admiration in her voice, we asked whether she would say that she admires the Core Member, and she answered decisively in the affirmative. And the admiration travels in the other direction as well: those with disabilities come to appreciate that Assistants can be lovable, admirable "human beings" too.

L'Arche has a tradition of celebrating birthdays and milestones (say, the fifth or tenth anniversary of a member's joining the community) by telling stories about the Core Member or Assistant who is being honored. These stories point out the excellences of the member and her or his importance in the community with narrative illustrations. The authors witnessed one such celebration in a US l'Arche community. This intentional ceremony, even ritual, drew attention to the excellences and importance of the individual member. It was a prolonged exercise in admiration. By training attention on the personal excellences of the members one by one, they heighten the mutual appreciation of members of the community, thus binding it together, reminding one another of the beauty of each community member and of the good each one brings. Incidentally, they also remind the community again and again of the traits that it cherishes in its members, and thus the nature of the community.

Homeboy Industries is a physical space located at 130 W. Bruno St., Los Angeles, California, and various nearby locations. Members of the community talk about the "door" (the front door of the main building) through which gang members who want relief from terrors and violence and false understandings of self in relation to others can walk into a different world, a place of indiscriminate welcome, compassion, reconciliation, and mutual caring. The act of walking through the door and of being greeted inside is the first of many acts of cooperation that characterize the daily life and work of Homeboy Industries. Eventually, the gang member who successfully integrates into the new community will find himself working side by side with others who may very well have been his enemies in the other world. The face-to-face and shoulder-to-shoulder proximity, and the activities of co-labor and co-education and playing together that he pursues indoors put him in a position something like that of the flight attendant as she strolled in her imagination on Alex's guided tour. The rival gang tattoos that, on the outside, might have provoked a gunshot from him, become almost invisible as he begins to be able to see, even with eyes of admiration, the virtues and humanity of the people who accompany him.

Our thesis that reliable admiration of exemplars requires virtue in the admirer has an implication for the nature of moral formation by way of admiration. Namely, admiration as an emotion can be only part of the story of moral development. It is a process by which the person who already has some virtue may grow, but it is not the beginning of virtue. A theoretical thesis also seems to follow, namely, that admiration of exemplars cannot be foundational for ethics; it presupposes ethics, so to speak. Morally successful admiration—admiration that picks out and understands what is genuinely admirable—is itself a moral phenomenon, a product of moral formation. Admiration is not conceptually prior to moral concepts, but mature admiration contains and depends on a system of moral distinctions.

Conclusion

Notable results that emerge from the present discussion are these:

In the exemplarity relationship, the excellence that is admired can be not only the virtues, but the basic humanity of the exemplar; thus not only canonical exemplars like Father Gregory Boyle and Jean Vanier, but also "ordinary" people, can be admired as exemplars. This possibility is especially salient and important where cultural externals obscure the humanity of the potential exemplar. Admiration is the central emotion involved in the exemplarity relation, but not all admiration is virtuous; in particular, some admiration mediates the dehumanizing relationship that belongs to the social ethos that Jean Vanier calls "the Normal," and some admiration is of outright evil. We have suggested that inspiration may be a better word than admiration for the mode in which the recipient is morally influenced by the exemplar, and that the most effective admiration involves a sense of belonging with the exemplar, an affectionate sense of kinship. Virtuous admiration presupposes as well as fosters virtues in the admirer; this fact implies that admiration cannot be the unique foundation, either of moral development or of moral concepts.

Notes

1. We are grateful to the Templeton Religion Trust and the Institute for the Study of Human Flourishing at the University of Oklahoma for support that made this chapter possible. The opinions expressed in it are the authors', and not necessarily those of the Templeton Religion Trust.
2. The *Oxford English Dictionary* doesn't support this sense of the word. In fact, the only two senses it endorses are 1) "the theory that things in the world exist as imperfect copies or approximations of abstract or eternally existing patterns or archetypes" and 2) "the doctrine that the atonement of Christ is of value to humanity purely as a moral example." "Exemplarist," according to the OED, just means, of or pertaining to exemplarism in one of these two senses. Linda Zagzebski (2010 and 2017) is responsible for initiating the recent flurry of interest in "exemplarism" and "exemplarist" moral theory.
3. "(1) A *virtue* is a trait we admire in an exemplar. It is a trait that makes a person like that admirable in a certain respect. (2) A *good motive* is a motive we admire in an exemplar. It is a motive of a person like that. (3) A *good end* is a state of affairs that exemplars aim to bring about. It is the state of affairs at which persons like that aim. (4) A *virtuous act* is an admirable act, an act we admire in a person like that. (5) An *admirable life* is a life lived by an exemplar. (6) A *desirable life* (a life of flourishing) is a life desired by an exemplar. (7) A *right act* for person A in some set of circumstances C is what the admirable (more specifically, practically wise) person would take to be most favored by the balance of reasons for A in C. (8) A *duty* in some set of circumstances C is an act an exemplar demands from both herself and others. She would feel guilty if she did not do it, and she would blame others if they do not do it" (Zagzebski, 2017, Chapter 1.5). Zagzebski calls these formulas "definitions." "Like that" is Zagzebski's way of indicating an act of ostention or pointing to a particular person.
4. Thanks to Chris Franklin for raising this issue.

References

Aristotle. (1980). *Nicomachean ethics* (W. D. Ross, Trans. and J. L. Ackrill & J. O. Urmson, Ed. and Revised). Oxford: Oxford University Press.
Boyle, G. (2010). *Tattoos on the heart*. New York, NY: Free Press.
Descartes, R. (2015). *Les passions de l'âme*. Seattle, WA: CreateSpace Independent Publishing Platform.
Kierkegaard, S. (1995). *Works of love* (Howard and E. Hong, Trans). Princeton, NJ: Princeton University Press.
Miller, W. (2008). *President Lincoln: The duty of a statesman*. New York, NY: Alfred A. Knopf.
Reimer, K. (2009). *Living l'arche*. London and New York, NY: Continuum.
Roberts, R. (2003). *Emotions: An essay in aid of moral psychology*. Cambridge: Cambridge University Press.
Roberts, R. (2013). *Emotions in the moral life*. Cambridge, MA: Cambridge University Press.
Roberts, R. (2017). Varieties of virtue ethics. In J. Arthur, D. Carr, & K. Kristjánsson (Eds.), *Varieties of virtue ethics* (pp. 17–34). London: Palgrave Macmillan.

Roberts, R., & Spezio, M. (2019). Self-other concept in humble love. In J. Wright (Ed.), *Humility: Reflections on its nature and function*. Oxford: Oxford University Press.

Roberts, R., & West, R. (2017). Jesus and the virtues of pride. In J. A. Carter & E. C. Gordon (Eds.), *The moral psychology of pride* (pp. 99–121). Lanham, MD: Rowman and Littlefield.

Roberts, R., & Wood, W. J. (2007). *Intellectual virtues: An essay in regulative epistemology*. Oxford: Oxford University Press.

Slote, M. (2001). *Morals from motives*. Oxford: Oxford University Press.

Smith, A. (1976/1783). *The theory of moral sentiments* (E. G. West, Intro.). Indianapolis, IN: Liberty Classics.

Spezio, Michael (2016). Forming identities in grace: Imitatio and habitus as contemporary categories for the sciences of mindfulness and virtue. *Ex Auditu, 32*, 125–141.

Vanier, J. (1989). *Community and growth*. Mahwah, NJ: Paulist Press.

Vanier, J. (1997). *Our journey home* (M. Parham, Trans). London: Hodder and Stoughton.

Vanier, J. (1998). *Becoming human*. Mahwah, NJ: Paulist Press.

Vanier, J. (2011). *Leur regard perce nos ombres*. Paris: Librairie Athème Fayard.

Watson, G. (1997). On the primacy of character. In O. Flanagan & A. Rorty (Eds.), *Identity, character, and morality* (pp. 449–469). Cambridge, MA.: MIT Press.

West, R. (2015). Contempt and the cultivation of character: Two models. *Journal of Religious Ethics, 43*(3), 493–519.

Wolf, S. (1982). Moral saints. *Journal of Philosophy, 79*, 419–439.

Zagzebski, L. (2010) Exemplarist virtue theory. *Metaphilosophy, 41*(1–2), 41–57. https://doi.org/10.1111/j.1467-9973.2009.01627.x

Zagzebski, L. (2017). *Exemplarist moral theory*. Oxford: Oxford University Press.

6 Achieving Deep Integration Across Disciplines
A Process Lens on Investigating Human Flourishing

Christine D. Wilson-Mendenhall, John Dunne, and Paul Condon

Multi-disciplinary collaborations are often challenging. They require an openness and patience that can run counter to the productivity valued in today's society. Under the right conditions, we suggest that deep integration across disciplines is well worth the time-consuming effort. Deep integration can be a powerful path to illuminate assumptions, cultivate insight, and energize change. How does this work? This is not a trivial question. We often focus on products without reflecting on process. Here we turn our attention to process in the hopes that some of what we have learned may be useful to others. We draw on our recent work as part of the Self, Motivation, and Virtue initiative, which focused on flourishing in relationships, to illustrate key considerations for collaborative work through deep integration.

We start by examining prerequisites for deep integration. In our experience, cultivating certain conditions and engaging in a kind of "pre-work" fosters progress during multi-disciplinary collaboration. We are often eager to dig into what we perceive will be most transformative, but it is important to build a foundation that supports this work. We then turn to construct mapping across disciplines. A significant process element that emerged during this phase was addressing disciplinary assumptions that are either overlooked or remain stagnant. Making assumptions explicit in each discipline contributed to generating insights emerging at their intersection. The final section of the chapter examines translation of these insights into an empirical approach, including disciplinary assumptions around the value of particular methods.

Prerequisites for Deep Integration

Research projects emerge in various ways, but in the context of one that involves the deep integration of divergent disciplines, certain prerequisites are essential. The first is so obvious that it could be overlooked: as a research team forms, they must share the conviction that deep integration, despite the time and effort involved, will be worthwhile. And this raises the question of what we mean by that term. In brief, deep integration involves more than simply deploying multiple disciplinary approaches within a research context. Instead, it requires an encounter aimed at transforming its participants in the assumptions, theories, and methods that they bring to their research. This transformation does not occur by the participants gaining expertise in a new discipline; our psychologists did not become experts in Buddhism, nor did our scholar of Buddhist contemplative practices become a psychologist. Deep integration also does not create some new discipline that is a hybrid of the researchers' expertise. Rather, we understand deep integration to involve the emergence of a shared or blended conceptual space that is constituted by the interaction of the explanatory models and methods of our individual disciplines. Within that space, the concrete focus of our research—in our case, flourishing in dyadic romantic relationships—guides the conversation toward the generation of a research agenda, with its hypotheses, methods, and underlying theories. Through that conversation within that shared space, our interactions transform our perspectives in a way that generate novel ideas, hypotheses, methods, and so on. And this is precisely the greatest value of deep integration: that it produces fresh and transformative insights that are otherwise obscured by disciplinary assumptions, histories, and agendas. At the same time, that shared conceptual space is not itself the place to work out the details of research, precisely because it does not constitute some kind of new, hybrid discipline itself. Instead, the fresh insights and novel approaches that emerge in the shared space of deep integration must be translated back into the methods, theories, and literatures of one or more specific disciplines within which the actual research will be conducted.

The conviction that the process just described is worth extra time and effort forms a crucial foundation for a research team to make an attempt at deep integration. Yet we have also identified additional prerequisites that seem to be key ingredients for success. Here, the choice of an appropriate research focus is crucial. Ideally, participants see the topic as having the potential to answer significant questions within their disciplines, and at the same time, they see how their own expertise can contribute concretely to that endeavor. Likewise, for conversations within the integrated space to be effective, no single discipline can play a hegemonic role. In straightforward terms, an atmosphere of mutual trust and respect is a key element in sustaining that shared space.

A shared research focus of keen interest and an atmosphere conducive to deeply integrated collaboration are crucial, yet the research team needs another skill: the capacity to communicate across disciplines. Again, it is not necessary—nor even desirable—for participants to become "experts" in each other's discipline, but some basic knowledge of others' disciplines is essential. In our case, team members have been developing that cross-disciplinary knowledge over several years, in part through earlier collaborations (e.g., Condon, Desbordes, Miller, & DeSteno, 2013; Hasenkamp, Wilson-Mendenhall, Duncan, & Barsalou, 2012; Lutz, Jha, Dunne, & Saron, 2015). And while developing the required cross-disciplinary knowledge need not take several years, it does require some time.

Finally, even with these other ingredients in place, the process of deep integration can collapse under the weight of miscommunication. More specifically, the constructs and terminology of one discipline, if not sufficiently examined, may trigger misunderstandings in another discipline. One example we encountered is the notion of "positive emotion" in psychology. For our scholar of Buddhism, this term was troublesome for two reasons. First, the term "emotion" itself is absent in Buddhist theoretical systems, and it appears to carry cultural assumptions about, for example, the separation of cognition and affect (for a recent discussion drawing on both Buddhism and psychology, see Barrett, 2017). Perhaps more troubling, within positive psychology, a typical list of positive emotions includes pride (Fredrickson, 2001), yet pride is considered to be a *negative* affective state in the usual Buddhist accounts (Thompson & Dreyfus, 2007). To communicate adequately about such a term, our team needed to pause and reflect on the assumptions within our disciplines, and this points to another key element: conversation. Much of the time and effort required for deep integration manifests in an ongoing and often lengthy conversation within the research team's shared conceptual space. We needed some time to work out the implications of a term like "positive emotion," but that process was highly fruitful. In particular, it is the kind of process that often manifests in the mapping of constructs across disciplines—a process that yields precisely the type of fresh insights and novel approaches that make deep integration worthwhile.

Construct Mapping Across Disciplines

Integrating Buddhist philosophy with psychological science to inform theoretical perspectives on virtue and flourishing in relationships formed the first aim of our project. Because constructs are the building blocks of theory, we first identified key constructs in each discipline and then worked to map them onto one another. Where did they converge and diverge? A process theme emerged as we engaged in this work: construct mapping across disciplines reveals assumptions of each discipline that often go unnoticed. To illustrate this theme, we provide examples of assumptions in each discipline. Identifying assumptions supported fully interrogating the conceptual space to develop an integrated framework. We summarize this framework briefly at the end of the section, with further detail available elsewhere (Condon, Dunne, & Wilson-Mendenhall, 2018).

Assumptions in the Psychology Literature

At the turn of the twenty-first century, the positive psychology movement challenged the status quo of focusing on suffering and psychopathology (Seligman & Csikszentmihalyi, 2000; Seligman, Parks, & Steen, 2004). This movement advocates for studying well-being and flourishing as positive functioning beyond the absence of detrimental mental health symptoms. The complimentary focus on psychological well-being set the stage for meaningful new collaborations with the humanities, including Buddhist philosophies of human flourishing (Ekman, Davidson, Ricard, & Alan Wallace, 2005; Wallace & Shapiro, 2006). The assumptions revealed by cross-disciplinary collaboration invite an examination of prevalent psychology constructs with greater nuance.

Core Self Is Essential

Given the unraveling of coherent self-concepts in psychopathology (Cicero, 2017; Cicero, Martin, Becker, & Kerns, 2016), an assumption is that "core self" plays a role in flourishing, including flourishing in relationships. Mapping to constructs in Buddhist accounts, however, suggests that this as an assumption worth interrogating more deeply.

Responsiveness (in Psychology Accounts)

Perceived partner responsiveness is an example of a construct in which this assumption is embedded (Reis, 2007, 2012). Responsiveness involves an intention to understand, validate, and care for the needs and best interests of a partner, and the perception of this intention as responsive by the partner (Reis & Clark, 2013; Reis & Gable, 2015). The first component is *understanding*, which refers to understanding the partner's core self. The second component is *validation*, which refers to respect for or valuing the partner's view of the self. Both of these components are built on the premise of a "core self," which refers to the various values, goals, traits, and attributes that best represent who one is (Reis, 2007). The third component is *caring*, which refers to expressing affection, warmth, and concern for the partner's well-being.

Mapping to Compassion (in Buddhist Accounts)

Compassion is a form of engagement with the world that is focused entirely on relieving others' suffering and ensuring their well-being. Responsiveness and compassion share several characteristics: the intention to understand and care for the needs and best interests of a partner, general positive regard (warmth and concern), and a self-transcending element (i.e., with a focus on another's needs, actions can come at a cost to the self). Divergences, though, highlight the assumption of a "core self." In Buddhist accounts, compassion is understood in the context of wisdom. Wisdom involves realizing that essentialism of a core "self" (and core "other") fosters suffering (Williams, 2008). In various ways, Buddhist philosophers point to the painful nature of experiencing oneself as an autonomous, independent agent, and they promote the benefits—and the philosophical coherence—of experiencing oneself as a contingent person embedded in multiple, overlapping contexts. On this account, one's sense of identity or "self" is highly context sensitive, variable, and capable of being deliberately transformed through various practices. Moreover, this transformation in the sense of identity or self is a key component in leading a life of flourishing, since the tendency to cling to a static, dysfunctional sense of self is considered a primary source of suffering (Gethin, 1998). Thus, Buddhist accounts suggest that "core self" may need to be questioned, not validated. In the integrated framework section, we explore how this could occur compassionately with warmth and concern.

Positive Is Beneficial

A burgeoning literature illustrates instances in which positive emotions and thinking are beneficial (Cohen & Pressman, 2006; Fredrickson, 2001, 2013; Sin & Lyubomirsky, 2009). The field often ascribes to an underlying assumption that positivity—construed primarily in terms of the positive valence of affective states—is a sign of flourishing. This assumption is increasingly being made explicit and context emphasized (Gruber, Mauss, & Tamir, 2011; McNulty & Fincham, 2012; Seligman & Pawelski, 2003). Mapping to Buddhist philosophy encourages this direction and provides hypotheses about the contexts in which positive experiences are beneficial.

Positive Illusions (in Psychology Accounts)

In couples, interpreting a partner's prosocial behavior as indicative of a stable and positive trait is often seen as protective (Gottman, 1998). Further, one account is that positive illusions about one's partner are beneficial for the relationship (Murray, Holmes, & Griffin, 1996b, 2003). Positive illusions refer to seeing one's partner in a more positive light than one's partner sees his or herself. In this perspective, a tight, coherent, evaluatively consistent story about one's partner prevents troubling doubts and thus bolsters relationship satisfaction (Murray et al., 2003).

Mapping to Wisdom (in Buddhist Accounts)

In Buddhist accounts, wisdom is orthogonal to valence; that is, whether it feels positive or negative. Wisdom consists in "seeing things as they are" (Skt., *yathābhūtadarśana*). As an ordinary being, one is said to be caught in the grips of "ignorance" (Skt. *avidyā*), whereby one is deluded about the nature of reality, especially the fixed nature of one's own (and others') identity (Gethin, 1998; Williams, 2008). Wisdom and social construction perspectives in psychology like positive illusions share an emphasis on the constructed nature of mental states, including the "stories" we construct about self, other, and relationships. Further, both perspectives recognize that one cannot have an absolute true story but that, as an ordinary individual (non-Buddha), one needs to construct a story to navigate the world. The two perspectives diverge, however, in how these stories promote flourishing. Whereas psychological theories often focus on content, Buddhist accounts focus on a self-aware stance. Positive illusions are about content: illusions are assumed to be beneficial as long as they are positive, because this positivity prevents troubling doubts. In contrast, Buddhist accounts suggest that one's self-aware stance is most important for well-being—that is, the ability to flexibly see a story as a construction (even when it is positive). Further, flourishing involves exercising wisdom in the context of other-focused compassion. In the integrated framework section, we explore how this manifestation of wisdom may occur in relationships, such that individuals do not become apathetic or distant.

Assumptions in Buddhist Accounts

The integration of Buddhist theories or contemplative techniques into psychology is an ongoing enterprise that dates from at least the early twentieth century (Harrington & Dunne, 2015), if not before (Lopez, 2008). Nevertheless, with some notable exceptions (Dalai Lama XIV Bstan 'dzin rgya mtsho, 2005; Hasenkamp & White, 2017), this exchange has primarily involved the appropriation or examination of Buddhist theories and practices within psychology, rather than an attempt to examine the assumptions of Buddhism from the standpoint of psychology (McMahan, 2008). Our project, however, revealed a number of assumptions in the Buddhist material that we drew upon, and here we point to some key assumptions in two areas: attitudes about dyadic romantic relationships and the approach to individual differences.

Relationships in Buddhist Accounts

Our project drew especially on Buddhist theories and practices as found in the Tibetan traditions, and for these traditions, human relationships are vitally important. For all Tibetan Buddhists, the highest spiritual goals require the cultivation of compassion, and this requires a concrete and authentic relationship with others. Ethical codes for monastics and lay people are also rooted in relationships, in part because the foundation of Buddhist ethics is "non-harm" (Sanskrit, *ahiṃsā* toward living beings (Keown,

2001). Despite this emphasis on relationships, traditional Buddhist authors generally avoid any systematic, theoretical engagement with the topic of romantic relationships, and this is largely due to an emphasis on monasticism as the paradigm of a spiritual life, even in Tibetan Buddhism, where lay practice traditions are robust (G. B. J. Dreyfus, 2003; Powers, 2007). It appears that the underlying assumption here is that romantic relationships are almost inevitably caught up in *saṃsāra*, the ordinary world of suffering, and disentangling oneself from those relationships, as illustrated by the life story of the Buddha himself, is often treated as necessary for the most rapid spiritual advancement (Gethin, 1998).

Attention to Dyadic, But Not Romantic Relationships

The Tibetan traditions in particular do thematize one form of dyadic relationship: the spiritual bond between a teacher and a student. This topic is discussed at length in dozens of works, and in these discussions wisdom and compassion are clearly central to healthy relationships. Nevertheless, while the student-teacher bond clearly involves mutual care, respect, and even love, it is specifically not romantic (Tsong kha pa, 2002). Likewise, it involves an asymmetry of power, with authority placed in the hands of the teacher, that need not typify romantic relationships.

Mapping to Romantic Relationships (in Psychology Accounts)

Romantic relationships are the iconic relationship in many cultures, especially Western cultures. Psychological science indicates that close relationships are instrumental to health and flourishing (Cohen, 2004; Feeney & Collins, 2015; Pietromonaco, Uchino, & Dunkel Schetter, 2013). People who lack social ties or social integration suffer from higher rates of diseases, including cardiovascular disease and cancer (Holt-Lunstad, Smith, & Layton, 2010). This literature suggests that constructs in Buddhist accounts would benefit from further development and grounding in the context of close relationships. People in close relationships inevitably experience conflict, for example (Mischel, Desmet, & Kross, 2006). Interpersonal conflicts of this nature offer a salient cultural context in which to exercise wisdom and compassion.

Buddhist Approach to Individual Differences

In Buddhist accounts, ordinary beings already possess the core constituents of Buddhahood. Thus, becoming a Buddha—the state of maximal flourishing—does not require one to construct or acquire new virtues; instead, one cultivates core human capacities that are already present, if sometimes only to a slight degree, in all humans. The important implication for our project is that wisdom and compassion—capacities that we claim are key ingredients for flourishing in romantic relationships—can be understood as dispositions that are already present in humans (Dunne, 2011, 2015; Ruegg, 1989). This universal claim also comes with a clear recognition that individuals vary in their capacities, and Buddhist traditions generally target practices for certain types of persons so as to develop these capacities most effectively.

Determining Individual Differences in Buddhist Accounts

The notion that individuals vary significantly in their psychological capacities and dispositions is a central part of nearly every Buddhist tradition, and this notion is accompanied by recommendations for different types of philosophies, meditative practices, and lifestyles that are suited to these various personality types. For example, different objects for mindfulness meditation are recommended for persons with different dispositions—the breath, for instance, is recommended as the object for persons who experience a high level of discursive thinking (Gethin, 1998). And methods for determining these differences are also suggested, with details about observing posture, diet, and so on (Buddhaghosa, 1976). While these approaches to assessing differences are robust, they nevertheless take an approach that assumes strict categories separating individuals, without a clear assessment of the degrees of difference within or across categories. In short, the approach, while keenly observational, does not recognize the utility of quantification, whether in the case of observations or other contexts.

Mapping to Individual and Dyadic Differences (in Psychology Accounts)

Quantifying individual differences is recognized as an important endeavor across many fields of psychology. In relationship science, there is a complimentary focus on differences that characterize those in close relationships, at the level of the dyad. It has been shown, for example, that physiological synchrony—the degree to which a physiological signal rises and falls in coordination with a partner's physiological signal—is associated with relationship quality (Levenson & Gottman, 1983; Saxbe & Repetti, 2010). The value of quantifying individual and dyadic differences demonstrated by psychological science inspires further attention to quantifying such differences in compassion and wisdom in Buddhist accounts.

An Integrated Framework

Through the deep integration process of mapping constructs and identifying assumptions, we developed a theoretical framework that bridges Buddhist philosophy and psychological science (Condon et al., 2018). Whereas the balance of wisdom and compassion in Buddhist accounts goes beyond existing constructs in the psychological literature, the context-specific instantiation of wisdom and compassion in close relationships goes beyond discussions in Buddhist accounts.

In this framework, wisdom and compassion facilitate the process of constructing a highly flexible narrative such that a person can engage in the world and in relationships in a manner conducive to flourishing. Compassion helps construct a relational narrative of self and other, even if that narrative is not ultimately real. Meanwhile, wisdom prevents any narrative from becoming fixed and thus a source of suffering when violated. A brief summary of this perspective is provided here. Additional details, including elaborated integration with psychological literature, can be found in Condon et al. (2018).

Buddhist philosophy emphasizes the need to integrate and balance wisdom and compassion. Wisdom consists in "seeing things as they are" (Skt., *yathābhūtadarśana*). A small but crucial step toward wisdom occurs when one experiences one's own thoughts as contingent mental events, rather than objective representations of the world—which we call "dereification" (Lutz et al., 2015). By cultivating wisdom, an ordinary being can come to see that one's sense of autonomous agency and permanence are illusory. Compassion is a form of engagement with the world that is focused entirely on relieving others' suffering and ensuring their happiness.

This other-oriented style of engagement replaces the self-focused engagement of the ordinary being, and along with wisdom, it constitutes the state of Buddhahood. Yet the two alone can pose specific dangers. Wisdom without compassion can lead to apathy in which thoughts are experienced as pointless, even kind thoughts toward others. Compassion without wisdom can lead to suffering if one's concern for another's well-being is attached to a single model of success or well-being, such as a parent's view of success for a child.

Wisdom supports the recognition that one's perception and narrative about self and other are dynamic constructions that represent only a limited aspect of reality. These representations are ultimately a story, or a fiction that aids in the navigation of the world and one's relationships. The story that one holds about another—the traits, attributes, values—ultimately represents only a limited aspect of the other's existence and nature. In a moment of dereification, one recognizes the limited nature of ones' perceptions, and can entertain flexible perceptions of the self and other, dynamically adjusting to the ebb and flow of life and the nature of relationship. Whereas dereification supports the ability to see through stories of the self and other, there is a clear need to adopt some story to function in the world.

Compassion represents the construction of a story that helps dissolve the reified self and promotes a healthier engagement with the world that includes a focus on the needs of others. For example, in secular compassion programs inspired by Buddhism, such as cognitively based compassion training (Reddy et al., 2013), participants learn reason-based arguments that all people seek happiness and all people seek relief from suffering or dissatisfaction. This stance can provide an observer with flexibility to construct a story about another's actions, thereby responding to another with care and lessening the grip of habitual negative reactions. The ability to see the self and another in a more flexible manner through compassion might also give rise to growth within a relationship. Through compassion, an individual could have the courage and resolve to question or challenge a partner while also communicating care. Compassion can also enhance relationship flourishing by leading a partner to construct a narrative of their relationship within a broader community and societal context. Such couples might view their relationship as a foundation that supports engagement in the world and as a means to contribute positively to others more broadly—similar to the process of self-expansion (Aron, Aron, & Smollan, 1992).

Constructing an Empirical Approach

Upon developing an integrated theoretical framework, our project aimed to construct an empirical test. Two deep integration process themes emerged as we translated conceptual development into empirical development. First, we recognized that the precision resulting from interrogated constructs across disciplines needed to translate into measurement. Second, we navigated disciplinary value systems (and assumptions) underlying methodological choices.

Fine-Grained Measurement

Conceptual development revealed that we should carefully consider the precision of our empirical approach. Although Buddhist accounts do not approach empirical data in the same way that scientists do, it is important to acknowledge the rich first-person empirical traditional of observation developed over centuries (G. Dreyfus, 1997; Dunne, 2004). This approach inspired thinking carefully about precision as we pursued designing an empirical study in a traditional Western lab setting.

CONCEPTUAL PRECISION

Our theoretical work highlighted conceptual precision of constructs. A good example is the psychology construct of responsiveness. Self-report measures of responsiveness often integrate caring with components of understanding and validation or average the three components of caring, understanding, and validation (Maisel & Gable, 2009; Reis, Crasta, Rogge, Maniaci, & Carmichael, 2017). The integrated framework described earlier suggests separating these components. For example, it is especially important to separate the caring component from validation and understanding components to address assumptions around core self. Accumulating literature suggests that responsiveness is associated with relationship satisfaction and well-being (Reis & Gable, 2015; Selcuk & Ong, 2013; Selcuk, Stanton, Slatcher, & Ong, 2017), but it is unclear how each component contributes.

METHODOLOGICAL PRECISION

The traditional self-report questionnaires used frequently in psychology are well suited for assessing beliefs, mindsets, and intuitive theories. More recent experience sampling methods (ESM; also referred to as ecological momentary assessment, or EMA) are ideal for studying what people actually experience in everyday life (Conner, Tennen, Fleeson, & Barrett, 2009). This type of measurement is different from traditional self-report in that it assesses experience in the moment, as it is occurring, which removes the bias involved in reflecting across days or weeks. Interestingly, this approach is closer to the first-person methods described in Buddhist accounts, which describe making an observation in the moment instead of sitting back and reflecting (Anālayo, 2003; dBan-phyug-rdo-rje, 2009).

In current implementations of this method, participants are typically sent alerts on a mobile device, which prompt answering questions about what they are experiencing at that moment in time (or in the very recent past) (Christensen, Barrett, Bliss-Moreau, Lebo, & Christensen, 2003). Recent studies demonstrate that socio-emotional patterns captured with this method are related to important mental and physical health outcomes (aan het Rot, Hogenelst, & Schoevers, 2012; Conner & Barrett, 2012). In the relationship literature specifically, choice of methodology is also raising interesting questions. For example, the seminal studies suggesting that positive illusions are associated with relationship satisfaction used traditional self-report methodology (Murray et al., 1996b; Murray, Holmes, & Griffin, 1996a). More recent studies that integrate experience sampling methods are producing more complex, mixed evidence in support of this perspective (Seidman & Burke, 2015).

Integrating Methods

The prevailing approach to design and analysis in psychology is quantitative. In this approach, data are expressed as numbers and thus easily processed and analyzed (by those with the requisite statistical knowledge). This sustains a disciplinary expectation of publishing articles frequently as a demonstration of productivity.

As we continued to engage in deep integration during study design, the humanities perspective called into question taking an exclusively quantitative approach. An example is the design of experience sampling questions. Categories or rating scale(s) are typically provided in response to a question, which are easily transformed into numbers, but can bias how people report on their experience. An alternative is asking people to respond in an open-ended manner (without providing any categories), which makes far fewer assumptions about what people are experiencing. This more unconstrained approach, however, often requires time-intensive coding procedures before any type of quantitative analysis can be attempted. After extended discussion, we ultimately moved forward with a hybrid approach in which we included questions of both types. An example from our project was asking people about how they wanted their partner to feel. Including categories like "cared for" or "understood" only provided positively oriented options, when it is possible that a person wants their partner to feel something more negative, like regret. Because we lacked knowledge about the potential diversity of people's intentions, we decided to keep this question open-ended and unconstrained by categories.

Conclusions

Although deep integration requires more time than disciplinary-specific approaches, we find it to be a fruitful and fulfilling approach that has enhanced our work. The Self, Motivation, and Virtue Project that funded our work is unique in valuing deep integration. Addressing prerequisites, constructing mapping, and constructing an empirical approach were important phases of our process. Engaging in these activities revealed disciplinary assumptions that, when made explicit, supported pursuing novel conceptual and empirical approaches. Perhaps the greatest testament to the process described here is that our team continues to work together.

References

aan het Rot, M., Hogenelst, K., & Schoevers, R. A. (2012). Mood disorders in everyday life: A systematic review of experience sampling and ecological momentary assessment studies. *Clinical Psychology Review*, *32*(6), 510–523. https://doi.org/10.1016/j.cpr.2012.05.007

Anālayo, B. (2003). *Satipaṭṭhāna: The direct path to realization*. Birmingham, AL: Windhorse.

Aron, A., Aron, E. N., & Smollan, D. (1992). Inclusion of other in the self scale and the structure of interpersonal closeness. *Journal of Personality and Social Psychology*, *63*(4), 596–612. https://doi.org/10.1037/0022-3514.63.4.596

Barrett, L. F. (2017). *How emotions are made* (Air Iri OME ed.). London: Macmillan.
Buddhaghosa. (1976). *The path of purification: Visuddhimagga* (B. Ñāṇamoli, Trans.). Berkeley, CA: Shambhala Publications.
Christensen, T. C., Barrett, L. F., Bliss-Moreau, E., Lebo, K., & Christensen, T. C. (2003). A practical guide to experience-sampling procedures. *Journal of Happiness Studies*, 4(1), 53–78. https://doi.org/10.1023/A:1023609306024
Cicero, D. C. (2017). Self-concept clarity and psychopathology. In J. Lodi-Smith & K. G. DeMarree (Eds.), *Self-concept clarity* (pp. 219–242). Cham, Switzerland: Springer. https://doi.org/10.1007/978-3-319-71547-6_12
Cicero, D. C., Martin, E. A., Becker, T. M., & Kerns, J. G. (2016). Decreased self-concept clarity in people with Schizophrenia. *The Journal of Nervous and Mental Disease*, 204(2), 142–147. https://doi.org/10.1097/NMD.0000000000000442
Cohen, S. (2004). Social relationships and health. *American Psychologist*, 59(8), 676–684.
Cohen, S., & Pressman, S. D. (2006). Positive affect and health. *Current Directions in Psychological Science*, 15(3), 122–125. https://doi.org/10.1111/j.0963-7214.2006.00420.x
Condon, P., Desbordes, G., Miller, W. B., & DeSteno, D. (2013). Meditation increases compassionate responses to suffering. *Psychological Science*, 24(10), 2125–2127. https://doi.org/10.1177/0956797613485603
Condon, P., Dunne, J., & Wilson-Mendenhall, C. (2018). Wisdom and compassion: A new perspective on the science of relationships. *Journal of Moral Education*, 48(1), 98–108. https://doi.org/10.1080/03057240.2018.1439828
Conner, T. S., & Barrett, L. F. (2012). Trends in ambulatory self-report: The role of momentary experience in psychosomatic medicine. *Psychosomatic Medicine*, 74(4), 327–337. https://doi.org/10.1097/PSY.0b013e3182546f18
Conner, T. S., Tennen, H., Fleeson, W., & Barrett, L. F. (2009). Experience sampling methods: A modern idiographic approach to personality research. *Social and Personality Psychology Compass*, 3(3), 292–313. https://doi.org/10.1111/j.1751-9004.2009.00170.x
Dalai Lama XIV Bstan 'dzin rgya mtsho. (2005). *The universe in a single atom: The convergence of science and spirituality*. New York, NY: Morgan Road Books.
dBan-phyug-rdo-rje. (2009). *Mahamudra, the ocean of true meaning the profound instructions on coexistent unity, the essence of the ocean of true meaning, and light radiating activity* (H. Havlat, Trans.). Münster: Verl.-Haus Monsenstein und Vannerdat.
Dreyfus, G. B. J. (1997). *Recognizing reality: Dharmakīrti's philosophy and its Tibetan interpretations*. Albany, NY: State University of New York Press.
Dreyfus, G. B. J. (2003). *The sound of two hands clapping: The education of a Tibetan Buddhist monk*. Berkeley, CA: University of California Press.
Dunne, J. D. (2004). *Foundations of Dharmakīrti's philosophy*. Boston, MA: Wisdom Publications.
Dunne, J. D. (2011). Toward an understanding of non-dual mindfulness. *Contemporary Buddhism*, 12, 71–88. https://doi.org/10.1080/14639947.2011.564820
Dunne, J. D. (2015). Buddhist styles of mindfulness: a heuristic approach. In B. D. Ostafin, M. D. Robinson, & B. P. Meier (Eds.), *Handbook of mindfulness and self-regulation* (pp. 251–270). New York, NY: Springer.

Ekman, P., Davidson, R. J., Ricard, M., & Alan Wallace, B. (2005). Buddhist and psychological perspectives on emotions and well-being. *Current Directions in Psychological Science*, 14(2), 59–63. https://doi.org/10.1111/j.0963-7214.2005.00335.x

Feeney, B. C., & Collins, N. L. (2015). A new look at social support: A theoretical perspective on thriving through relationships. *Personality and Social Psychology Review*, 19(2), 113–147. https://doi.org/10.1177/1088868314544222

Fredrickson, B. L. (2001). The role of positive emotions in positive psychology. *The American Psychologist*, 56(3), 218–226.

Fredrickson, B. L. (2013). Positive emotions broaden and build. In *Advances in experimental social psychology* (Vol. 47, pp. 1–53). Oxford: Elsevier. https://doi.org/10.1016/B978-0-12-407236-7.00001-2

Gethin, R. (1998). *The foundations of Buddhism*. New York, NY: Oxford University Press.

Gottman, J. M. (1998). Psychology and the study of marital processes. *Annual Review of Psychology*, 49(1), 169–197. https://doi.org/10.1146/annurev.psych.49.1.169

Gruber, J., Mauss, I. B., & Tamir, M. (2011). A dark side of happiness? How, when, and why happiness is not always good. *Perspectives on Psychological Science*, 6(3), 222–233. https://doi.org/10.1177/1745691611406927

Harrington, A., & Dunne, J. D. (2015). When mindfulness is therapy: Ethical qualms, historical perspectives. *American Psychologist*, 70(7), 621–631. https://doi.org/10.1037/a0039460

Hasenkamp, W., & White, J. R. (Eds.). (2017). *The monastery and the microscope: Conversations with the Dalai Lama on mind, mindfulness, and the nature of reality*. New Haven, CT: Yale University Press.

Hasenkamp, W., Wilson-Mendenhall, C. D., Duncan, E., & Barsalou, L. W. (2012). Mind wandering and attention during focused meditation: A fine-grained temporal analysis of fluctuating cognitive states. *NeuroImage*, 59(1), 750–760. https://doi.org/10.1016/j.neuroimage.2011.07.008

Holt-Lunstad, J., Smith, T. B., & Layton, J. B. (2010). Social relationships and mortality risk: A meta-analytic review. *PLoS Medicine*, 7(7), e1000316. https://doi.org/10.1371/journal.pmed.1000316

Keown, D. (2001). *The nature of Buddhist ethics*. Basingstoke: Palgrave Macmillan.

Levenson, R. W., & Gottman, J. M. (1983). Marital interaction: Physiological linkage and affective exchange. *Journal of Personality and Social Psychology*, 45(3), 587–597.

Lopez, D. (2008). *Buddhism & science: a guide for the perplexed*. Chicago, IL: University of Chicago Press.

Lutz, A., Jha, A. P., Dunne, J. D., & Saron, C. D. (2015). Investigating the phenomenological matrix of mindfulness-related practices from a neurocognitive perspective. *The American Psychologist*, 70(7), 632–658. https://doi.org/10.1037/a0039585

Maisel, N. C., & Gable, S. L. (2009). The paradox of received social support: The importance of responsiveness. *Psychological Science*, 20(8), 928–932. https://doi.org/10.1111/j.1467-9280.2009.02388.x

McMahan, D. L. (2008). *The making of Buddhist modernism*. New York, NY: Oxford University Press.

McNulty, J. K., & Fincham, F. D. (2012). Beyond positive psychology? Toward a contextual view of psychological processes and well-being. *The American Psychologist*, 67(2), 101–110. https://doi.org/10.1037/a0024572

Mischel, W., Desmet, A. L., & Kross, E. (2006). Self-regulation in the service of conflict resolution. In M. Deutsch, P. Coleman, & E. Marcus (Eds.), *The handbook of conflict resolution: Theory and practice*. San Francisco, CA: Jossey-Bass.

Murray, S. L., Holmes, J. G., & Griffin, D. W. (1996a). The benefits of positive illusions: Idealization and the construction of satisfaction in close relationships. *Journal of Personality and Social Psychology*, 70, 79–98.

Murray, S. L., Holmes, J. G., & Griffin, D. W. (1996b). The self-fulfilling nature of positive illusions in romantic relationships: Love is not blind, but prescient. *Journal of Personality and Social Psychology*, 71(6), 1155–1180. https://doi.org/10.1037/0022-3514.71.6.1155

Murray, S. L., Holmes, J. G., & Griffin, D. W. (2003). Reflections on the self-fulfilling effects of positive illusions. *Psychological Inquiry*, 14(3/4), 289–295.

Pietromonaco, P. R., Uchino, B., & Dunkel Schetter, C. (2013). Close relationship processes and health: Implications of attachment theory for health and disease. *Health Psychology: Official Journal of the Division of Health Psychology, American Psychological Association*, 32(5), 499–513. https://doi.org/10.1037/a0029349

Powers, J. (2007). *Introduction to Tibetan Buddhism* (Revised ed.). Ithaca, NY: Snow Lion.

Reddy, S. D., Negi, L. T., Dodson-Lavelle, B., Silva, B. O., Pace, T. W. W., Cole, S. P., . . . Craighead, L. W. (2013). Cognitive-based compassion training: A promising prevention strategy for at-risk adolescents. *Journal of Child and Family Studies*, 22(2), 219–230. https://doi.org/10.1007/s10826-012-9571-7

Reis, H. T. (2007). Steps toward the ripening of relationship science. *Personal Relationships*, 14(1), 1–23. https://doi.org/10.1111/j.1475-6811.2006.00139.x

Reis, H. T. (2012). Perceived partner responsiveness as an organizing theme for the study of relationships and well-being. In L. Campbell & T. J. Loving (Eds.), *Interdisciplinary research on close relationships: The case for integration* (pp. 27–52). Washington, DC: American Psychological Association. https://doi.org/10.1037/13486-002

Reis, H. T., & Clark, M. S. (2013). Responsiveness. In J. Simpson & L. Campbell (Eds.), *The Oxford handbook of close relationships* (pp. 400–423). New York, NY: Oxford University Press. Retrieved from www.oxfordhandbooks.com/view/10.1093/oxfordhb/9780195398694.001.0001/oxfordhb-9780195398694-e-018

Reis, H. T., Crasta, D., Rogge, R. D., Maniaci, M. R., & Carmichael, C. L. (2017). Perceived Partner Responsiveness Scale (PPRS). In D. L. Worthington & G. D. Bodie (Eds.), *The sourcebook of listening research* (pp. 516–521). Hoboken, NJ: John Wiley & Sons, Inc. https://doi.org/10.1002/9781119102991.ch57

Reis, H. T., & Gable, S. L. (2015). Responsiveness. *Current Opinion in Psychology*, 1, 67–71. https://doi.org/10.1016/j.copsyc.2015.01.001

Ruegg, D. (1989). *Buddha-nature, mind and the problem of gradualism in a comparative perspective : On the transmission and reception of Buddhism in India and Tibet*. London: School of Oriental and African Studies.

Saxbe, D., & Repetti, R. L. (2010). For better or worse? Coregulation of couples' cortisol levels and mood states. *Journal of Personality and Social Psychology*, 98(1), 92–103. https://doi.org/10.1037/a0016959

Seidman, G., & Burke, C. T. (2015). Partner enhancement versus verification and emotional responses to daily conflict. *Journal of Social and Personal Relationships*, 32(3), 304–329. https://doi.org/10.1177/0265407514533227

Selcuk, E., & Ong, A. D. (2013). Perceived partner responsiveness moderates the association between received emotional support and all-cause mortality. *Health Psychology: Official Journal of the Division of Health Psychology, American Psychological Association*, 32(2), 231–235. https://doi.org/10.1037/a0028276

Selcuk, E., Stanton, S. C. E., Slatcher, R. B., & Ong, A. D. (2017). Perceived partner responsiveness predicts better sleep quality through lower anxiety. *Social Psychological and Personality Science*, 8(1), 83–92. https://doi.org/10.1177/1948550616662128

Seligman, M. E. P., & Csikszentmihalyi, M. (2000). Positive psychology: An introduction. *American Psychologist*, 55(1), 5–14. https://doi.org/10.1037//0003-066X.55.1.5

Seligman, M. E. P., Parks, A. C., & Steen, T. (2004). A balanced psychology and a full life. *Philosophical Transactions of the Royal Society B: Biological Sciences*, 359(1449), 1379–1381. https://doi.org/10.1098/rstb.2004.1513

Seligman, M. E. P., & Pawelski, J. O. (2003). Positive psychology: FAQs. *Psychological Inquiry*, 14(2), 159–163.

Sin, N. L., & Lyubomirsky, S. (2009). Enhancing well-being and alleviating depressive symptoms with positive psychology interventions: A practice-friendly meta-analysis. *Journal of Clinical Psychology*, 65(5), 467–487. https://doi.org/10.1002/jclp.20593

Thompson, E., & Dreyfus, G. (2007). Asian perspectives: Indian theories of mind. In P. D. Zelazo, M. Moscovitch, & E. Thompson (Eds.), *The Cambridge handbook of consciousness* (1st ed., pp. 89–113). Cambridge: Cambridge University Press.

Tsong kha pa. (2002). *The great Treatise on the stages of the path to enlightenment* (1st ed., Vol. 3). Ithaca, NY: Snow Lion Publications.

Wallace, B. A., & Shapiro, S. L. (2006). Mental balance and well-being: Building bridges between Buddhism and Western psychology. *The American Psychologist*, 61(7), 690–701. https://doi.org/10.1037/0003-066X.61.7.690

Williams, P. (2008). *Mahāyāna Buddhism: The doctrinal foundations* (2nd ed.). London and New York, NY: Routledge.

7 Toward an Integrated Psychology and Philosophy of Good Life Stories

Jack J. Bauer and Peggy DesAutels

Our aim for this interdisciplinary project was to derive and to advance an empirically grounded, normative theory of virtuous self-development. Virtue theory since Aristotle has been steeped in idealistic notions of virtues. Yet personal virtues emerge within actual persons, developing as those people live their lives in social contexts, which are generally not ideal. Social conditions may facilitate or thwart particular individuals' capacities to enact virtues, depending on, for instance, whether one is a member of a privileged or marginalized group in society. We began this project with the aim of seeking principles that underlie both the facilitation and thwarting of virtues in people's lives. We sought to build a path between the peaks and valleys of virtue and vice, tying life in the clouds to life on the ground, to construct a model of virtuous self-development from the ground up.

To do this, we designed a study featuring people's life stories. Life stories reveal how people construct meaning and self-identity in their lives (McAdams, 2008a). These meanings and identities rest on cultural virtues and notions of a good life (Taylor, 1989). Virtues serve as themes in people's life stories, not only motivating people's broad contours of action in life but also providing the basis for people's evaluations of their own lives in light of cultural ideals. In other words, we sought to investigate how people attempt to construct a good life story, all within the non-ideal contexts of living in a contingent social world.

Our Approach to Self, Motivation, and Virtue

Our project has offered an opportunity to combine the central questions of our lives' work on the psychology of eudaimonic self-development (Bauer, 2016) and the philosophy of non-idealized virtue ethics (DesAutels, 2016). Our primary investigative approaches emphasize narrative psychology and feminist philosophy. People's life stories and other personal narratives open a window to the empirical study of self, motivation, and virtue (McAdams, 1993; Taylor, 1989). Narratives also allow for an examination of lives in context—a longtime aim of feminist philosophers and psychologists (Chodorow, 1978; Gilligan, 1982; Nelson, 2001). Furthermore, master narratives guide social groups—from families to cultures—presenting individual members with ideal models of a good or virtuous life (McLean & Syed, 2016). Feminist scholars demonstrate how contemporary societies systematically present barriers to women's capabilities to live out many of those cultural ideals (Nussbaum, 2000; Tessman, 2005). With all this as our foundation, we designed a research project and defined terms that could contribute to our respective fields of psychology and philosophy—and integrated the methods and concepts of both fields (Nicolescu, 2007).

This project addresses the constructs of self, motivation, and virtue in a tradition of those philosophers and psychologists looking to scientific methods to arrive at a psychologically plausible understanding of normative ethics (e.g., Bauer & McAdams, 2010; Colby & Damon, 1992; DesAutels, 2012; Flanagan, 1991, 2007; Haybron, 2008; Kristjánsson, 2010; Nussbaum, 2000; Ryan & Deci, 2001; Snow, 2008; Tiberius, 2008; Waterman, 2013). We integrate two approaches to virtue that emphasized its inherent ties to self and motivation: the narrative self (in psychology, see McAdams, 1993; in philosophy, see Taylor, 1989) and eudaimonia (philosophy—Flanagan, 2007; psychology—Ryan & Deci, 2001), both situated within a culturally embedded, developmental framework (psychology—Erikson, 1950; philosophy—Nussbaum, 2000). Our project extends a model of eudaimonic growth, a dynamic process in which motivations for eudaimonic virtues (e.g., care, wisdom, self-actualizing) serve as themes of the narrative self (Bauer, 2016), grounded in an everyday world of social hierarchies that place limits on living out those virtues for oppressed groups (DesAutels, 2016). We use philosophical and psychological definitions and methods to inform each other (e.g., Nicolescu, 2007; Sripada & Konrath, 2011).

Virtue and Personhood

We take the position that both the study of virtue ethics and its situationist critique have focused on virtues in too abstract a manner.

Virtue ethics in philosophy and its counterparts in psychology tend to overemphasize the power of personality traits in predicting actual, virtuous behavior (Doris, 2002; Haidt, 2012). Likewise, situationist ethics tends to underemphasize the deeper aspects of personhood (such as meaningful motives and narrative self-identity), the person's longer-term development, and broader contexts of social institutions and culture (Narvaez, 2010; Snow, 2008). We maintain that our narrative model and methods are situated at the intersection of these concerns and are poised to advance the study of virtuous motives and self-development.

We approach virtues on three levels of personality, as in McAdams's personological model of personality (1995, 2013): the actor, the agent, and the author. At the level of the person as *actor* we find broad, dispositional *traits*, such as the Big Five traits of extraversion and neuroticism. Traits (as a technical term in this model) refer to highly generalized characteristics of the person, abstracted from specific contexts in life. To know a person's traits, we do not need to know much about how the person views the self subjectively. We just need to observe them and can infer their traits in as little as a few minutes (Tackett, Herzhoff, Kushner, & Rule, 2016). For example, the trait of openness to experience correlates with out-group tolerance (Sibley & Duckitt, 2008) and with—and is part of—wisdom (Staudinger & Glück, 2011). But openness to experience only begins to explain how virtues like tolerance and wisdom work in people's lives.

At the level of the *agent* we have *characteristic adaptations*, which include motives, personal values, and ego defenses. Characteristic adaptations are inherently more subjective—or "deeper"—than traits; they are largely known by knowing the person's views, not by merely observing the surface of their actions. At this level we find virtues—or at least virtues as individuals subjectively conceptualize them in their lives. At this level, personally valued virtues serve as motives of the subjective self, such as agentic motives for learning and wisdom or communal motives for care and compassion. Like traits, virtues at this level are abstracted from real-life contexts; virtues at this level refer to general tendencies to be motivated by particular virtues, as when virtues for fairness or care serve as characteristic motives for a person (on virtue-relevant, dispositional motives, see Fleeson & Jayawickreme, 2015; on dispositional virtues specifically, see Graham et al., 2011). However, to understand how virtues function more concretely in their real-life contexts, we turn to the study of stories from people's lives.

At the level of the *author*, *life stories* convey information about how the person creates a meaningful understanding of self over time—a narrative self. Notably, the narrative self ties abstract personal values (and virtues) to the concrete, lived events and people in one's life. Virtues are no longer viewed as traits or even as abstract motives, but rather as *contextualized* motives, bound to the actual actions and persons in one's life. We elaborate on the narrative self later, after describing our study's methods. But for now it is important to note that particular measures of traits, characteristic adaptations, and life stories do correlate with one another, but the narrative self is no mere byproduct of traits or motives, either conceptually (McAdams, 1995) or empirically (Adler, Lodi-Smith, Philippe, & Houle, 2016). In other words, if we know that a person is prone toward virtuous thoughts, feelings, or behavior (at the level of the actor), we still have no idea whether that person values a virtue in the abstract (at the level of the agent), much less how the person applies—or might be able to apply—the concept of that virtue (as a narrative theme—Bauer, 2016) to his or her lived events to interpret that action as meaningful (at the level of the author). It's one thing to say you value this or that virtue; it's another thing to incorporate a virtue into your routine interpretations of actual, lived events as meaningful.

The three levels of personality function within a social ecology (McAdams, 2013). We are especially interested in the development of virtues under conditions of oppression, particularly with regard to women's development in patriarchal societies (e.g., Nussbaum, 2000). When a culture values a set of virtues but places systematic impediments to enacting them, whether through politics or social norms, those virtues are "burdened virtues" (Tessman, 2005). Those individuals who experience and resist oppression are burdened because their freedoms to enact the virtues of their culture are hindered by that very culture via limited access to material resources, political power, and social standing. To make matters worse, additional psychological and moral burdens are leveled on those who resist power, particularly those who are the whistleblowers—those who call out the abuse, harassment, or neglect by those who have organizational power over those in positions of relatively less power (DesAutels, 2009).

Empirical Method

The project centered on interviews of 100 adults' life stories and a subset of their families' stories. The life stories and family stories featured some of the most personally meaningful events in their lives. Interviewees' ages range from 25 to 88, the vast majority being in mid-life. Life story interviews lasted approximately two hours. Family story interviews lasted approximately one and a half hours. Interviews were conducted via Skype, and audio recordings were transcribed.

The life story interview was modified from that of McAdams (2008b) to address the topic of virtue development. Questions were organized into five sections (A-E), with 20 questions total. *Section A: Life Chapters* asked interviewees to think of their life in chapters, to give each chapter a name, and to briefly describe each one. *Section B: Key Scenes* included seven episodes in the person's life—discrete events that happened on a particular day in a particular place. The episodes were, in order: high point in life, low point, turning point, major life decision in work, major life decision in relationships, an insight or realization event, and a gender event. *Section C: Life Challenges* included four questions: the most significant challenge that the interviewee has faced in his or her life, a significant interpersonal loss, a gender-based life challenge, and a social-justice challenge. *Section D: Personal Values and Beliefs* included three questions: a personal role model, religious or spiritual views, and political or social views. *Section E: Personal Development* included five questions: one's becoming oneself within one's family environment, a personal vice or weakness, a personal virtue or strength, a personal growth project in life, and a major life theme as a wrap-up question.

The family story interview had six questions modified from that of McLean (2015). Families were interviewed as a group, with two to four family members each. The questions were: (1) enjoyable family event, (2) difficult family event, (3) turning point for the family, (4) becoming yourself in this family, (5) gender in the family, and (6) a family theme or characteristic.

In addition to the interviews, participants completed an online survey with numerous measures of self, motivations, virtues, and other characteristics of personality and family. This method allows for the qualitative and quantitative study of how people's interpretations of self, motives, and virtues correspond to how their lives have turned out, particularly in non-ideal circumstances. Even in the most comfortable of circumstances, life presents detours and road blocks to the pursuit of virtues, with barriers such as gendered norms, illness, and the perpetual conflicts and balancing acts tied to love and work. In the following sections we examine the theoretical framework of our study, illustrated by excerpts from the life and family stories.

The Narrative Self

Self-narration is how people tie their actions to personal and cultural virtues (Taylor, 1989). In their life stories, people use cultural concepts of virtue not only to explain what they value and identify with but also to explain why they did this-or-that action. In other words, people view cultural values as motives in their lives, and these values serve as themes in their life stories (McAdams, 1993). In doing so, people use concepts of eudaimonic virtues such as wisdom and care as life-story themes to evaluate themselves and to plan their lives (Bauer, 2016). In other words, the narrative self contains motivational themes of virtue.

As in past research (e.g., Bauer, McAdams, & Sakaeda, 2005b), individual participants in our study featured different types and degrees of virtuous themes in their life stories. We focused on two broad themes of virtue: reflective growth themes, which have been shown to predict the more intellectual features of wisdom, and experiential growth themes, which have been shown to predict more socio-emotional concerns such as a sense of meaningfulness and well-being (reviewed in Bauer, King, & Steger, in press). Reflective growth themes focus on motives for learning and perspective-taking, whereas experiential growth themes focus on personally meaningful activities and relationships—eudaimonic, humanistic concerns, rather than egoistic or materialistic concerns for social status and appearances. The cultural ideal of self-actualization combines the themes of reflective and experiential growth (Bauer, Schwab, & McAdams, 2011). We see this ideal in the literary genre of the Bildungsroman, or character development story, where the protagonist struggles against mainstream values of conformity and materialism to forge an existentially authentic life (e.g., Guignon, 2004) of his or her own. The Bildungsroman serves as a cultural master narrative for eudaimonic growth (Bauer, 2016).

As an example of both kinds of growth themes in a story of self-actualization, one woman in her 40s talked about becoming a motivational speaker, traveling the world as a corporate personal trainer, which combined her passions for theater and helping others:

I saw a motivational speaker [. . .] I said, 'That's what I want to do.' [. . .] So I got to be on stage. But it's not [just that I was] the center of attention. I got to help people [figure out] their core values [. . .] Sometimes I changed lives [. . .] They were able to change their career paths.

This life story features several themes of experiential growth, such as pursuing a personally meaningful career and personally meaningful relationships, and making contributions to society (Bauer, 2016). The foregoing excerpt also hints at a form of reflective growth that involves examining and exploring one's deeper values in life. Elsewhere this participant's life story features themes of personally meaningful engagement with others (experiential growth) and of critical reflection on personal values and cultural expectations and ideals (reflective growth).

As another example, a man in his 50s said he left his small town, "like George Bailey wanted to do," saying:

It was hard to do. [I] was part of something [. . .] but I wanted to see the world [and] learn everything I could [. . .] But it was also an escape from [relationships]. 'Relationship' was code for 'conflict.' [. . .] I challenged myself to learn about my emotions [and] to accept myself.

This participant essentially explained the difficulties of pursuing ideals for eudaimonic growth within the real-life conflicts of life with others. Later in the interview, responding to a question on role models, this participant said, "No one's heroes should appear flawless," arguing that cultural ideals of perfection have little to do with people's actualities as they try to live a good life.

The Social Ecology of Virtues

While individuals and cultures may value wisdom and happiness, cultures will also impose limitations or extra burdens on certain classes of individuals who try to live them out, as when women wish to pursue a fulfilling career but are hampered by the gender-disproportionate assumption that they should care for family members (e.g., Bauer & DesAutels, in press). To examine this concern, we start by considering that individuals develop within various contexts and levels of a social ecology, which can be represented in concentric rings of systems (Bronfenbrenner, 1979). Rings expand outward from the ring of the *individual person* (which is a system in itself) to the *microsystem* (which includes groups such as the family and peers and everyday activities), the *exosystem* (which includes social institutions such as government, education, commerce, and religion), and finally the *macrosystem* (which includes cultural values, ideologies, and attitudes).

Macrosystem: Cultural Master Narratives

From a narrative perspective, cultural values and virtues are constructed and reconstructed over history through *cultural master narratives* (Hammack, 2011; Nelson, 2001; Thorne, 2004). These master narratives come in the form of culturally sanctioned stories in literature, religion, politics, and other social institutions. As with cultural mythologies, one of the functions of master narratives is to instruct an individual on how to live a good life (Campbell, 1973). One such master narrative, particularly in America, is of personal progress, which Nisbet (1980) traces to the ancient Greek notion of natural, organismic growth and to the ancient Jewish notion of the necessity of human flourishing. The cultural master narrative of redemption has roots in personal progress (McAdams, 2006). The Bildungsroman genre of literature—of character development, of coming-of-age or personal growth—is perhaps the greatest example of a cultural master narrative of eudaimonic growth (Bauer, 2016; Jeffers, 2005). These master narratives and their virtues, while culturally constructed, also reflect deep structures of value that are embedded evolutionarily in humans, such as norms of group participation, long before a modern sense of self had evolved (Boyd, 2013; Montoya & Pittinsky, 2013; Narvaez, 2013).

Individuals draw on these master narratives—notably their themes of virtue—to construct their own life stories and thus to shape the very meanings of their lives. Recently we (Bauer & DesAutels, in press) demonstrated how two women built their life stories upon a foundation of the virtue of care, and more specifically, upon a cultural master narrative of generativity and redemption (McAdams, 2006). Generativity involves one's contributing to the welfare of future generations (Erikson, 1950), whereas redemption involves a change from bad to good (e.g., rags to riches, sin to salvation, ignorance to enlightenment, sickness to health). Generativity served as a dominant theme for both women. For example, one woman in her 40s described her role in parenting children of a minority ethnicity in the US (this and the following two excerpts come from Bauer & DesAutels, in press):

> [My] kids [. . .] know that I will fight for them [. . .] and that I'm a very good advocate. And when I have seen injustice in their lives [. . .] I have made [people] re-think their decisions based on what I thought were discriminatory policies and practices that were impacting my kids. So then I've been successful on every front because I'm tenacious.

Here we see generativity in both a family context (concern for the welfare of her children) and a societal context (ethnic discrimination). However, generativity was not the only theme. Both women's life stories feature the virtue of self-actualization, notably where their paths to self-actualization had been detoured or blocked by life circumstances (illness, family problems) that forced them (and not the various men in their lives) to care for others at the expense of pursuing their own dreams. Such a scenario is the cultural expectation (and a master narrative) for women as caregivers (Tronto, 1993). For example, one woman, in her early 60s, described her caring for a sister with dementia in relation to forging a life of her own:

> But when my [older] sister got sick [. . .] everybody but my youngest sister [who was in high school] was married [. . .] I was the only one at that point who wasn't tied down with family and young kids [. . .] so I went and stayed with her. And that's been probably the most defining moment of my life up to that point. [. . .] I was 41. So it was the biggest thing. And so to look at getting married and having kids, it was not going to happen for me.

Despite such a major overhaul of her dreams and plans, she had repeated "redemption sequences" across the various stories in her life. As she said, "A door closes and another door opens." As a specific example:

> Well, when I was 30 I [. . .] almost got married. And we were together for about two and a half years. I found him cheating

on me [. . .] And I don't know if he was threatened by me going back to school or what was going on, but we had kind of grown apart. So it was really . . . it was a quick decision to break up because he was cheating on me, but it had been oncoming for several months [. . .] And it turns out it was a blessing in disguise.

The interpretation of one's life stories in terms of redemption not only reflects resilience but also correlates empirically with themes of generativity (McAdams & Guo, 2015).

Exosystem: Social Institutions and Non-Idealized Eudaimonic Growth

The capacity for a culture's social institutions to facilitate or thwart eudaimonic growth is considerable. Consider that social institutions (e.g., workplaces, churches or synagogues, community organizations) provide many of the activities that form the concrete, behavioral core of life stories and family stories. Social institutions and their activities are predicated on cultural values, which can enable or constrain the individual's eudaimonic growth (DesAutels & Walker, 2004; DesAutels & Whisnant, 2007). By interpreting those activities in terms of values, a life story inherently reflects how cultural values (the macrosystem) are filtered through social institutions (exosystem) to influence both family stories (microsystem) and the individual's own, value-laden self-identity.

Social institutions are typically structured hierarchically with a powerful few individuals having coercive control over the many or with one group-based identity having privileged status within these institutions. Institutions that perpetuate unjust social, political, and economic inequalities systematically advantage and exploit those who are vulnerable and powerless (Tessman, 2001). In addition, there is a significant risk that social institutions perpetuate and sustain particular individuals who abuse power in ways that significantly stunt the eudaimonic growth of those they abuse (DesAutels, 2016; Nussbaum, 2000).

Eudaimonia since Aristotle has been framed as resting on relatively ideal circumstances in one's life, such as the luxuries of material resources and social status. Those who experience oppression or abuse of power may foster their own eudaimonic growth despite non-ideal circumstances. Nussbaum (2000) portrays the scenario in terms of gender and poverty from a macro-, socioeconomic level. Our sample comes from a middle- and upper-middle-class population, but we are finding that the eudaimonia-thwarting effects of inequalities in gender, age, and ethnicity—filtered through social institutions—are surfacing despite these material luxuries. For example, one participant, a woman in her mid-40s, described her divorce from her husband in the context of religion. In response to the question on gender-based life challenges, she said:

> So probably the hardest thing [are] the [extremely conservative] churches that my husband has taken us to [. . .] I find as a female, you have no voice. It's of course elder-ruled, who are all men. The husband is consulted. The wife is never really talked to and even really considered.

Under these conditions, she describes an argument with her husband over yet another of his decisions to change churches:

> I said, 'My best friend has died, my mother has [advanced disease] and is probably gonna die in the next five years. My kids are happy here. My oldest is questioning whether she even is a Christian, and if you move her churches again, she doesn't even wanna go.' You know, and just pleading with him to just stop being difficult. And he doesn't even see it that way. He sees it that people aren't following the Bible and he's defending God.

This brief excerpt showcases her predicament as rooted in a social institution that has prescribed roles for men as not merely leaders but as defenders of a higher power. In this case, the woman, who works in a STEM field dominated by men, has decided—after much struggle—not to comply with the master narrative, instead forging a new path. This excerpt also hints at how cultural master narratives filter through social institutions and affect the lives and narratives of families.

Microsystem: Family Master Narratives

One of the primary contributions of this project to the study of virtue development is the interview narratives of families. Just as individuals have life stories that define the self, families have stories that serve as master narratives of the family's identity and micro-culture of values (McLean, 2015). Family stories are both given to the individual and are co-constructed with the individual. Dialogical patterns and styles of family narratives have an established impact on a child's development (Fivush, Bohanek, & Zaman, 2011). For instance, both fathers and mothers encourage greater elaboration in narrating the day's events from their daughters than from their sons. And gendered notions of what constitutes womanhood and manhood in cultural master narratives are filtered through family narratives. Furthermore, how individuals handle conflict in general—and not whether conflict merely arises—is key to the coherence of the individuals' relationships (Gottman, Coan, Carrere, & Swanson, 1998).

A smaller but growing body of research has focused on how individuals construct a narrative self within the context of family stories (Bohanek, Marin, Fivush, & Duke, 2006; Bohanek et al., 2009; Fivush, Haden, & Reese, 2006; McLean, 2015). In our current project, we extend this research by focusing on the development of eudaimonic virtues in two general ways. First, we are analyzing the family stories qualitatively and critically for particular kinds of values (e.g., justice, power, intimacy) and then in terms of the stories' positioning of social roles within the family as conflicting or consonant with individuals' beliefs and efforts within cultural roles. Second, in quantitative analyses, we are examining how individuals co-construct both self-identity and family identity in terms of eudaimonic virtue. For instance, either concordance or conflict between individuals and their families with respect to any one virtue may either help or hinder that virtue, depending on the individuals' personalities (on multiple levels) and family dynamics. Unlike past research with family stories, we also have in-depth life stories of a family's target member, so we can compare themes and structure to examine person–family concordance and conflict.

Some virtues have a dark side that becomes a dominant theme in a family master narrative. One instance is perfectionism, which is a central tenet of Aristotelian eudaimonia (Haybron, 2008) and surfaces in personal narratives as the "dark side of eudaimonic growth" (Bauer, in press). Consider this excerpt from a family story interview of three brothers, all in later mid-life at the time of the interview:

PAUL: She really was abusive, I mean physically and verbally, to an amazing extent.

JEFF: Well, so was I. I remember saying when she called . . . she called me sonofabitch and I said, "Well, what does that make you?" You know, of course, I ran out the door. [. . .]

PAUL: I remember defending Sam a couple of times when he was getting . . . hit or whatever. I hope it was just a short period of time, but I'm glad everything eventually resolved there, and it seemed like things were much better 10, 15, 20 years later. But you're right, that was traumatic, and I think it affected me—it made me [unsocial] you know, my self-esteem was probably not that good.

SAM: Well, I think a lot of our self-esteems suffered. She expected perfection; she expected us all to be the King of the World, and we didn't live up to that, the wrath came down.

JEFF: Well, I would say she expected us to be princes.

SAM: Yes.

JEFF: Princes of the queen.

SAM: Yes.

PAUL: Oh, I don't know about that.

SAM: I could go there. But yeah, she expected perfection from us, and her idea of perfection, and whenever that wasn't achieved, she would try to fix it.

JEFF: I dreaded bringing anybody home.

SAM: I rarely did. Yeah, none of us brought friends that . . . we went to friends' houses; we didn't really bring friends to our house.

Here we see two of the brothers employing the theme of perfection as a pernicious ideal of the family. Such master narratives hinder one's capacity for moral mindfulness *in situ* (DesAutels, 2004). Fortunately, during the period of their mother's terminal illness, they all had repaired their relationships with their mother, with whom they also had loving memories.

The Mesosystem: Links Between Life Stories and Family Stories

In Bronfenbrenner's (1979) ecological model of development, the mesosystem refers to links between or among systems. The present study offers a unique opportunity for comparing and contrasting individuals' life stories with their families' stories, both of which draw on cultural master narratives. To illustrate this dynamic, we pick up where we left off—on the role of perfectionism in people's lives.

Perfectionism comes in many forms, including the ideal to "have it all." This ideal is particularly salient for women, such as in expectations to somehow be a full-time mother and a full-time careerist (Tajlili, 2014). For example, one participant—in her life story interview—talked about the difficulty of living up to the ideal of her mother's volunteerism, helping others, and making a difference (the virtue of generativity—Erikson, 1950). However, unlike her mother, the participant had a full-time (and highly successful) career (Bauer & DesAutels, in press):

> I guess the insight [. . .] that I regularly have is that you can't be her. [. . .] I have the desire to be very involved in my kids' school and their activities, and I do quite a bit. But sometimes [. . .] I find myself trying to measure myself up to my mom and everything that she did. [But] she didn't have a career. I mean she didn't have to give at least 40 to 50 hours of her week to an institution, to an organization for payment, right?

Despite her knowing consciously that she has a career, whereas her mother did not, she *still* carried an enduring expectation or ideal that she should do everything her mother did *and* have a career. We note too that her career involved research and advocacy for children and others living in disadvantaged environments. In other words, the ideal of "having it all" diminished her sense of flourishing.

However, high expectations do not all come in the form of perfectionism and unrealistic ideals. Some high expectations are grounded in more humanistic concerns for personally meaningful activities and relationships, and even for making humane changes in society—that is, for various forms of eudaimonic growth (Bauer, 2016). Here's the twist: the same ideals and intergenerational dynamics in one's life can be simultaneously perfectionistic and humane. To illustrate, here is an excerpt from the family story of the same woman ("Lena") who struggled with perfectionistic images of her mother. They are responding to a question about gender in the family:

LENA: I mean, I think it's pretty clear that my mother has great leadership capabilities [. . .] I think she forgot to tell you that she joined the boys' golf team.
JESSICA: This was in 1951. [. . .] I was the only girl on the golf course too, for the most part, in this small town that I lived in.

LENA: So as you can imagine, as a girl growing up in this family, and I actually think [. . .] we are really not treated any differently [than the boys]. [My parents] had the same expectations for me educationally, socially, developmentally, as they did for my brothers. But the one thing, when you grow up with a strong woman, and a strong grandmother on top of it, you see your . . . you can turn a course for yourself and realize that you can break the ceiling. And I think that's probably . . . that it was maybe a subliminal message that oftentime was given off by my mom in . . .

JESSICA: Probably.

LENA: . . . because she just expected us to reach for the stars and to . . . and I think she showed us how to be strategic and how to be . . . to work hard, and that also came from our father. Their father was a hard worker. And, you know, to this day I'm grateful.

JESSICA: And I think I grew up in a family where I had a father who said, "You can do anything you want."

In this brief exchange we get a glimpse of how the ideal of changing the world for the better—here in terms of gender equality—are passed from one generation to the next and then the next. The perfectionistic and humane goals of both "having it all" and acting on one's most personally meaningful interests come together for both generations of women interviewed. The life story of Lena and her family's story both emphasized the importance of breaking "the ceiling" and changing society toward greater equality between women and men—all while enacting the generative concern of helping others.

By turning to cross-generational family stories (e.g., Fivush et al., 2011), we can observe just how powerfully cultural narratives about gender and a good life shape entire lives. Lena's mother broke ceilings throughout her life, although not in a full-time career. Lena did so in her career. The individual life stories and the shared family story of this mother and daughter were filled with struggles against society's prescribed roles for women, even if these struggles differed somewhat between their life stories, reflecting the changing roles regarding women and work across their generations. As Lisa said in her life story, "Watch out for a woman who has above-average intelligence and a work ethic" (Bauer & DesAutels, in press). Their family story interviews hint at how such qualities in life, notably conveyed as themes of eudaimonic growth in contexts of non-ideal life circumstances, extend over generations and develop for individuals and their families in the context of social history.

Concluding Reflections

This study offers numerous methodological innovations, including a focus on narrative measures of virtuous motivation, the coding of narrative themes of virtuous motives rather than mere word counts or action types (themes predict eudaimonic well-being better—Bauer, McAdams, & Sakaeda, 2005a), the statistical comparison of narrative and non-narrative data on virtues, the statistical nesting of life stories within family stories, the qualitative analysis of life and family stories in terms of cultural master narratives from the perspective of critical social inquiry, and the infusion of quantitative and qualitative methods. This chapter focuses on the qualitative study of narratives to shed light on how eudaimonic ideals actually work in people's non-ideal lives. However, we are currently coding the narratives quantitatively according to established protocols (see Bauer, 2016) to examine statistically how the prevalence of themes of eudaimonic virtues predict an array of personality characteristics and life conditions, not only concurrently but also prospectively over the course of years, since these data are part of a larger, longitudinal study of personality development. Thus, we are approaching our aims for the project simultaneously and conjointly in the fields of philosophy and psychology.

We wish we could impart some wisdom on what we learned about the process of this interdisciplinary work. But in our case, we are hesitant to prescribe any particular approach, other than to choose collaborators with whom you get along and with whom you share interests at a deep level rather than in a cursory or seeming manner—and then from compatible theoretical perspectives (e.g., in our case, eudaimonic, feminist, narrative). Even in such a compatible environment, differences in particular interests, theoretical perspectives, and methods will eventually surface, but impasses are less likely, yielding a dynamically constructive struggle that advances each other's work. Humility, curiosity, and an overarching desire for constructive integration—as simplistic as such characteristics or attitudes might sound—facilitate the process.

Plus, we each came into this project with relatively strong backgrounds in each other's primary discipline, so we did not have the interdisciplinary language barrier that might otherwise be the case. Early conversations were peppered more with comments like an excited "oh, *that's* the term for" such-and-such phenomenon, rather than "what on earth are you talking about?" So, like our approach to studying virtues, our approach to this project was person-centered. This approach has yielded years of data to analyze as well as hundreds and hundreds of real-life stories that will help us shape an understanding of how virtues motivate and develop in the stories of people's lives amid their virtue-fostering and virtue-hindering families and American culture.

References

Adler, J. M., Lodi-Smith, J., Philippe, F. L., & Houle, I. (2016). The incremental validity of narrative identity in predicting well-being: A review of the field and recommendations for the future. *Personality and Social Psychology Review*, 20, 142–175.

Bauer, J. J. (2016). Eudaimonic growth: The development of the goods in personhood (or: cultivating a good life story). In J. Vittersø (Ed.), *Handbook of eudaimonic well-being* (pp. 147–174). Cham, Switzerland: Springer.

Bauer, J. J. (in press). *The transformative self: Identity, growth, and a good life story*. Oxford: Oxford University Press.

Bauer, J. J., & DesAutels, P. (in press). When life gets in the way: Virtuous self-development along non-idealized paths in women's lives. *Journal of Moral Education*.

Bauer, J. J., King, L. A., & Steger, M. F. (in press). Meaning-making, self-determination theory, and the question of wisdom in personality. *Journal of Personality*.

Bauer, J. J., & McAdams, D. P. (2010). Eudaimonic growth: Narrative growth goals predict increases in ego development and subjective well-being three years later. *Developmental Psychology*, 46, 761–772.

Bauer, J. J., McAdams, D. P., & Sakaeda, A. R. (2005a). Crystallization of desire and crystallization of discontent in narratives of life-changing decisions. *Journal of Personality*, 73, 1181–1213.

Bauer, J. J., McAdams, D. P., & Sakaeda, A. R. (2005b). Interpreting the good life: Growth memories in the lives of mature, happy people. *Journal of Personality and Social Psychology*, 88, 203–217.

Bauer, J. J., Schwab, J. R., & McAdams, D. P. (2011). Self-actualizing: Where ego development finally feels good? *The Humanistic Psychologist*, 39, 121–136.

Bohanek, J. G., Fivush, R., Zaman, W., Depore, C. E., Merchant, S., & Duke, M. P. (2009). Narrative interaction in family dinnertime conversations. *Merrill-Palmer Quarterly*, 55, 488–515.

Bohanek, J. G., Marin, K. A., Fivush, R., & Duke, M. P. (2006). Family narrative interaction and children's sense of self. *Family Processes*, 45, 39–54.

Boyd, B. (2013). *On the origin of stories: Evolution, cognition, and fiction*. Cambridge, MA: Belknap.

Bronfenbrenner, U. (1979). *The ecology of human development: Experiments by nature and design*. Cambridge, MA: Harvard University Press.

Campbell, J. (1973). *Myths to live by*. New York, NY: Bantam.

Chodorow, N. (1978). *The reproduction of mothering*. Berkeley, CA: University of California Press.

Colby, A., & Damon, W. (1992). *Some do care: Contemporary lives of moral commitment*. New York, NY: Free Press.

DesAutels, P. (2004). Moral mindfulness. In P. DesAutels & M. U. Walker (Eds.), *Moral psychology: Feminist ethics and social theory* (pp. 69–81). Lanham, MD: Rowman and Littlefield.

DesAutels, P. (2009). Resisting organizational power. In L. Tessman (Ed.), *Feminist ethics and social and political philosophy: Theorizing the non-ideal* (pp. 223–236). New York, NY: Springer.

DesAutels, P. (2012). Moral perception and responsiveness. *Journal of Social Philosophy, 43*, 334–346.

DesAutels, P. (2016). Power, virtue, and vice. *The Monist, 99*(2), 128–143.

DesAutels, P., & Walker, M. U. (Eds.). (2004). *Moral psychology: Feminist ethics and social theory*. Lanham, MD: Rowman and Littlefield.

DesAutels, P., & Whisnant, R. (Eds.). (2007). *Global feminist ethics*. Lanham, MD: Rowman and Littlefield.

Doris, J. M. (2002). *Lack of character: Personality and moral behavior*. Cambridge: Cambridge University Press.

Erikson, E. H. (1950/1994). *Childhood and society*. New York, NY: Norton.

Fivush, R., Bohanek, J. G., & Zaman, W. (2011). Personal and intergenerational narratives in relation to adolescents' well-being. *New Directions for Child and Adolescent Development, 2011*(131), 45–57.

Fivush, R., Haden, C. A., & Reese, E. (2006). Elaborating on elaborations: Role of maternal reminiscing style in cognitive and socioemotional development. *Child Development, 77*, 1568–1588.

Flanagan, O. (1991). *Varieties of moral personality: Ethics and psychological realism*. Cambridge, MA: Harvard University Press.

Flanagan, O. (2007). *The really hard problem: Meaning in a material world*. Cambridge, MA: MIT Press.

Fleeson, W., & Jayawickreme, E. (2015). Whole trait theory. *Journal of Research in Personality, 56*, 82–92.

Gilligan, C. (1982). *In a different voice*. Cambridge, MA: Harvard University.

Gottman, J. M., Coan, J., Carrere, S., & Swanson, C. (1998). Predicting marital happiness and stability from newlywed interactions. *Journal of Marriage and the Family, 60*, 5–22.

Graham, J., Nosek, B. A., Haidt, J., Iyer, R., Koleva, S., & Ditto, P. H. (2011). Mapping the moral domain. *Journal of Personality and Social Psychology, 101*, 366–385.

Guignon, C. (2004). *On being authentic*. New York, NY: Routledge.

Haidt, J. (2012). *The righteous mind: Why good people are divided by politics and religion*. New York, NY: Pantheon.

Hammack, P. L. (2011). *Narrative and the politics of identity: The cultural psychology of Israeli and Palestinian youth*. New York, NY: Oxford University Press.
Haybron, D. (2008). *The pursuit of unhappiness*. New York, NY: Oxford University Press.
Jeffers, T. L. (2005). *Apprenticeships: The bildungsroman from Goethe to Santayana*. New York, NY: Palgrave.
Kristjánsson, K. (2010). Positive psychology, happiness, and virtue: The troublesome conceptual issues. *Review of General Psychology, 14*, 296–310.
McAdams, D. P. (1993). *The stories we live by: Personal myths and the making of the self*. New York, NY: Morrow.
McAdams, D. P. (1995). What do we know when we know a person? *Journal of Personality, 63*, 365–396.
McAdams, D. P. (2006). *The redemptive self: Stories Americans live by*. New York, NY: Oxford University Press.
McAdams, D. P. (2008a). Personal narratives and the life story. In O. P. John, R. W. Robins, & L. A. Pervin (Eds.), *Handbook of personality: Theory and research* (3rd ed., pp. 242–262). New York, NY: Guilford.
McAdams, D. P. (2008b). *The life story interview*. Unpublished manuscript. Retrieved from www.sesp.northwestern.edu/foley/instruments/interview/
McAdams, D. P. (2013). The psychological self as actor, agent, and author. *Perspectives on Psychological Science, 8*, 272–295.
McAdams, D. P., & Guo, J. (2015). Narrating the generative life. *Psychological Science, 26*, 475–483.
McLean, K. C. (2015). *The co-authored self: Family stories and the construction of personal identity*. New York, NY: Oxford University Press.
McLean, K. C., & Syed, M. (2016). Personal, master, and alternative narratives: An integrative framework for understanding identity development in context. *Human Development, 58*, 318–349.
Montoya, R. M., & Pittinsky, T. L. (2013). Individual variability in adherence to the norm of group interest predicts outgroup bias. *Group Processes & Intergroup Relations, 16*, 173–191.
Narvaez, D. (2010). Moral complexity: The fatal attraction of truthiness and the importance of mature moral functioning. *Perspectives on Psychological Science, 5*, 163–181.
Narvaez, D. (2013). Development and socialization within an evolutionary context: Growing up to become "a good and useful human being". In D. Fry (Ed.), *War, peace and human nature: The convergence of evolutionary and cultural views* (pp. 341–358). New York, NY: Oxford University Press.
Nelson, H. L. (2001). *Damaged identities, narrative repair*. Ithaca, New York, NY: Cornell University Press.
Nicolescu, B. (2007). *Transdisciplinarity as methodological framework for going beyond the science-religion debate*. Paper presentation at the Metanexus Institute Conference, Philadelphia.
Nisbet, R. (1980). *History of the idea of progress*. New York, NY: Basic Books.
Nussbaum, M. C. (2000). *Women and human development: The capabilities approach*. Cambridge: Cambridge University Press.

Ryan, R. M., & Deci, E. L. (2001). On happiness and human potentials: A review of research on hedonic and eudaimonic well-being. *Annual Review of Psychology, 52*, 141–166.

Sibley, C. G., & Duckitt, J. (2008). Personality and prejudice: A meta-analysis and theoretical review. *Personality and Social Psychology Review, 12*, 248–279.

Snow, N. E. (2008). Virtue and flourishing. *Journal of Social Philosophy, 39*, 225–245.

Sripada, C. S., & Konrath, S. (2011). Telling more than we can know about intentional action. *Mind & Language, 26*, 353–380.

Staudinger, U. M., & Glück, J. (2011). Psychological wisdom research: Commonalities and differences in a growing field. *Annual Review of Psychology, 62*, 215–241.

Stewart, A. J., & Vandewater, E. A. (1999). "If I had it to do over again. . .": Midlife review, midcourse corrections, and women's well-being in midlife. *Journal of Personality and Social Psychology, 76*, 270–283.

Tackett, J. L., Herzhoff, K., Kushner, S. C., & Rule, N. (2016). Thin slices of child personality: Perceptual, situational, and behavioral contributions. *Journal of Personality and Social Psychology, 110*, 150–166.

Tajlili, M. H. (2014). A framework for promoting women's career intentionality and work-life integration. *The Career Development Quarterly, 62*, 254–267.

Taylor, C. (1989). *Sources of the self: The making of modern identity*. Cambridge: Cambridge University Press.

Tessman, L. (2001). Critical virtue ethics: Understanding oppression as morally damaging. In P. DesAutels & J. Waugh (Eds.), *Feminists doing ethics* (pp. 79–99). Lanham, MD: Rowman and Littlefield.

Tessman, L. (2005). *Burdened virtues: Virtue ethics for liberatory struggles*. New York, NY: Oxford.

Thorne, A. (2004). Putting the person into social identity. *Human Development, 47*, 361–365.

Tiberius, V. (2008). *The reflective life: Living wisely within our limits*. New York, NY: Oxford University Press.

Tronto, J. C. (1993). *Moral boundaries: A political argument for an ethic of care*. New York, NY: Routledge.

Waterman, A. S. (Ed.). (2013). *The best within us: Positive psychology perspectives on eudaimonic functioning*. Washington, DC: American Psychological Association.

8 Reflections on Our Sociological-Philosophical Study of the Self, Motivation, and Virtue Among LGBTI Conservative Christians and Their Allies

Theresa W. Tobin and Dawne Moon

A sociologist and a philosopher, we are studying the growing conservative Christian movement in the United States to end the so-called culture wars. A network of overlapping conservative Christian organizations has emerged since the 1990s, working to change how conservative churches treat lesbian, gay, bi+, transgender, and intersex (LGBTI) people,[1] to apologize for damage they have caused, and to try to convince other evangelical and fundamentalist Protestants that Christian love does not mean shunning people or refusing to listen to them. Conventionally, the church and its members have often consciously dispensed shame, treating it almost as a sacrament (a tangible sign of God's presence) in these cases, in an effort to bring "same-sex attracted" or gender-variant people closer to God.[2] Examining this movement, our collaborative philosophical and sociological study, to culminate in a book, explores the harm caused by what we call *sacramental shame*, how targets of this form of shaming resist and overcome this form of spiritual violence, and what motivates perpetrators of this violence to change their views and come to see their shaming treatment of LGBTI people as morally wrong and as incompatible with Christian love. We examine how perpetrators and victims are motivated to overcome these institutional abuses and cultivate virtues such as humility and love. We analyze data from participant observation, document analysis, and semi-structured interviews with LGBTI and heterosexual, cisgender[3] Christians in conversation about their churches' abuses of LGBTI and other people and their routes to reconciliation and intersectional justice.

By integrating sociological methods of data collection and analysis with philosophical methods of analysis and moral argumentation, we both offer a nuanced portrait of how victims experience the spiritual violation of sacramental shame and provide empirically grounded, dynamic accounts of how people find the motivation to love other people well while they forge a Christian understanding of social justice rooted in solidarity across racial, gender, and sexual diversity. Recognizing the partiality of our own disciplines from the outset and speaking a shared language of feminist scholarship, our collaboration has allowed us to develop insights that would otherwise have been difficult to see—or to say.

Self, Motivation, and Virtue

We espouse a developmental perspective whereby the *self* is produced constantly throughout the course of life, in social interactions and shaped by institutions (Blumer, 1969; Holstein & Gubrium, 2000; Mead, 1934). By *social*, we refer to the interactional and institutional processes that constitute people's daily lives and shape what kinds of persons it is possible to be and how people experience and navigate the questions and problems that confront them. Our definition of the self is fairly standard in sociology, and Mead's pragmatist views of the self (coming from a philosopher regarded as a key progenitor of the mainstream microsociological approach) are not incompatible with a neo-Aristotelian understanding of human beings as social creatures who learn morality, virtue, and vice in and through relationship with others embedded in a particular social and cultural context.

We use *motivation* to refer to what compels people to change beliefs and behaviors that yield new ways to be loving, to be humble, and to have self-respect. We study moral motivation at the level of social processes, interpersonal interactions, and the phenomenology of emotional experience—by which we mean people's emotional experiences as they understand those experiences and describe them. We consult scholarship in psychology, philosophy, and gender/sexuality studies to build our understanding of particular emotions. However, starting from a sociological perspective that attunes us to how culture and institutions shape individuals, we are interested in the interactional processes that shape people's self-concepts and their experiences of faith and relationships.

Early on, Moon had begun to explore the large-scale historical processes that have fostered conservative Christians' motivations to change their understandings of gender and sexuality, all rooted in capitalism: the nineteenth-century invention of "sexuality" as definitive of selfhood (Foucault, 1978); late capitalism's mobility of people and information that make it unfeasible to many people that they alone could have already accessed every facet of God's ultimate truth (Harvey, 1989), and thus the openness to new information; neoliberalism's acceptance of white, middle-class normative forms of gay and lesbian partnerships and subjectivity and its attendant media images of gay men and lesbians as "normal" (Walters, 2001; Duggan, 2003; Stryker, 2008). These socio-historical factors shape the conditions for motivational possibilities, so we began with the premise that social context bears on the possibilities of virtue development.

Tobin had already considered the social contexts in which people become selves as crucial to understanding morality. Previously, she had focused on how people's religious or cultural worldviews, and their identities as members of oppressed or privileged groups, influenced their conceptions of the good and their capacities for moral agency. Our combined emphasis on various aspects of social context helped us to ground our claims about obstacles to virtue and the motivation to overcome those obstacles *in situ*, in the embodied, lived social worlds in which people negotiate right and wrong and experience thriving or its opposite.

Virtue was a concept foreign to Moon as a sociologist, so we use virtue concepts from philosophy, and in particular from neo-Aristotelian, Christian, and feminist conceptions of virtue. From the neo-Aristotelian tradition, we borrow the broad notion of virtues as habitual dispositions that enable a person to act well in a certain domain of activity, and of moral virtues as enduring traits that enable a person to live well as a human being (Aristotle, 1999; Snow, 2010). We assume that virtues (and vices) develop over time through activity and shape a person's moral perception, provide moral motivation, and frame justification for action. One piece of the neo-Aristotelian tradition that we have assumed is that virtues are necessary (though insufficient) for human flourishing.

We borrow from Roberts (2007, 2009, 2012, 2016; Roberts & Wood, 2007) and Hauerwas and Pinches (1997) to frame particular virtue concepts within a Christian tradition, the tradition of those we study. However, the literature we've encountered in Christian virtue ethics accounts for the virtues and their development by assuming a religious environment in which people are not routinely spiritually abused or demeaned. So we have also turned to feminist conceptions of virtue, including Tessman (2005) and Card's (1996), which explore virtue development and barriers to it under conditions of oppression. We have also turned to feminist affect theory (Ahmed, 2015; Shotwell, 2011), which examines the politics of emotional experience, and specifically how emotional experience functions either to maintain or rupture social power dynamics. This work has been vital for understanding virtue development and obstacles to it in religious environments that are spiritually violent. Bringing these literatures on virtue ethics into conversation with sociological perspectives provides a robust theoretical framework to study social and interpersonal forces influencing the development of the moral and spiritual self of LGBTI and heterosexual, cisgender Christians in the conservative Protestant movement to overcome spiritual violence in this particular social context at this particular historical moment.

Whereas *virtue* is a concept foreign to sociology, sociologists are very much concerned with social inequality, oppression, and the social formation of selves and habitual dispositions in conditions of inequality (Bourdieu, 1989). Attending to virtue will help sociologists to appreciate and account for forms of despair that are not objectively measurable. A virtue perspective that links traits to human flourishing gives us the freedom to make normative claims about traits that undermine it. It provides a richer account of the social and moral effects of oppressive ideologies and self-contradictory languages of domination and yields the ability to name them. Finally, by using virtue concepts developed within Christianity and feminism, we can engage people's moral arguments in their own terms and make our own normative claims within those debates based on what we have learned from them.

Developing Our Key Terms

The key terms for our project include *shame, sacramental shame, spiritual violence, humility, pride, love*, and *relationship*.

Shame

We came to our conclusions about sacramental shame as spiritual violence early on, but while we had heard discussions of shame, we still hadn't found a satisfactory definition of the word. To address this need, we spent months reading extensively from the philosophical (Taylor, 1985; Lehtinen, 1998; Woodward, 2000; Velleman, 2001; Manion, 2002; Calhoun, 2004; Mason, 2010;

Shotwell, 2011; Deonna, Rodogno, & Teroni, 2012; Flanagan, 2013; Ahmed, 2015; Thomason, 2015), sociological (Lynd, 1958; Scheff, 1990, 2000; Stein, 2006; Turner & Stets, 2007; Gould, 2009), queer theoretical (Sedgwick, 2003; Halperin & Traub, 2009; Gould, 2009), psychological (Lewis, 1971; Bradshaw, 1988; Lewis, 1992; Tangney, 2007; Karlsson & Sjoberg, 2009; Narvaez, 2014), and theological (Fowler, 1996; Pattison, 2000; Brownson, 2013) literatures and assembled a working definition that best reflected and illuminated the experiences of our participants. We came to define *shame* as a social emotion incorporating a painful feeling of being exposed as a flawed self, fear of rejection by others on the basis of that exposure, and powerlessness over one's identity in the eyes of others who matter. This definition contributes to both our fields' notions of shame as a social emotion with ethical roots and implications. These literatures have also helped us frame complex understandings of the role of shame in moral motivation, by enabling us to chart different types of shame, different temporal and spatial dynamics of shame experiences, and the difference between shame as an emotional experience and chronic shame that gets instilled as a disposition.

Sacramental Shame as Spiritual Violence

The term *spiritual violence* was coined by Christians as an umbrella term for a variety of practices that use religious means to degrade or demean a person spiritually and harm their relationship with God (Manson, 2010; Truluck, 2001). Tobin's research had aimed to clarify the nature of this mode of violence and its impact on spiritual and moral development (Tobin, 2016). Spiritual violence is violence in the sense of violation of persons (Brison, 2003; Galtung, 2007; Garver, 2007). It is distinctively spiritual in terms of its means—it uses religious texts, teachings, symbols, and rituals, for example, as spiritual weapons—and in terms of its target—it harms a person's spiritual self and relationship with God.

Before we began working together, Moon had started to notice that shame was treated almost as a special sacrament (tangible sign of God's presence) for LGBTI people. As we began to collaborate, we realized that *sacramental shame* is a form of spiritual violence; by demanding constant displays of shame from LGBTI people, other church members were effectively demanding they constantly acknowledge their unworthiness of relationship with

God and other people. Sacramental shame is consciously dispensed by the church and its members in an effort to bring a same- (or multi-) sex–attracted or gender-variant person closer to God, so it is ironical that this shame actually attacks people's ability to relate to God and other people. The results are toxic. Constantly displaying unworthiness made it impossible for our LGBTI participants to serve God and other people, but even those who fasted daily, beseeched God constantly, slept on a church altar nightly for years, enrolled in reparative therapy programs over and over, and/or were subject to repeated (sometimes violent) efforts at exorcism or faith healing—never achieved the desired changes, and over time came to feel that God's back had been turned on them. This is spiritual violence: the use of religious means—in this case sacramentalized shame—to lead a person to experience God as hostile, and diminishing a person's capacities to participate in religious life and to know and love God, self, and others. The shame and subsequent efforts to fix themselves attacked their capacity not only to relate to others sexually, but also to relate to others, including God, *at all*.

Our project investigates how the self is harmed by the spiritual violence of sacramental shame, as well as how perpetrators and victims can both overcome these institutional abuses and acquire the motivation to cultivate such virtues as humility and Christian love that can serve as counterforces to this form of violence. At some point, the LGBTI respondents who came to this movement realized, at least to some extent, that they were just as God intended them to be. Some lesbian and gay people might believe celibacy was their only option and others might believe that a same-sex relationship could be God's intention for them, but they all had to accept that they simply *were* LGBTI, and that describing themselves that way was not rejecting God's plan, but embracing God's plan *for them*.

Pride and Humility

Our respondents dwell in contexts where shame is widespread and regarded as a path to Christian humility and redemption, yet our LGBTI participants experience shame as toxic. For many, shame was instilled as a disposition, distorting humility into extreme self-abnegation and self-deprecation, sometimes to the point of annihilation. We found that one important antidote to this toxic shame is pride, but we needed to reconcile LGBTI notions of pride as life-giving with Christian notions of it as a deadly sin and a gateway to perdition. We turned to Edman's queer theological understandings of "queer pride" (Edman, 2016) as the recognition of the humanity and lovability of other sexual and gender Others as a path to accepting one's own humanity and lovability, and as crucial to Christianity.

To challenge the Christian tendency to *define* pride as hubris, we also drew from philosophical understandings that link virtuous humility and virtuous pride (Snow, 1995; Whitcomb, Battaly, Baehr, & Howard-Snyder, 2015), as a realistic sense of one's limitations, coupled with the acknowledgment that improvement is possible, that others can help us to improve, and that our flaws do not impinge definitively on our basic worth as persons. Proper pride that enables a person to have confidence in their basic worth prevents humility from sliding into self-abnegation or self-deprecation. We thus came to affirm recent philosophical and psychological accounts that see humility and proper pride as two sides of a single virtuous disposition (Whitcomb et al., 2015).

Whereas toxic shame seemed to distort humility in the experience of LGBTI participants, humility helped explain the positive motivational role of a different type of shame experience among heterosexual, cisgender church members who discuss coming to feel ashamed of their prior shaming treatment of LGBTI church members and became allies. However, accounting for this testimony we found limitations in philosophical definitions (including those that link humility and pride) that too narrowly construe humility as an emotion of self-assessment, a form of self-knowledge about one's limitations and shortcomings. Our heterosexual, cisgender ally respondents' expressions of humility led us to redefine humility as a virtuous disposition of openness to others that is anchored in concern to protect relationship; humility is the disposition that makes a person open to receiving self-knowledge from encounters with others and vulnerable to possibilities for self-transformation in light of these encounters. That Spezio, Peterson, and Roberts (2019) found a similar conception of humility as openness to others in their study of intentional communities seems a significant outcome of the SMV project.

Love and Relationship

The themes of relationship and love—both well-meaning but misguided claims to love and authentic expressions of love—emerge in several parts of our project. First, the sacramental shaming dynamic often arises under the guise of love, as church members attempt to "love the sinner and hate the sin." When Christians express love by shaming others for their "failure" to live up to Christian ideals of the self, they break relationship with LGBTI people, blame them for the rupture, and leave them with the sense that there is nothing they can do to restore relationship until and unless they "fix" themselves. Queer theoretical perspectives on the relationship between love and shame were the most useful for understanding precisely how communal forms of love, which include shared ideals of the self that "stick" a community together, make people vulnerable to shame in both good and bad ways (Sedgwick, 2003; Shotwell, 2011; Ahmed, 2015).

Moon had previously come to the conclusion that contemporary sociology is lacking to the extent that it neglects Buber's (1923/1971) conception of *relationship* as unbounded connection and radical equality with another—distinct in its capacity to transform a person's sense of self in the world—in contrast to experiences where the boundaries of the ego are preserved. We began this project with the hypothesis that relationship in this sense would be key to the motivation to virtue, and our findings have enriched our understanding of relationship. In this movement, we have observed that many come to realize that some of what Christians (and others, no doubt) call "love" is not rooted in openness to being transformed by the other but a one-sided feeling (or effort to control) an object. Whereas the sacramental shaming dynamic expresses sincere attempts to love that miss the mark, we found that relationship in Buber's sense of *I-thou* intimate connection with LGBTI people is a significant catalyst for heterosexual, cisgender church members coming to see their treatment of LGBTI Christians as failed attempts to love, to apologize, and to work to become allies. This type of shame experience inspired heterosexual, cisgender respondents to rethink the meaning of same-sex sexual conduct in light of their own sexual sin and struggle for virtuousness, removing double-standards against LGBTI people. In other cases, recognition that a loved one was LGBTI prompted a rereading of Scripture, recognizing that prior teachings about homosexuality impinged not on some monstrous others driven by perversion but on people they knew and loved, driven—like themselves—by a desire for intimacy and love.

Furthermore, our respondents have made it clear that their understandings of Christian love have changed as a result of their experiences and reflections on them. "Love" no longer refers to simply a good feeling or desire to help but must be accompanied by work to truly welcome people for who they are and to end systemic institutional violence. Love can no longer be seen to motivate only charity; it must motivate justice (Moon & Tobin, 2019). Many respondents came to understand that a desire to be "nice" is fruitless if it neglects a context where people are being systematically harmed and their lives systematically devalued. These understandings have come to clarify our own definitions. The work of loving others in this way often requires painful self-scrutiny and self-transformation, a willingness to "die" to old ways of being and thinking that may be accompanied by a sense of loss even as they usher in more authentically loving and just forms of relationship and community.

Aligning Disciplinary Goals

We began as two scholars engaged with the interdisciplinary field of gender/sexuality studies, where we both often read and taught work from a wide range of fields. Neither of us had any notion that our own discipline had *the* definitive method for ascertaining truth; we both had already seen the value of examining social problems from a range of perspectives. We both thus began with a sense of intellectual humility, that each had something to learn from the other, that our own disciplines lacked something we would find helpful. Qualitative sociological methods and standards of evidence structure the project, and we use qualitative evidence to support both sociological and philosophical arguments. Philosophical ethics is represented in central arguments of several papers taking a normative stand on these issues and/or contributing directly to debates in moral philosophy, for example, about the value of shame as a motivator for self-improvement and moral repair (Tobin & Moon, 2019).

Theoretical Innovation

The definition work just discussed constitutes some of our theoretical innovation. In addition, we contribute to the phenomenology of emotions by underlining the social nature of and connections among shame, virtuous pride, and humility. We have made three theoretical innovations in the study of shame, pride, and humility as moral and political emotions.

First, we introduce a previously untheorized form of shame into scholarly taxonomies of shame: *sacramental shame* names a shaming dynamic in which churches require LGBTI members to constantly acknowledge their unworthiness or relationship and constantly display shame about their sexual attractions or gender experience: (1) as proof that they have not turned their backs on God, (2) as a necessary condition for church membership, and (3) as a necessary condition for their salvation. This type of shame is distinctive because it paradoxically makes an emotion that typically signals threat of rejection into a requirement of belonging, thereby exacerbating an already abusive shaming dynamic.

Second, our collaboration makes theoretically new contributions to debates about the moral value of shame as a catalyst for self-improvement (Tobin & Moon, 2019; Moon & Tobin, 2019). The moral value of shame is often defended on grounds that a liability to feel shame indicates the presence of humility, a person's acknowledgment that their self-concept does not define their identity and that they may be wrong about who they think they are. Our research affirms a link between shame and humility but complicates this picture by showing that a liability to feel shame does not by itself indicate the presence of humility; rather, the way a community encourages in certain groups a liability to feel shame—either as an occasional experience or chronically—influences whether they develop humility or instead become excessively self-abnegating, servile, and/or self-deprecating.

Third, our project has led to a cluster of theoretical innovations around the nature of pride and humility, their relationship to each other as well as to shame, and their role in moral and spiritual healing and transformation. We have developed a new philosophical definition of humility as a virtuous disposition of openness to others that is grounded in concern to prioritize relationship. The toxicity of the shaming many LGBTI conservative Christians have endured calls out for an alternative (Moon & Tobin, 2018, 2019). The need to navigate conservative Christianity's categorization of "pride" as vicious called for us to specify the virtue of a realistic assessment of one's strengths as well as limitations, leading us to conceptualize healthy pride and humility as two sides of the same virtuous disposition, which we call *humility-pride* (Tobin & Moon, 2019).

We have also made several theoretical innovations in sociology of religion and gender and sexuality studies. Conventional "culture wars" discourse establishes false dichotomies of conservative vs. liberal in two ways: conservative vs. social justice and conservative vs. gay. The reflection necessary to articulate an identity as an LGBTI conservative Christian leads many to also question the dichotomy of Christianity vs. social justice. They come to see social justice as not in tension with Christianity but as a mandate of following in the footsteps of Jesus (Moon & Tobin, 2016). Such conclusions may seem to lend credence to many conservative Christians' fears that critical thought about certain topics constitutes the first step down a slippery slope to liberalism. But we have found that many of these actors retain crucial elements of what made them conservative all along, such as a "high view" of Scripture, a personal relationship with Jesus. They don't believe they have turned "liberal," but see themselves following more closely in the footsteps of Jesus.

But some see themselves as LGBTI conservative Christians without embracing social justice. We have observed this tension between, and sometimes within, the organizations we've studied and will conceptualize them in our book. In addition, we have found it valuable to watch movement actors hold space for people just entering the movement for social justice who are afraid of saying the wrong thing. We have argued that their actions in this regard may be instructive for other social justice movements who seem more accustomed to dispensing their own forms of shame (Moon & Tobin, 2016; Moon, Tobin, & Sumerau, 2019).

Our respondents' own words and actions have led us to challenge false dichotomies between conservative Christians and LGBTI politics. For instance, our findings from within this movement for LGBTI recognition and social justice called us to explore how not just religious conservatives, but *everyone*—including feminists and queer theorists—may employ partial conceptualizations of gender and sexuality in critical analyses and that we need to keep a holistic conception of sex/gender/sexuality in mind if we hope to produce pathways to a more complete form of liberation. Participants' Scripture-based challenges to conventionally conservative understandings of sex, gender, and sexuality have led us to argue that we must understand sexism (giving men freedom, power, and authority over others), cissexism (privileging the experiences of those whose genitals at birth consistently match their gender identity in later life), heteronormativity (positing male and female as made for each other and complete only when together), monosexism (rendering invisible and illegitimate the experiences of those for whom binary gender does not dictate sexual attraction), and mononormativity (defining sexual activity as legitimate and moral only within the privatized confines of monogamous marriage) as mutually reinforcing modes of oppression (Moon et al., 2019). By challenging the complementarian interpretations of Scripture at the roots of sexism, cissexism, heteronormativity, monosexism and mononormativity, this movement gives us evidence to weigh in on recent sociological debates, showing that people can consciously work to "undo" gender (Deutsch, 2007; West & Zimmerman, 2009; Connell, 2010).

Methodological Innovation, Expansion, and Limitations

Hybrid Methodology Expands Knowledge

We integrate sociological methods of data collection and analysis with philosophical methods of analysis and moral argumentation. These methods mutually inform one another, creating new ways of knowing, but also creating potential limits. We are using qualitative data collection methods of sociology to identify themes and patterns. Moon trained Tobin in these methods, but our different disciplinary lenses lead us to ask different questions or frame issues differently. These differences have enriched our data by enabling different conversations with movement participants.

We also use philosophical methods of conceptual analysis and moral argumentation to analyze data, employing qualitative observations in making ethical arguments about claims to virtue in the movement we are studying. Both researchers analyzed evidence by identifying people's presuppositions, but distinctly philosophical analysis in this study includes clarifying the various virtue concepts people use, investigating how these concepts are explained, and locating convergences and inconsistencies in those explanations. Philosophical moral argumentation uses logic and conceptual analysis within a specific ethical framework, in this case Christian and feminist virtue ethics, to make normative arguments about claims to virtue.

By using the dynamic observational methods of sociology, including qualitative interviewing and participant-observation, we create a rich and nuanced portrait of precisely how victims experience spiritual violation and how they define ethical and virtue terms

(Moon & Tobin, 2018, 2019). When Tobin began studying spiritual violence, she started by trying to formulate a working definition of it as the use of sacred or religious mediators (e.g., texts such as sacred Scripture, objects such as a crucifix or altar, places such as a sanctuary, rituals including individual and communal prayer, or religious teachings) to violate a person in their spiritual formation. But getting at the nature of this harm beyond this thin definition required situating the question, because of the variety of ways people experience spirituality and faith and the variety of contexts in which this kind of harm is inflicted. Any answers we propose are likewise situated, fitted to this context. However, we are also beginning to see ways in which lessons drawn from this context may have broader import and value. For instance, Catholics for whom "guilt" may be more salient than shame have expressed that our findings from within conservative Protestantism resonate with them as well, but with some variation. Likewise, heterosexual/cisgender women, and men, have in different ways expressed that constant shame has shaped their lives as well. Future research should map the similarities and differences between these cases and that which we study now.

Our integrated methods of data collection and analysis enable us to observe in people's own narratives and interactions where their ethical motivations come from, as we can ask them to articulate their thought processes. For instance, Tobin's philosophical conjecture had been that experiencing spiritual violence makes people vulnerable to moral and spiritual injury, erecting obstacles to virtue development, and analysis of published testimony supports this conjecture. Now, we can draw from sometimes rawer public testimonies and ask interviewees specific questions about their experiences to help to refine our understanding of the specific kinds of harm caused by spiritual violence. These methods allow us more systematically to chart the terrain of this category, and to express more richly the nature of its violation.

In addition to refining philosophical concepts with qualitative data, we also treat participants as co-creators of knowledge. Qualitative social scientific methods are by nature open to epistemological challenge; serious qualitative researchers expect that their way of approaching their research questions will be revised in conversation with the people they study (Emerson, Fretz, & Shaw, 1995; Holstein & Gubrium, 2008; LaRossa, 2005; Strauss & Corbin, 1998). For example, Moon coined the term "sacramental shame" to name a phenomenon in which these communities treat shame as a special, unspoken sacrament just for LGBTI people. Mentioning the possibility to respondents in the field, she was often (as we would both be later) met with wide-eyed responses of "YES!" and "I have a lot to say about that!" Respondents' explanations for why and how this is the case are helping us develop the concept; in addition, respondents have expressed appreciation for having a term to name and make intelligible some of what they have experienced but might not have named. Collaboratively, researchers from two disciplines and non-academics in the communities we are interacting with are developing the concept of sacramental shame in a way that deepens our understanding of this form of violence as it manifests in this community, and that may have some beneficial use for people in these movements working to stop this violence.

Many ethnographers will share drafts of their work with certain people in the community they studied; we do this as well, allowing some respondents to challenge us when they thought we got it wrong, to refer us to experts, readings, and friends of theirs whose insights would help us better to understand. We also submit our papers to the consultants and other members of these communities for critical feedback. This aspect of the method has been humbling sometimes, as when an interviewee helped one of us to see how her claims linking data as evidence for a certain view were too quick, and that she needed to explore another possible explanation. This process strengthened our argument and showed us how some of our own views may have obscured alternative explanations. Some of these respondents have written within the very movement we are studying, and we came to see our own study as potentially contributing, in our own way, to that conversation.

We have also collaborated with movement participants in gathering data. As two white women, we hired a consultant from the movement to run focus groups and conduct interviews with people of color who are members of these communities and who may have been uncomfortable talking with outsiders or with white researchers. The richness and complexity of the data from these interviews and observations calls attention to the limits of the abstract solitary thinking conventional among philosophers. But it has also helped us appreciate the value of philosophical definitions (even imperfect ones) and attempts to clarify concepts such as spiritual violence and sacramental shame, which help participants to clarify the harms they have been working to articulate.

Normative Judgment as Methodological Limitation

Framing sociological data in terms of virtue allows us to overcome the sometimes-debilitating relativism of social scientific inquiry. As a sociologist, Moon had examined the logic of opposing Protestant perspectives on homosexuality and the images of the divine that anchored each, but was not positioned to weigh the ethical claims (Moon, 2004, 2005a, 2005b). Her work could go so far as to say that people seemed to be contradicting themselves, but could make no ethical judgments. Using moral frameworks from philosophy we can distinguish true virtue from false virtue, thus producing empirically grounded, dynamic accounts of how people find the motivation to love and to overcome the spiritually violating impact of sacramental shame. This engagement with others' normative claims situates the normative claims we defend, and at the same time, we do not purport to settle the moral disputes in the communities we are interacting with, but to make a normative contribution to these ongoing debates. In this sense, we may contribute to the movement we have been studying not as observers from some mythical Archimedean point, but as situated observers with the ethical tools of philosophy at our disposal.

The difficulties our disciplines posed for our project were sources of intellectual challenge and growth, but also limitation. While many subfields of sociology tend to assume a particular and often unacknowledged stance with regard to their objects of inquiry, in the sociology of religion the long-standing assumption has tended not to examine the substance of religion itself, and it runs against the grain to find fault with religious actors or to make normative judgments about actions that countervene their stated goals.

Conversely, moral philosophers using analytical methods and logical argumentation do consider and respond to objections to the views they defend; it is not customary (or common) for philosophers to engage in dialogue with specific non-academic persons or communities in order to improve understanding of the issue they are studying, including perspectives from the lived experiences of people who disagree with them. For instance, LGBTI Christians who maintain that same-sex sex is always sinful advocate celibacy for all lesbian and gay people, and for bisexuals who fall in love with someone of their same sex. In the movement we are studying, this perspective is known as "Side B," in contrast to the "Side A" perspective that sees same-sex marriage as compatible with Christian teaching. We have felt resistance from a Side B participant who read drafts of our work and disagreed with our normative framework that endorsed more of a Side A perspective (which we did because of the toxic shame some formerly Side B people reported). These discussions were not easy (though it was easy to blame it on the philosopher!), but they helped the respondent to make their own views clearer, even as they might have lost some faith in our project or our ability to "get it right" from their perspective. This theoretical innovation is thus a methodological limitation of our hybrid analytical approach—those who disagree with our normative evaluations may be less inclined to participate in future studies. We are thus committing to studying largely those who are not put off by our analyses.

One challenge has been to write papers capable of conveying the depth of what we are learning through this methodological innovation while staying within journal word count limits. We have found it difficult to discuss all relevant literatures from both disciplines and find adequate space to develop new concepts with the rigor and depth they merit in under the 10,000 words usually allowed by the most generous journals. However, by bringing our disciplines into conversation, we are developing new understandings that will benefit both our disciplines.

Notes

1. While the terms *lesbian* and *gay* are probably familiar to readers, other terms may be less so. *Bi+* refers to people who may be attracted to others regardless of gender, with the + indicating multiple identity categories that people use to indicate such attractions (bisexual, ambisexual, pansexual, sexually fluid). *Transgender* refers to people who disagree to any extent with the sex they were assigned at birth, including those who feel that they are of the other binary category and those who feel they are neither, or in between. *Intersex* refers to people whose bodies at birth defied simple categorization into either conventional gender category. Intersex people are not always treated as LGBT people, but can be; not all intersex people identify with LGBT people, but those we have spoken to had similar experiences so we include them here.
2. Brownson 2013, Wolkomir 2006; see also Conley 2016, Lee 2012, Pasquale 2015, VanderWal-Gritter 2014.
3. *Cisgender* means agreeing with the sex assignment one was given at birth, or not transgender.

References

Ahmed, S. (2015). *The cultural politics of emotion*. New York, NY: Routledge.
Aristotle. (1999). *Nicomachean ethics* (T. Irwin, Trans. and Ed.). Indianapolis, IN: Hackett.
Blumer, H. (1969). *Symbolic interactionism: Perspective and method*. Berkeley, CA: University of California Press.
Bourdieu, P. (1989). Social space and symbolic power. *Sociological Theory, 7*(1), 14–25.
Bradshaw, J. (1988). *Healing the shame that binds you*. Deerfield Beach, FL: Health Communications Inc.
Brison, S. (2003). *Aftermath: Violence and the remaking of a self*. Princeton, NJ: Princeton University Press.
Brownson, J. V. (2013). *Bible, gender, sexuality: Reframing the church's debate on same-sex relationships*. Grand Rapids, MI: Eerdmans.
Buber, M. (1923/1970). *I and thou* (W. Kaufman, Trans.). New York, NY: Simon & Schuster.
Calhoun, C. (2004). An apology for moral shame. *The Journal of Political Philosophy, 12*(2), 127–146.
Card, C. (1996). *The unnatural lottery: Character and moral luck*. Philadelphia, PA: Temple University Press.
Conley, G. (2016). *Boy erased: A memoir*. New York, NY: Riverhead Books.
Connell, C. (2010). Doing, undoing, or redoing gender? Learning from the workplace experiences of transpeople. *Gender and Society, 24*(1), 31–55.
Deonna, J. A., Rodogno, R., & Teroni, F. (2012). *In defense of shame: The faces of an emotion*. New York, NY: Oxford University Press.
Deutsch, F. (2007). Undoing gender. *Gender and Society, 21*(1), 106–127.
Duggan, L. (2003). *The twilight of equality?: Neoliberalism, cultural politics, and the attack on democracy*. Boston, MA: Beacon Press.
Edman, E. M. (2016). *Queer virtue: What LGBTQ people know about life and love and how it can revitalize Christianity*. Boston, MA: Beacon Press.
Emerson, R. M., Fretz, R. I., & Shaw, L. (1995). *Writing ethnographic fieldnotes*. Chicago, IL: University of Chicago Press.
Flanagan, O. (2013). The shame of addiction. *Frontiers in Psychiatry, 4*(Article 120), 1–11. https://doi.org/10.3389/fpsyt.2013.00120
Foucault, M. (1978). *History of sexuality, volume I: An introduction*. New York, NY: Vintage.
Fowler, J. W. (1996). *Faithful change: The personal and public challenges of postmodern life*. Nashville, TN: Abingdon Press.
Galtung, J. (2007). Violence, peace, and peace research. In V. Bufacchi (Ed.), *Violence: A philosophical anthology* (pp. 78–109). London: Palgrave MacMillan.
Garver, N. (2007). What violence is. In V. Bufacchi (Ed.), *Violence: A philosophical anthology* (pp. 170–182). London: Palgrave MacMillan.
Gould, D. (2009). *Moving politics: Emotion and ACT UP's fight against AIDS*. Chicago, IL: University of Chicago Press.
Halperin, D., & Traub, V. (2009). *Gay shame*. Chicago, IL: University of Chicago Press.
Harvey, D. (1989). *The condition of postmodernity: An enquiry into the origins of cultural change*. Malden, MA: Wiley Blackwell.

Hauerwas, S., & Pinches, C. (1997). *Christians among the virtues: Theological conversations with ancient and modern ethics.* Notre Dame, IN: University of Notre Dame Press.

Holstein, J. A., & Gubrium, J. F. (2000). *The self we live by: Narrative identity in a postmodern world.* New York, NY: Oxford University Press.

Holstein, J. A., & Gubrium, J. F. (2008). *Handbook of constructionist research.* New York, NY: Guilford.

Karlsson, G., & Sjoberg, L. G. (2009). The experiences of guilt and shame: A phenomenological-psychological study. *Humanistic Studies, 32,* 335–355.

LaRossa, R. (2005). Grounded theory methods and qualitative family research. *Journal of Marriage and Family, 69,* 845–862.

Lee, J. (2012). *Torn: Rescuing the gospel from the gays-vs.-Christians debate.* New York, NY: Jericho Books.

Lehtinen, U. (1998). How does one know what shame is? Epistemology, emotions, and forms of life in juxtaposition. *Hypatia, 13*(1), 56–77.

Lewis, H. (1971). *Shame and guilt in neurosis.* New York, NY: International Universities Press.

Lewis, M. (1992). *Shame: The exposed self.* New York, NY: The Free Press.

Lynd, H. (1958). *On shame and the search for identity.* New York, NY: Science Editions.

Manion, J. C. (2002). The moral relevance of shame. *American Philosophical Quarterly, 39*(1), 73–90.

Manson, J. L. (2010, July 10). New norms are much more than a PR disaster [editorial]. *National Catholic Reporter.* Retrieved from http://ncronline.org/blogs/new-norms-are-much-more-pr-disaster

Mason, M. (2010). On shamelessness. *Philosophical Papers, 39*(3), 401–425.

Mead, G. H. (1934/1967). *Mind, self, and society from the standpoint of a social behaviorist.* Chicago, IL: University of Chicago Press.

Moon, D. (2004). *God, sex, and politics: Homosexuality and everyday theologies.* Chicago, IL: University of Chicago Press.

Moon, D. (2005a). Discourse, interaction, and testimony: The making of selves in the US protestant dispute over homosexuality. *Theory and Society, 34*(5–6), 551–577.

Moon, D. (2005b). Emotion language and social power: Homosexuality and narratives of pain in church. *Qualitative Sociology, 28*(4), 327–349.

Moon, D., & Tobin, T. W. (2016). *Overcoming shame, practicing love: LGBTQ evangelicals' strategies for social justice, carpenter series on religion and sexuality.* Fordham University, New York, NY, March.

Moon, D., & Tobin, T. W. (2018). Sunsets and solidarity: Overcoming sacramental shame in conservative Christian churches to forge a queer vision of love and justice. *Hypatia,* forthcoming.

Moon, D., & Tobin, T. W. (2019). Humility: Rooted in relationship, reaching for justice. *Political Power and Social Theory, 36,* 101–121.

Moon, D., Tobin, T. W., & Sumerau, J. E. (2019). Alpha, omega, and the letters in between: LGBTQI conservative Christians undoing gender. *Gender & Society, 33*(4), 583–606.

Narvaez, D. (2014). *Neurobiology and the development of human morality.* New York, NY: Norton.

Pasquale, T. B. (2015). *Sacred wounds: A path to healing from spiritual trauma.* St. Louis, MO: Chalice Press.
Pattison, S. (2000). *Shame: Theory, therapy, theology.* Cambridge: Cambridge University Press.
Roberts, R. C. (2007). *Spiritual emotions: A psychology of Christian virtues.* Grand Rapids, MI: Eerdmans Publishing Company.
Roberts, R. C. (2009). The vice of pride. *Faith and Philosophy*, 26(2), 119–130.
Roberts, R. C. (2012). Unconditional love and spiritual virtues. In P. Moser & M. McFall (Eds.), *The wisdom of the Christian faith* (pp. 156–72). New York, NY: Cambridge University Press.
Roberts, R. C. (2016). Learning intellectual humility. In J. Baehr (Ed.), *Intellectual virtues and education: Essays in applied virtue epistemology* (pp. 184–201). New York, NY: Routledge.
Roberts, R. C., & Wood, J. (2007). *Intellectual virtues: An essay in regulative epistemology.* Oxford: Clarendon Press.
Scheff, T. J. (1990). Socialization of emotions: Pride and shame as causal agents. In T. D. Kemper (Ed.), *Research agendas in the sociology of emotions* (pp. 281–304). Albany, NY: SUNY Press.
Scheff, T. J. (2000). Shame and the social bond: A sociological theory. *Sociological Theory*, 18(1), 84–99.
Sedgwick, E. K. (2003). *Touching feeling: Affect, pedagogy, performativity.* Durham NC: Duke University Press.
Shotwell, A. (2011). *Knowing otherwise: Race, gender, and implicit understanding.* University Park, PA: Penn State University Press.
Snow, N. (1995). Humility. *Journal of Value Inquiry*, 29, 203–216.
Snow, N. (2010). *Virtue as social intelligence: An empirically grounded theory.* New York, NY: Routledge.
Spezio, M., Peterson, G., & Roberts, R. C. (2019). Humility as openness to others: Interactive humility in the context of l'Arche. *Journal of Moral Education*, 48(1), 27–46.
Stein, A. (2006). *Shame/less: Sexual dissidence in American culture.* New York, NY: NYU Press.
Strauss, A. C., & Corbin, J. M. (1998). *Basics of qualitative research: Techniques and procedures for developing grounded theory* (2nd ed.). Thousand Oaks, CA: Sage.
Stryker, S. (2008). Transgender history, homonormativity, and disciplinarity. *Radical History Review*, 100, 145–57.
Tangney, J. P. (2007). Self-relevant emotions. In M. R. Leary & J. P. Tangney (Eds.), *Handbook of self and identity* (pp. 184–201). New York, NY: Guilford Press.
Taylor, G. (1985). *Pride, shame and guilt.* Oxford: Oxford University Press.
Tessman, L. (2005). *Burdened virtue: Virtue ethics for liberatory struggles.* Oxford: Oxford University Press.
Thomason, K. (2015). Shame, violence, and morality. *Philosophy and Phenomenological Research*, 91(1), 1–24.
Tobin, T. W. (2016). Spiritual violence, gender, and sexuality: Implications for seeking and dwelling among some Catholic women and LGBT Catholics. In *Seekers and dwellers: Plurality and wholeness in a time of secularity*. Ed. Philip

J. Rossi in the Cultural Heritage and Contemporary Change Series VIII. *Christian Philosophical Studies*, *20*, 133–167.

Tobin, T. W., & Moon, D. (2019). The politics of shame in the motivation to virtue: Lessons from the shame, pride, and humility experiences of LGBT conservative Christians and their allies. *Journal of Moral Education*, *48*(1), 109–125.

Truluck, R. (2001). Spiritual violence [article in online magazine]. *Whosoever*. Retrieved from www.whosoever.org/v5i6/violence.html

Turner, J. H., & Stets, J. E. (2007). Moral emotions. In J. E. Stets & J. H. Turner (Eds.), *Handbook of the sociology of emotions* (pp. 544–566). New York, NY: Springer.

VanderWal-Gritter, W. (2014). *Generous spaciousness: Responding to gay Christians in the Church*. Grand Rapids, MI: Brazos Press.

Velleman, D. (2001). On the genesis of shame. *Philosophy and Public Affairs*, *30*(1), 27–52.

Walters, S. D. (2001). *All the rage: The story of gay visibility in America*. Chicago, IL: University of Chicago Press.

West, C., & Zimmerman, D. (2009). Accounting for doing gender. *Gender & Society*, *23*(1), 112–122.

Whitcomb, D., Battaly, H., Baehr, J., & Howard-Snyder, D. (2015). Intellectual humility: Owning our limitations. *Philosophy and Phenomenological Research*, *91*(1), 509–539.

Wolkomir, M. (2006). *Be not deceived: The sacred and sexual struggles of gay and ex-gay Christian men*. New Brunswick, NJ: Rutgers University Press.

Woodward, K. (2000). Traumatic shame, televisual culture, and the cultural politics of emotion. *Cultural Critique*, *46*(Autumn), 201–240.

9 Integrating "Cultures of Reasoning"
Interdisciplinary Research on Motivating the Self to Wisdom and Virtue

Ricca Edmondson, Michel Ferrari, Monika Ardelt, and Hyeyoung Bang

Many of the most interesting and important contemporary problems demand interdisciplinary research: they cannot be examined effectively within the confines of a single discipline. This team addressed one such question: *How do people motivate themselves to behave as virtuously and wisely as they can, and how do nation, religious faith, age, and/or wisdom contribute to this?* We examined virtue and wisdom together because, historically and theoretically, they have been seen as integrally connected. To be good involves knowing when and how to make virtuous efforts, which are governed by wisdom; wisdom itself involves virtue (Aristotle, *Nicomachean Ethics*; Schwartz & Sharpe, 2006). Yet people of different nations, cultures, and faiths, or different ages in adulthood, might well have very different understandings of what this entails.

Our specific project emerged in response to a call for proposals to examine motivating the self to virtue within interdisciplinary teams. It struck Michel Ferrari, on the basis of both his prior research experience and his conceptual analysis of the problems involved, that, to be addressed with any scope and depth, this topic demanded scholars working in psychology, philosophy, sociology, and political science, and could even extend to theological issues. Because this is a question that is salient to both individuals and to social and cultural groups, a specialist in cross-cultural psychology was also needed to compare across cultures. New measurement methods using computer simulations might also provide a novel way to address the complex and multifaceted dimensions of this topic. But, even so—retrospectively, in his own estimation—his initial framing of the project and methods to address it was rather unsophisticated. It was only as the different disciplinary sensibilities of the various team members were incorporated into the final proposal that a project of greater depth and potential interest began to take shape.

As we then formulated it, our project was designed to compare Canadians (in a historically Christian nation) and South Koreans (in a historically Buddhist nation) of four different faith conditions (Christian, Muslim, Buddhist, atheist). In other words, we were going to explore two highly contrasting overall settings, but within those settings we were aiming at as broad a coverage of faith conditions as possible. We envisaged that two studies were needed to accomplish this: The first aimed to compare older and younger adult lay people belonging to these four faith conditions in both countries; the second to focus in detail on a smaller number of exemplary individuals in both countries from these same traditions. How did we succeed in marshalling our interdisciplinary team in these endeavors?

This chapter starts by exploring a range of types and degrees of interdisciplinary cooperation that are possible for this type of project; we did not so much choose between them at the outset as *discover* which were appropriate and productive for us. Secondly, we examine the impact of the team members' disciplinary and personal academic experience on how the project took shape. Because this impact developed over time, it is most appropriate to describe it chronologically. This also underlines the processual nature of interdisciplinary inquiry. Thirdly, we found that our different approaches led to negotiations about what should be regarded as data and how to collect it, impacting on the shape our project eventually took. This applies also, fourthly, to interpreting the material we had collected; then too, our differences in approach impacted the shape the project took. Thus, fifthly, we argue that our divergences, which were always complemented by key realms of agreement and, just as importantly, by personal willingness to adapt and learn (Lélé & Norgaard, 2005), indicate the presence of what we call different "cultures of reasoning" (Edmondson, 2015) in specific approaches in the behavioral sciences. Moreover, these cultures and approaches may or may not coincide with disciplinary boundaries as conventionally understood. They are, more fundamentally, differences in relation to the theory of science. Then, we draw some conclusions about interdisciplinarity and what we have learned about it in the present project, which may have implications beyond our own work.

Our Funding Environment and Interdisciplinarity Beginnings

There are many different levels and forms of interdisciplinary cooperation, some of which can be described as "methodologically conservative" (Callard & Fitzgerald, 2015, pp. 4–5). In these cases, each colleague may simply contribute to a project from within their own discipline on a particular topic, with no fundamental attempt to modify their normal work processes; an instance might be an engineer who supplements her construction of a bridge with an exhibition based on a historian's description of the history of bridges in that district. (Even in such a case, one might reflect, such an engineer might reflect elements of this history at least in visual aspects of her design.) Alternatively, the epistemological and methodological practices in the project may be dominated by one discipline—whether for reasons dictated by the project's intrinsic demands, on the basis of funding parameters, or because of the relative social status of one of the disciplines or researchers involved. There are fashions and power structures in the academic world as in all others, and the relative influence of particular disciplines waxes and wanes, partly reflecting wider social, economic, and political developments. In other words, "modes of thinking and working" are "strongly inflected by particular arrangements of institutions, funders, and cross-disciplinary debates" (Callard & Fitzgerald, 2015, p. 6), not to mention the conventions and expectations of the "target community" for the research (Callard & Fitzgerald, 2015, p. 25; cf. Büttner & Leopold, 2016). In contrast to these conservative approaches, and despite the potential obstacles identified by Callard and Fitzgerald, a much more active form of sharing across disciplinary boundaries is demanded by research areas such as our own, one highly promising for innovation and knowledge development (Andersen & Wagenknecht, 2013; Dunbar & Fugelsang, 2005). Its discussion over the centuries has identified it as incapable of confinement within a single intellectual arena.

Funding environments are inescapably influential in setting the tone and style of research processes. In our case, we were fortunate enough to be permitted considerable leeway in the choice of colleagues and methods—in fact, the call for projects targeted deep integration across disciplines to address motivation to virtue, and a rigorous selection process was put in place through which ten interdisciplinary teams were finally selected. Although the overall project seemed to be leaning toward the discipline of psychology, partly because of the preponderance of empirical psychological research into virtue and wisdom today, its integration was rooted deeply within the project's design, examination of the quantitative and qualitative protocols, and analyses of the data as well as the writing processes. In other words, the project has aimed to reflect colleagues' conceptual and empirical responses to its central questions, rather than being oriented to more pragmatic considerations such as the availability of established work routines or institutional connections. Importantly, too, the overall funding call did not impose the "projectification" of research (Boltanski & Chiapello, 2005) that appears to demand flexibility and creativity but in practice confines these at a superficial and essentially instrumental level (Eliasoph, 2011). Nor was the call connected with any attempt to harness interdisciplinarity to specific forms of economic enterprise (cf. Barry, Born, & Weszkalnys, 2008). Researchers were free to pursue knowledge for the sake of understanding the phenomena involved.

The authors of this paper—to say nothing of the rest of the team—are of four different nationalities, work in three different countries, and stem from disciplines which are in principle cognate but whose differences became apparent as the project progressed. Two are psychologists, both with experience in mixed-methods studies, but with a different emphasis in their training (Hyeyoung Bang's training is more cross-cultural and with an educational psychology background, whereas Michel Ferrari—although also engaged in educational and developmental psychology—is particularly interested in person-centered and indigenous approaches). Two are sociologists, one a mixed-methods sociologist and life course researcher with a history of cooperation within psychology and long-term experience of questionnaire composition and analysis (Monika Ardelt), and the other a qualitative and ethnographic researcher with a background in philosophy and political science (Ricca Edmondson). All of these core colleagues had considerable interdisciplinary experience and commitment even before the project started—to the extent that it would actually be misleading to categorize them simply as "psychologists" or "sociologists." (For this reason, we have continued to use colleagues' given names in this paper; see the List of Contributors for details about their professional experience.) We should also note that all of us have experience living for extended periods in countries/cultures other than those in which we were born. The rest of the team embodies the rich combination we have already indicated, which extends to Jesuit Christian theology (Gilles Mongeau); cognitive science (John Vervaeke) (both of whom tended, possibly for partly logistical reasons, to communicate in more detail with Michel than with the other team members); and computer science and simulation (Michael Connell, whose contribution are explored later in this chapter). Even so, we found ourselves working within an overall research environment in which administering questionnaires and analyzing their results is taken for granted, a situation familiar to three of us but less so to Ricca, accustomed to working more ethnographically.

Working together over a series of team meetings and side conversations entailed what we see as a deep and active, rather than a conservative, form of interdisciplinarity. Grappling with these differences seems to us to have been creative and fruitful, but, like Callard and Fitzgerald, we consider it crucial to explore interdisciplinary tensions if we are to extract its full potential from interdisciplinary work. For example, from our initial meeting, Ricca's ethnographic leanings made her adamant that we needed to ask questions that would allow participants to tell us in their own terms what they understood by virtue and how that manifested in their own lives, in a way that extended beyond their personal ideas and actions (the focus of psychological studies more familiar to Michel and Hyeyoung) to the social and institutional contexts within which they acted. For her, meaning is enacted in interaction with social settings, in fluctuating ways, and individuals' capacities to report on their motives and ideals should not be exaggerated. We therefore needed several Skype discussions to iron out an interview protocol that was acceptable to everyone, especially since Monika and Hyeyoung also wanted to perform statistical analyses based on the answers to standardized questions and scales. Ricca was critical of standardized scale items and answer categories, because, as she pointed out, the meaning of these items and answer categories seemed likely both to differ significantly among respondents and to fail to capture what they regarded as more central aspects of their lives. While Monika and Michel acknowledged this possibility, they also emphasized that the answers to individual scale items are less relevant in quantitative research than the overall reliability of the scale and the relationship patterns between the variables for the groups of participants involved. For Ricca, the problems she saw meant that scales might be reliable in terms of consistency, but still lack validity as measures of wisdom and virtue. There are ripostes and counter-ripostes to arguments like this, not least that carrying this objection to its extreme would prohibit the use of scales altogether. As we explain, deep integration remained an aspiration, requiring compromises on all sides to adapt to the requirements of different disciplinary methods and practices.

Chronological Origins of Cooperation: Early Positions

Our chronology can begin before the project itself, since many of us had worked together or been in contact with one another before, having collaborated on a variety of other projects. Michel and Monika, for example, had already conducted an international study of understanding of wisdom (but not virtue) in Canada, the USA, Serbia, Ukraine, China, and India, using a mixed-methods approach similar to our current project. Michel and his graduate student Nic Weststrate had edited a book with chapters from Monika, Ricca, and John. Michel, Ricca, Monika, John, and Gilles had also been centrally involved in a workshop on wisdom and its meaning within different disciplines, and many of us were very familiar with Hyeyoung's published studies, comparing the USA, Korea, and China, using Monika's wisdom scale. Michael was brought in serendipitously, when Michel happened to hear him talking about a computer simulation he had developed to assess wisdom in several rounds of a task designed to provoke active problem solving under uncertain environmental conditions—which seemed an innovative method that could add significantly to the project. (It is perhaps no coincidence that Michel had previously co-authored a paper surveying educational simulations useful in training students for success in the workplace [Ferrari, Taylor, & VanLehn, 1999].)

Once we formally launched the project, we found—probably in common with many projects—that initial debates about how to collect data were less contentious than those concerning how to interpret them would later prove to be. The former could be solved using the principle of generosity: trying to include as much as possible that each researcher wanted. Eagerly we imagined what we might be able to ask our respondents, and were relatively charitable toward one another's wishes in this respect. Ricca, for example, felt that we were asking far too many questions, but did not raise this issue as energetically as she might have done if she had not *also* been keen to insert new kinds of questions about community and what recipients thought about *other* people's wisdom and virtue, that *she* felt were crucial! But, of course, data collection and data analysis are always intertwined. Several Skype meetings were required to arrive at a clear understanding of what different disciplines would eventually require of the data collected. Used to statistical analyses that identify group differences and patterns among variables, Monika, Michel, and Hyeyoung worried that the method of recruiting participants advocated by Ricca (essentially, to collect as wide a variety as possible within each faith condition) would result in too wide a range of individuals to be identified as a single group. For example, Michel worried that if our Canadian Christian participants included Catholics, Protestants, Evangelicals, and many other subgroups of Christian religion, are they really all Christian in the same way? For Ricca, that was exactly the point; she felt the term "Christian" by itself means little, and encouraged us to maximize diversity, for fear of limiting the meaning of "Christian" or "Buddhist," say, in an artificial manner that in the end led us to generalize about these faith positions from minority samples. Subgroups within, say, Christianity, are traditionally distinguished specifically with regard to their motivational structures: Catholics, for instance, are (rightly or wrongly) held to be more community-oriented and Protestants more individualistic. Nonetheless, the logic of statistical group comparisons requires a certain number of relatively homogenous people in each group. This tension remained unresolved, although—as happens in many projects—the pragmatic challenges of finding respondents itself exercised a key influence on what sorts of individuals we talked to. As a tension, the aspiration to wide coverage versus statistical group comparisons counts as a qualitative strength of the project but a quantitative limitation.

It is crucial to recognize here that quantitative and qualitative, or large-scale and ethnographic, approaches to data are *not merely* different-scale versions of the same type of inquiry. Some commentators assume that ethnography, for example, simply goes into "more detail" about situations described in more general terms using other methods: a sort of filling-in process. In fact, ethnography is intended (among other things) to discover more, and different types of items, about how respondents create and perform certain practices, and this takes place on the basis of distinct conceptions of the human being and human communication. It is based on the assumption that, ultimately, the meaning of language can only be discovered with the help of finding how people behave. For a range of reasons we cannot simply ask people for their views; much of what we think is obscure even to ourselves and constructed only in interaction. Recently, for example, Ricca repeat-interviewed a person she had previously conversed with in connection with wisdom. He talked at length about his gratitude for his life; for him, this gratitude demanded open-mindedness, generosity and tolerance toward others, even though these virtues are not semantically entailed by the word "gratitude" (Edmondson & Woerner, 2018, pp. 60–61). This finding could not have been predicted or deliberately sought in advance; although, after the event, other methods might be used to probe whether comparable associations arise elsewhere. In ethnography, therefore, it is important to allow data collection to proceed in a relatively open direction, without defining its destination too narrowly at the start, whereas quantitative survey research can only analyze the variables that have been included a priori in a questionnaire. Thus, these different methods entail genuinely radical (albeit sometimes productive) differences in conception of the entire project, and our team continuously sought to create an exploration that allowed for more than one conception of the project and its data. The simulation platform was largely unknown to us as a research team and we, perhaps naively in retrospect (see subsequent section), hoped it would be easily accommodated to a familiar qualitative or quantitative methodology.

What Are the Data? A Processual Approach to Project Development

In the initial phase, drawing up the methods for the project and discussing what we wanted to discover, the various questions that might underlie what we intended to do were not discussed in intricate detail. Partly, this was because it is difficult to discuss matters of principle in the abstract, without reference to the concrete empirical results that only the project itself can generate; partly because some methods, such as ethnographic ones, are envisaged as generating fundamental questions simultaneously with the progression of the work; partly because the urgent task at the time was to formulate a project that outlined the topics we all considered significant and timely and that at the same time conformed to the professional expectations that projects are expected to satisfy within a very limited timeframe of two years. We could not lose too much time at the beginning debating foundational principles and assumptions, so we tried to be inclusive of any disciplinary concerns that arose, with the thought that ultimate aims would emerge in the course of interaction among us and that dogmatism at the start would be misplaced and counterproductive. This approach was inevitable given our disciplinary differences, but it also allowed for maximum creativity and collegiality in developing the project.

Nonetheless, disciplinary tensions emerged despite every effort at collegiality, since particular interview questions betrayed differences in methodological approaches to meaning: for example, around the issue whether meaning can be regarded as fixed at the time of collection or best sought in reference to the individual or their communities. Ricca's previous interdisciplinary cooperation with ethnographers, and in particular a psychiatrist/psychotherapist, resulted in the conclusion that meaning is not fixed at the time of collection. This practitioner regularly asks her patients, "How do you feel about what you said yesterday? Does that seem the same way to you?" That is, the fact that "data" were submitted on a particular day by a particular person cannot necessarily be taken to be a permanent account of their position (Pearce, 2013). Different kinds of utterances about different kinds of topics might be expected to have different kinds and degrees of impermanence, certainly, but later in the project (looking at the experimental simulation data) we had reason to believe that people's accounts of what they think wisdom is may be strongly influenced by context. On the other hand, colleagues from psychology, like Michel and Hyeyoung, and Monika from sociology, argued that while all this may be true in principle, in the pragmatic world of data collection, we still needed to analyze the information we actually have rather than the data it might potentially become, and that the point of asking a group of people the same questions was to account for this potential variability at the time of data collection. Ricca would accept this, out of necessity, but would prefer to preserve a relatively tentative attitude to what counts as "data" and how it is treated, even when considering the groups as a whole. Of course, one solution to this problem, asking the same group of people the same questions over an extended period (Salthouse &

Nesselroade, 2010), would have required more time and resources than our project had available.

In addition, part of the difficulty emanates from differences in philosophical anthropology. Are human beings' attitudes chiefly cognitive items, locatable in their heads, so that they can be reported fairly straightforwardly? Or are they a fluid congeries of partly behavioral tendencies and practices, dependent on local languages for their expression and subject to change in different circumstances? How fixed is linguistic meaning, and how difficult to interpret accurately? While these questions can be debated, other differences are hard even to diagnose, since they derive from sub-conscious perceptual habits. This led to a fruitful tension over whether to locate our unit of analysis at the level of the individual or at the level of experienced social interactions by individuals within their socio-cultural groups. Over the course of several Skype meetings and side meetings, and in line with her generally constructionist approach to meaning (Edmondson, 2015), Ricca made a strong case for including questions that asked about participation at the level of interpersonal relationships and group membership, a welcome corrective to the project's initial frame of reference, which was almost exclusively imagined in terms of individual psychological motivation, choices, and understanding, but within the constraints of a specific national and religious context. Monika would caution, however, that even these questions are subject to the same criticism Ricca had about the changing meaning of language: letting people talk about interpersonal relationships and group membership is not equivalent to observing people during social interactions. The focus of attention is still the individual, rather than an interactional unit.

Much of the foregoing discussion happened during our research meeting in Oxford before the Study 2 phase began. Study 2 planned to interview moral nominees with the same interview protocols and measurement items that were administrated in Study 1. Ricca, Michel, and Hyeyoung met at Oxford University (since Hyeyoung was already visiting Oxford), and extensively discussed what the data from the Study 1 phase had revealed, what else we wanted from the data, and how we could adjust to add deep understanding of the reality between participants' words, behaviors, and recognition. As discussed earlier, although the integration efforts had been exercised in each step of the project, Ricca still felt some results from Study 1 did not prevail enough on the ethnography side. Ricca emphasized that meaning is conveyed by the full gamut of human (inter-)behavior, while the results of the data, in a way, are more artificial. The interview protocol collects only one aspect of behavior—speech—and divests it of its context, so that it can be difficult to know what interviews of this sort really convey. Thus, this discussion greatly affected the Study 2 phase.

In this second phase, we significantly changed the frame of data collection to include observing exemplary participants' interactions in communities and social settings. Originally, we had wanted to observe the moral exemplars nominated by the participants in Study 1. However, there was a serious research design limitation (limited time, too many participants to observe and interview, and too many structured interview questions) to apply Ricca's suggestions of using more in-depth ethnographic data collection for Study 2. Thus, we selected moral exemplars whom Hyeyoung, Michel, and their research assistants knew, or who had been nominated by closer friends of the research team, so that we could freely engage with them in their social settings. For example, Hyeyoung interviewed a Buddhist monk who was a friend of one of Hyeyoung's friends, and she was able to spend an entire day not only with the participant, but also with the participant's own friends, and observed and actively participated in the interactions and the conversations. The resulting interview was a fascinating and deeply contextual account of wisdom and virtue in the context of healing that showed how Korean understanding of the concepts of wisdom and virtue are bound up with deep-seated cultural beliefs, such as karma, that are essential to helping suffering people to become more virtuous (Bang, 2017).

As another Korean example, a research assistant selected one of her colleagues as a moral exemplar, someone who was actively engaged in social work and missionary work in the Christian church. She was able to attend a dinner with the participant along with the participant's church friends to observe their interactions. In Canada, we interviewed Gretta Vosper, a United Church minister who is an avowed atheist and yet whose church community has followed her in this unorthodox approach to religious practice, which emphasizes community and social justice in place of faith in an immaterial, ultimate God—in some ways returning to what some consider the origins of Christianity, before Christ became God, as explained by Ehrman (2014), whose work she knows well. This generated an ideological battle within the United Church over whether such a person should be allowed to continue to be a minister in the Church that is still unresolved. Qualitative data analysis now under way that includes notes of ethnographic participation and interviews is expected to provide the greatest insight into participants' perceptions and understanding of this unique situation surrounding motivation to virtue that borders both atheism and Christianity.

Interpreting the Data

In the interpretation phase of the research, it became necessary to develop more definite ideas of the aim of interpretation and what it involves. Are we trying to reconstruct the "webs of meaning" people share? To explore their identities and views of themselves? To discover patterns of behavior and predict change? Research and interpretation procedures are different in all these cases. For instance, in content analysis (Stemler, 2001), it is acceptable to start with the question, "What shall we code for?" even before having seen the data; this method aims to be "a systematic, reliable technique for compressing many words of text into fewer categories based on explicit rules of coding" developed in advance. From a more Grounded Theory approach (Glaser & Strauss, 1967), this seems shocking: codes must *arise from the data*, precisely without being influenced by what researchers hope or expect to find on the basis of their own linguistic worlds.

For Ricca, the question of meaning is central to interpretation; for her, meaning is contextual and fluid rather than fixed, demonstrated via use rather than definition, thus understood incrementally through the hermeneutic analysis of how terms are used. So we had to proceed hermeneutically, examining interviews by scrutinizing minute forms of utterances, but always going back to the overall interview, then back to the minute utterance. These issues arose very clearly when Michel, Ricca, and Monika met in Berlin in the spring of 2017 to analyze the interviews of Christian participants who scored the highest and lowest on Monika's wisdom scale. This experience was very important for all of us in demonstrating the essential need for collegiality in practice in the process of interpretation. It seemed that we learned far more about the people speaking when discussing them together than when reading interviews alone; the back and forth of debate about what a person might have meant, supported by a return to the original audio recordings of the interviews to gauge the tone of what was said, conjured up that individual in much richer detail than a one-person-interpreted reading could have done. This richness arose in large part because Monika, Ricca, and Michel had very different training in qualitative analysis of interviews and, as previously mentioned, very different starting ideas about what to look for in the interviews, and what would count as evidence of having found it—all of which made for productive and mutually enlightening discussions.

In relation to one of the most surprising interviews—a case we will call Cynthia—our impression changed as her interview evolved over the course of two sessions' meeting between the interviewer and herself. She had been selected as a maximally contrastive case of low wisdom (the lowest scorer on Monika's wisdom scale) for the older Canadian Christian group, and at first seemed to bear this out as someone whose relation to others was somehow obstructed—for example, her moral exemplar was a friend who had simply supported her in an office conflict, but she said this was something she had never experienced before. It was only at the end of the second interview that it became clear that her life had been a struggle, not least in response to the ongoing unresponsiveness, even neglect, of her parents, especially of her father, whom she still looked to as wise, but whose "wisdom" included sayings such as "Never trust anyone, not even your own father." Thus, she no longer seemed just a "low scorer" on the wisdom scale, but someone engaged in a perhaps desperate emotional and moral struggle, reflected in the actual help she offered to neighbors in need, which she recounted in stories framed in terms of being somewhat demanding to her. This was an important experience for us, not least because the revelation about this respondent's father came right at the end of the second of two interviews. The interview could easily have been broken off earlier, in which case we would never have obtained this new perspective. This raises the question about what else we are missing from all our interviews, given the relatively minute slivers of our respondents' lives we have obtained; for Ricca, this constitutes an additional argument for the appropriateness of tentativeness in interpretation.

There were more questions about what interpretation is and how it should be carried out. For Ricca, the interviews were central, and their interpretation should be regarded as the basis of our data; she tends to regard questionnaire data as highly speculative, unless the topics are bounded and concrete, which is not the case here. For Monika, the questionnaire data, particularly from the Three-Dimensional Wisdom Scale (3D-WS; Ardelt, 2003), with which she has been working for many years, helps to discover patterns of relationships among the variables, with cases, such as Cynthia's, illustrating the differences between the extreme ends of the scale. It follows that it makes sense to select respondents who scored highest and lowest on the scale for a contrasting in-depth analysis of the qualitative interviews to gain additional insight into the respondents' lives and their understanding of wisdom and moral virtue. Monika viewed these extreme cases as in-depth illustrations of the quantitative data whereas, to Ricca, this position appears circular, as if searching for details that could justify a judgment which actually ought to be regarded as suggestive or—again—tentative. She prefers to interpret the interviews in all their complexity (or as much of it as time and opportunity allow), and only then ask how the respondents had replied to the items in the Wisdom Scale questionnaire, comparing the two sources for different types of insight into the respondents' positions. Michel had hoped for a position midway between these two poles, in which the entire set of questionnaire data for respondents might produce some sort of typology of different kinds of more or less wise and moral prototypes.

Each of these positions had larger implications for the project. For example, expediency required that we draw on graduate students to conduct the 240 interviews scheduled in our design in Canada and South Korea—a standard practice in psychological studies, but one that worried Ricca, who felt that students might miss the nuances of the situation. This same concern extended to data analysis, with Monika, Hyeyoung, and Michel much more willing to instruct a team of graduate students to look for key ideas and tabulate their frequency in the interviews. In fact, it would not have been possible to do without the help of these students within the time-scale of the project. On occasion we wished they had had the confidence to probe certain answers of the respondents a little more subtly or in a little more detail, but we felt that by and large they helped the respondents to provide rich and informative data that could not have been obtained without them.

It might be pointed out that familiarity and practice influenced differences of opinion about gathering and interpreting data, in addition to divergences in principle. On the occasions—as yet relatively few—where we compared "blind" interpretations to those yielded by the 3D-WS, they have seemed compatible, or at least to indicate promising relationships. More work along these lines seems thus to be indicated as constructive.

At the time of this writing, we are just beginning to explore these points across the cultures of Canada and South Korea and similar issues are arising, but with the additional difficulty of language allowing for new concepts, and possible cultural differences in how people respond to self-report scales (and, of course, the translations of those scales). As mentioned earlier, Michel, Ricca, and Hyeyoung met in Oxford in late 2016 to discuss these issues before launching the second phase of the study, interviewing exemplars of wisdom and virtue, and Hyeyoung came to Toronto and joined a group meeting to discuss this with the entire team before launching Phase 1. Both of these meetings allowed us to better understand what would be easy to transport to South Korea unchanged, and what needed to be adapted to that particular cultural context. Despite these efforts, Hyeyoung encountered many problems in deploying the study in South Korea. For example, when translating some of the spirituality and religiosity items into Korean, the subtlety disappears and there is little difference in the content of the scales. Thus, after a Skype consultation with Michel after data collection was under way in Korea, Hyeyoung decided to streamline the questionnaire portion of the study by dropping some scales assessing religious practices that in their Korean version seemed entirely redundant.

Nonetheless, some challenges might affect the compatibility of interdisciplinary research. When analyzing quantitative results, we tested measurement invariance to provide either confidence in the interpretation of the data or explanations for cultural differences in the meaning of items or subscales. However, in ethnographic data collection and analysis, the different cultural settings might complicate the interpretation of the data. As already mentioned, Hyeyoung was able to find a way to pay closer attention to the interdisciplinary research objectives, but there are still unknown challenges because of the linguistic issue. Because Hyeyoung is the only person who speaks and understands Korean on the research team (not counting some Korean graduate students who have been able to assist her), it is not possible for other research members to interpret the qualitative data without Hyeyoung's help and through her lens. Although some Korean interviews have been translated into English, it is impossible to understand the nuanced meaning of these interviews without returning to the original Korean. Thus, there will be more discussions on interpreting the data, which will certainly lead to more learning opportunities for all our team members.

To move to a separate aspect of the project, a simulation game was devised by Mike Connell in another context, but we were given access to its use in conjunction with our interviews. The game attempts to trace wise decisions in practice, which in principle extends our access to respondents' capacities, by offering participants a linked series of practical problems of resource management envisaged as taking place in two imaginary countries, where ministers needed to make decisions about industry and the environment, with the possibility of discussing their decisions between them. Because this type of dynamic assessment of wisdom is still under development, the simulation was restricted; opportunities offered players for decision-making were extremely circumscribed. This made it hard for other team members to understand how the algorithms for the game could reasonably assess participants' degrees of wisdom, based on "scores" given at the end of a game, without a deeper understanding of how and why these allocations took place. Mike was also reluctant to stand behind these assessment scores in any definitive way, but did agree that the dialogue between participants and their definitions of wisdom might contribute something to the interdisciplinary project.

In one of our initial interdisciplinary efforts to interpret the data, graduate students in Florida worked with Monika to use her Three-Dimensional Wisdom Model (3D-WM)—consisting of cognitive, reflective, and compassionate (affective) dimensions (Ardelt, 1997, 2003, 2004)—to code respondents' definitions of wisdom after completing the simulation task. Pairs of students were assigned to code one of the three dimensions independently. After each student coded the answers, coding pairs met to discuss and resolve coding discrepancies.

Unfortunately, as the result of a misunderstanding between Michel's team conducting the interviews and Mike's team running the simulation, in the data received, the identifiers of the simulation task were not related to the identifiers on the surveys and qualitative interviews. Because we had not anticipated this problem we had not thought to have players specifically identify themselves at the start, which has made it so far impossible to link the simulation performance to the interview or questionnaire data—despite a significant effort to match players to interviews using the data on the times of their interviews. This incident illustrates the difficulty of working across disciplines with methods about which the principal investigator (Michel) and team members know very little, since our seemingly small oversight during data collection led to this major problem later during data analysis. It also demonstrates that what might have appeared too obvious to state to one set of researchers—that we needed to regard the data as generated by *people* whose reactions could be traced throughout their progress through the simulation—seemed by no means self-evident from another point of view.

Nevertheless, we were still able to analyze the simulation data independently, and results showed that 60.8% (48 of the 79) of participants in the simulation task who provided a wisdom definition mentioned a cognitive characteristic when defining wisdom, and about half (50.6%) specifically mentioned the ability to make important decisions—a main focus of the simulation task itself. Only 16.5% defined wisdom as a reflective characteristic (perspective-taking), and 31.6% used a compassionate characteristic to describe wisdom. Surprisingly, 27.8% (22/79 participants) mentioned neither cognitive, reflective, nor compassionate characteristics of wisdom. Lastly, the amount of time spent on the simulation task was unrelated to any of the three-dimensional wisdom codings. In other words, we are not yet in a position to interpret participants' performance in the game or to coordinate it with the interview or questionnaire data, so we are still grappling with how to integrate the rest of the simulation data into the larger project.

"Cultures of Reasoning": Argumentative Conventions and Membership of Academic Communities

Scientific work has not been consistently corralled into rigid disciplinary areas throughout the whole of its history (Barry et al., 2008); many current disciplinary barriers were originally erected during the professionalization of university research as late as the nineteenth century, as much in the interests of professional self-protection as from intrinsic logic or need (Dixon, 2003). Abandoning them can on occasion renew traditions in intellectual history that should never have been obscured. As we navigate between the islands of an "archipelago" of disciplines and interests, evolving relationships among them can also demand re-thinking the structure of the knowledge involved (Ette, 2004). As we have discovered in our own case, melding disciplinary approaches can alter the nature of their original constituents; that is, each of us has come to appreciate more of what drives the others' perspectives, and this has affected our own practice in the course of this project. However, some of this understanding has developed through aspects of interpersonal interaction rather than (or in addition to) explicit debate. In this section, we reflect on some of the less obvious pathways that have enhanced our mutual comprehension. We suggest that they point to differences between (parts of) disciplines as *cultural* differences about what scientific *reasoning* can be taken to be.

As a result of the different historical pathways followed in academic research communities, researchers in different (sub-) disciplines now have somewhat different theoretical expectations of what constitutes reliable knowledge; however, our work together has highlighted the fact that these expectations about reasoning are often communicated through *styles* rather than stated in so many words. For example, in psychology, concision and definiteness are taken as signs of competence, whereas tentativeness is taken as unnecessarily vacillating, tending in the end simply to waste time or signal continued confusion or ignorance. For Ricca and other ethnographers—and (uncharacteristically, as a psychologist) for Michel, too—by contrast, being consistently definite is merely a sign of the unreliability of colleagues' understanding of the theory of science, and tentativeness is both ethically and epistemologically demanded. For Monika, the statement that "it could be otherwise" is a given in scientific research, since research can never *prove* that a theory, hypothesis, or conclusion is correct, but she believes that the task of the researcher is to make sense of the quantitative and qualitative data and present a definite plausible set of explanations and conclusions to the reader about "what is going on." In Ricca's approach, certainly one needs to try to make sense of what is going on: but this needs to foreground the views and behaviors of respondents rather than the researcher. In other words, "what is going on" is an expression that means different things to different researchers. This exemplifies the fact that colleagues have different "epistemic preferences": contrasting expectations of what counts as (useful) knowledge. Communicative styles are in practice taken to indicate these preferences, with their varying values, emphases, and epistemological and moral positions. While not necessarily stated explicitly, different styles of argumentation became apparent to us as the project unfolded. We needed to negotiate a shared style in order to proceed with analysis and interpretation that all team members could support, even if it did not always match their own preferred styles. However, as in non-academic cultural settings, adjusting one's style to that of others can have the effect of making their more formal views easier to access.

"Styles" such as precision versus tentativeness concern colleagues' ways of doing things. But they have correlates in terms of perceptions: what people from different disciplines actually perceive. We saw this when Michel worked with John Vervaeke to supervise an MA student, Juensung Kim, whose thesis on exemplars of wisdom and virtue grew out of the project, using the same extreme contrast examples examined by Monika, Ricca, and Michel in Berlin. John, being trained as a philosopher, was very interested in the arguments advanced, while Michel was extremely concerned about the empirical support for the claims that were made in accordance with the conventions of psychological research. For each of them, there were different salient features of what was on the page.

In effect, therefore, within different (regions of) different disciplines, "cultures of reasoning" (Edmondson, 2015, 2012) have evolved which define what items of evidence count as most relevant, what networks of respected work can be drawn upon, and what styles of inference should be brought into play. In some areas within the humanities (such as in some approaches to historical studies), anything that smacks of the "theoretical" or "philosophical" tends to be dismissed, perceived as unduly tenuous; perhaps we might try to explain this on the grounds that the links between steps in theoretical reasoning are conventionalized and orderly, but in ways that may not be apparent to those untrained in that discipline. Individual researchers' personal ranges remain relatively limited, and possible reasons for this are worth examining. In sociology, for example, it is rare to find anyone equally skilled in qualitative and quantitative methods. There are grounds for this not only in terms of the time it takes to acquire and practice complex skills but also in the career paths and associated social interactions that emerge from possessing them; other important reasons are epistemological and ontological. It is possible to imagine an ethnographer engaged in a hermeneutic exchange with the members of a particular locality, from which emerges a version of inhabitants' shared understandings of how life-courses, say, develop under the specific conditions obtained there. Someone skilled in survey construction might find it natural to ask how general this set of attitudes is. The hermeneuticist, in turn, might feel affronted by the implication that the work in question involved detecting a set of standard items in a social region, such that one could sensibly assume that the distribution of *similar* items could automatically be measured elsewhere. It would need to be explored, rather than assumed, in how far similar phenomena arise and what is importantly distinctive about other situations. This does not mean that hermeneutic methods could not, in principle, be combined in projects with quantitative ones; but, to achieve this, researchers would need to devise ways of coming to terms with divergent conceptions of human beings and about what their "attitudes" are. In real life, proponents of such different views usually solve the problem simply by avoiding one another, but in an interdisciplinary project, this stalemate cannot be allowed.

These cultural differences go some way to explaining what other authors have noticed in terms of what Callard and Fitzgerald (2015, pp. 21 & 30) term the importance of "co-location"—at least on visits, not least so that members can familiarize themselves with aspects of one another's work and taken-for-granted assumptions and procedures that may be difficult to describe in so many words; and so that collegiality and friendliness can induce a relatively charitable interpretation of differences within the team (see also Cummings & Kiesler, 2005). This was certainly true for our project. We have managed to be physically together on a number of occasions in the UK (Oxford), Canada (University of Toronto), Germany (Berlin), and the US (San Francisco), and via Skype meetings and phone conferences, though not as many as we had hoped. Given members' other commitments, bringing an international team together for protracted periods proved very challenging. (In the case of Mike Connell and his colleague, we did not succeed in meeting in person, which may have affected our ability to predict and circumvent problems.) This highlights the fact that time is a considerable issue in interdisciplinary work, and may circumscribe its production overall (cf. Leahy, Beckman, & Stanko, 2017). We felt that the direct interaction we did achieve was extremely important and constructive to creating a meaningful project that spanned the concerns of our respective disciplines (and indeed that colleagues who had not been physically integrated in this way also became intellectually somewhat distanced from others' concerns). Our interpretation of the significance of "cultures" of reasoning, which are like other cultures in needing to be communicated via interaction, helps to explain *why* "co-location" is so significant.

We can explore links between academic style and reasoning further, for example, by observing that in fields that differ between (sub-)disciplines, "approaches" are partly characterized by singling out particular (sets of) items as significant—meaning rather than causation, or lived experience rather than social structure, for example. This is understandable, at least insofar as it would be impossible to perceive patterns within a field at all, if all its constituents seemed equally important. Perceived scales of significance are not, however, mere disagreements about where items stand on a list (as on a Likert scale); in effect, they alter the field. To argue for the significance of local interpretations of concepts concerned with virtue and wisdom entails getting readers not only to entertain vivid images of respondents' lived contexts but to grow accustomed to accepting these images *as paradigmatically communicative* in textual arguing, rather than as mere illustrations. Interpretive texts are hence replete with literary operations (such as mimesis, on the small scale, or narrative on a larger one), which act to persuade readers to accept relevant descriptions *as salient* to conveying meaning—to care about them, to accept them as reflecting significant features of the social world which demand explication (Edmondson, 1984, 2007).

The fact that conventions of thought and debate differ between (sub-)disciplines has far-reaching implications. In general, authors of academic texts need to make efforts to establish an "ethos" sufficient for them to be taken seriously (Edmondson, 1984, 2007; cf. Goffman, 1959). They try to show that they respect their audiences, are well equipped to find arguments taking readers' interests into account, and are both motivated and able to deal with the difficulties their arguments are designed to confront. But different professions generate highly conventionalized modes of discourse which are taken to convey such effects, though members are often unaware that they are doing more than reasoning *tout court*. It is not unreasonable for readers to seek indications that writers have read the appropriate texts in the field, can demonstrate correct use of central concepts, and can show familiarity with what other people are arguing in salient debates; making demonstrations of this kind, and doing so using the linguistic terms and scripts accepted as up to date in the field, can take up much of the argument in short texts such as journal articles. The capacity for this type of discursive fluency is developed, often painfully, in the course of academics' individual socialization, and hence it commands considerable loyalty once acquired. For this reason, however, the work of colleagues following conventions acquired in other academic terrains can appear to bear the signs of unreliability or incompleteness. Interdisciplinary projects bear the burden of trying to convince readers that new sets of conventions must be accepted.

Under these circumstances, even apparently trivial conventions of debate may acquire not only authority but their own independent meaning. Referencing conventions are a case in point. Philosophical footnotes tend to be relatively discursive, since authors often feel obliged to say why they are referring to another text: for instance, because it discusses some particular problem in a manner which is satisfactory in certain respects or suggests additional questions. In sociology or politics, authors also refer to other writers who have made contributions to areas they discuss. This is usually done by simply supplying the reference (name and date) in brackets; it is not mentioned, for example, whether the writer referred to is held to be entirely competent or otherwise. In psychology, in particular, this form of referencing can lead to the unspoken implication that the reference is counted as *referring to satisfactory support*, often additional empirical support, perhaps even implying that this demonstrates the validity of the first writer's concerns. To this extent, supplying another author's name can be read as legitimizing the writer's own argument, though there may be few rational reasons for this assumption; indeed, the practice can lend somewhat spurious solidarity to the text. It simultaneously endorses a crispness of style which itself conveys the impression that tentativeness is to be discouraged and that knowledge of the social world is more definite than—from a hermeneutic point of view—it really seems to be.

In terms of our project, these different cultures of reasoning led to some uneasiness about how conclusions were being drawn out or written up that sometimes needed prolonged discussion among different members of the team to articulate what it was they were concerned about. Nonetheless, becoming aware of them enables us to appreciate in much more depth how the priorities of different (sub-)disciplines are constituted, learning to make explicit the implicit argumentation involved.

Conclusions: Coping With Interdisciplinarity

Although we are still in the process of articulating the full set of findings from our project, we feel that our interdisciplinary work has been fruitful and must be treated as an intercultural project with several levels of difference, from dissimilarities in the ways we collect and interpret data, to variations in what we accept as appropriate scientific methods. Our own approach to dealing with these features of interdisciplinarity have been based on learning that it takes time to understand others' methods and assumptions—starting by seeing them as *needing* to be interpreted (or even recognized) rather than dismissed as simple mistakes. This cannot be taken for granted. Nikander (2007, p. 50) documents what she terms tightrope-walking during meetings of hospital interdisciplinary teams, as members try to avoid utterances which they believe will appear meaningless, misleading, or inappropriate to one another. As a result, they take refuge in relatively non-committal personal stances, since "departures from neutralism are sometimes understood as a breach of sound professional practice" (Nikander, 2007, p. 50). Such flights to neutrality can be observed in many or most settings where interdisciplinary cooperation is required: it is an unintended consequence of intercultural misunderstanding to entice participants to refrain from interventions that might, potentially, have been significant but that are, in the press of interaction, interpreted as embarrassing or confusing. This occurs partly because of researchers' own feelings of diffidence or reluctance to appear ill-informed; cracks are papered over rather than excavated. Callard and Fitzgerald (2015) refer to the emotional life of interdisciplinary researchers, the possible confusion and irritation that may arise from this type of work, and the "affectively fuzzy domain" and various forms of anxiety it may generate (p. 112; cf. also Rabinow & Bennett, 2012; Lélé & Norgaard, 2005).

This is not a feature of research to which much attention is normally accorded, but it is undoubtedly significant in the success or failure of interdisciplinary research teams in general. In our case, we benefited from the gentle and open-minded mediation of Michel Ferrari—whose readiness to find constructive ways out of disagreement was enormously beneficial—but also of our entire team, who entered the project with a spirit of engaged inquiry that naturally cuts through convention and reaches out to discover what other disciplines have to offer. Moreover, our project was located within an overall research landscape in which open-minded interdisciplinarity was specifically supported rather than treated with suspicion. Indeed, a criticism by our funders at a very early stage of our project development was that it was not interdisciplinary *enough*.

These factors allow us to draw a number of conclusions about what can be learned from our project. Firstly, we felt free to identify and express disciplinary divergence arising from the research heterogeneity we have described, excavating it down to a fundamental level in terms of the theory of science. Secondly, we identified features in terms of what we have called "cultures of reasoning" that expressed and intensified this divergence. We were able to recognize these features as stemming partly from differences in biography, temperament, and training, but partly also as expressing (in compressed form) the genuine differences of opinion to which we have already referred. This enabled us both to keep patience with one another and to gain insight into our own methodological convictions which could, we believe, be extended to benefit even teams working in projects that are not specifically interdisciplinary. Thirdly, working through these factors enabled us to flourish within a project whose aim was to investigate other people's culture—in a way that allowed us to deal more responsively with our colleagues' and our own.

Acknowledgment

All the authors are grateful for a grant from the Templeton Religion Trust [311678]. Ricca Edmondson is grateful for support in interdisciplinary research at the Centre for Advanced Studies in the Ludwig Maximilian University, Munich, in spring 2017.

References

Andersen, H., & Wagenknecht, S. (2013). Epistemic dependence in interdisciplinary groups. *Synthese*, *190*(11), 1881–1898.

Ardelt, M. (1997). Wisdom and life satisfaction in old age. *The Journals of Gerontology, Series B: Psychological Sciences and Social Sciences*, *52B*, 15–27. https://doi.org/10.1093/geronb/52B.1.P15

Ardelt, M. (2003). Empirical assessment of a three-dimensional wisdom scale. *Research on Aging*, *25*, 275–324.

Ardelt, M. (2004). Wisdom as expert knowledge system: A critical review of a contemporary operationalization of an ancient concept. *Human Development*, *47*, 257–285. https://doi.org/10.1159/000079154

Aristotle. (1984). Nicomachean ethics. In J. Barnes (Ed.), *The complete works of Aristotle: The revised Oxford translation* (Vol. 2). Princeton, NJ: Princeton University Press.

Bang, H. (2017). Buddhism and Up (Karma): A Buddhist priest's wisdom to help suffering: A conversation with Ji-Gong Bob-Sa. *Journal of Global Mental Health and Traditional Healing*, 1, 85–102.

Barry, A., Born, G., & Weszkalnys, G. (2008). Logics of interdisciplinarity. *Economy and Society*, 37(1), 20–49.

Boltanski, L., & Chiapello, È. (2005). *The new spirit of capitalism*. London: Verso.

Büttner, S., & Leopold, L. (2016). A "new spirit" of public policy? The project world of EU funding. *European Journal of Cultural and Political Sociology*, 3(1), 41–71.

Callard, F., & Fitzgerald, D. (2015). *Rethinking interdisciplinarity across the social sciences and neurosciences*. Houndmills: Palgrave Macmillan.

Cummings, J. N., & Kiesler, S. (2005). Collaborative research across disciplinary and organizational boundaries. *Social Studies of Science*, 35(5), 703–722.

Dixon, T. (2003). *From passions to emotions: The creation of a secular psychological category*. Cambridge: Cambridge University Press.

Dunbar, K., & Fugelsang, J. (2005). Scientific thinking and reasoning. In K. J. Holyoak & R. Morrison (Eds.), *Cambridge handbook of thinking & reasoning* (pp. 705–726). Cambridge: Cambridge University Press.

Edmondson, R. (1984). *Rhetoric in sociology*. London: Macmillan.

Edmondson, R. (2007). Rhetorics of social science: Reflexive sociology, disciplinary boundaries and the paradigmatic role of methodologies. In W. Outhwaite & S. Turner (Eds.), *The handbook of social science methodology* (pp. 479–498). London: Sage.

Edmondson, R. (2012). Practical reasoning in place: Tracing "wise" inferences in everyday life. In R. Edmondson & K. Hülser (Eds.), *Politics of practical reasoning: Integrating action, discourse and argument* (pp. 111–130). Lanham, MD: Lexington.

Edmondson, R. (2015). *Ageing, insight and wisdom: Meaning and practice across the life course*. Bristol: Policy Press.

Edmondson, R., & Woerner, M. (2018). Socio-cultural foundations of wisdom. In R. J. Sternberg & J. Glück (Eds.), *Handbook of wisdom* (pp. 40–68). Cambridge: Cambridge University Press.

Ehrman, B. (2014). *How Jesus became God: The exaltation of a Jewish preacher from Galilee*. New York, NY: HarperOne.

Eliasoph, N. (2011). *Making volunteers: Civic life after welfare's end*. Princeton, NJ: Princeton University Press.

Ette, O. (2004). *Überlebenswissen: Die aufgabe der philologie*. Berlin: Kulturverlag Kadmos.

Ferrari, M., Taylor, R., & VanLehn, K. (1999). Adapting work simulations for school: Preparing students for tomorrow's workplace. *Journal of Educational Computing Research*, 21(1), 25–53.

Glaser, B. G., & Strauss, A. L. (1967). *The discovery of grounded theory: Strategies for qualitative research*. London: Weidenfeld and Nicholson.

Goffman, E. (1959). *The presentation of self in everyday life*. New York, NY: Random House.

Leahy, E., Beckman, C., & Stanko, T. (2017). Prominent but less productive: The impact of interdisciplinarity on scientists' research. *Administrative Science Quarterly*, 62(1), 105–139.

Lélé, S., & Norgaard, R. (2005). Practicing interdisciplinarity. *BioScience*, 55(11), 967–975.

Nikander, P. (2007). Emotion categories in meeting talk. In A. Hepburn & S. Wiggins (Eds.), *Discursive research in practice* (pp. 50–69). Cambridge: Cambridge University Press.

Pearce, J. (2013, June). Wisdom and some creative processes. Unpublished paper from *International symposium on wisdom: Wisdom and the common good*. University of Potsdam, Potsdam, Germany.

Rabinow, P., & Bennett, G. (2012). *Designing human practices: An experiment with synthetic biology*. Chicago, IL: Chicago University Press.

Salthouse, T. A., & Nesselroade, J. R. (2010). Dealing with short-term fluctuation in longitudinal research. *The Journals of Gerontology: Series B: Psychological Sciences and Social Sciences*, 65B(6), 698–705. https://doi.org/10.1093/geronb/gbq060

Schwartz, B., & Sharpe, K. E. (2006). Practice wisdom: Aristotle meets positive psychology. *Journal of Happiness Studies*, 7(3), 377–395.

Stemler, S. (2001). An overview of content analysis. *Practical Assessment, Research and Evaluation*, 7(17), 1–6.

Contributors

Monika Ardelt is Professor of Sociology in the Department of Sociology, and Criminology and Law at the University of Florida. She received her *Diplom* in Sociology from the Johann Wolfgang Goethe University in Frankfurt, Germany, where she studied the representativeness of survey data, using log-linear models. She earned her PhD in Sociology from the University of North Carolina—Chapel Hill, examining the role of wisdom in successful aging from a life-course perspective through structural equation models. Her mixed-method quantitative and qualitative research focuses on successful human development across the life course, with particular emphasis on the relations among wisdom, psychological well-being, spirituality, aging well, and dying well.

Hyeyoung Bang holds an undergraduate degree in Elementary Education (Busan National University, South Korea) and taught elementary school children in Busan, South Korea. She also earned two master's degrees in Education (Bukyung National University, South Korea, and the University Of New England, Australia) and a PhD in Educational Psychology, Oklahoma State University (Stillwater, Oklahoma). She is currently an Associate Professor, and teaches Educational Psychology, Human Growth and Development, and Cross-Cultural Human Development in the School of Educational Foundations, Leadership, and Policy at Bowling Green State University (Ohio). Bang utilizes quantitative, qualitative, mixed-methods, and Q methodology in research. Her research agenda is on wisdom in the development of self; morality, virtue, and contemplation in life; acculturation, resilience, and schooling; Q methodology; and international and minority students in the United States.

Contributors

Jack J. Bauer, PhD, is Professor of Psychology at the University of Dayton. His forthcoming book, *The Transformative Self: Identity, Growth, and a Good Life Story* (Oxford), explains how people's life stories draw on cultural ideals of growth to facilitate well-being, wisdom, and moral virtue. He is the co-editor of *Transcending Self-Interest: Psychological Explorations of the Quiet Ego* (APA Books).

Bradford Cokelet, PhD, (Northwestern University, 2009) is a Visiting Assistant Professor of Philosophy at the University of Kansas. His work focuses on the nature of virtue and good human lives, with an emphasis on cross-cultural and empirically informed philosophic inquiry. He has published articles in *Ethics*, *European Journal of the Philosophy of Religion*, *Oxford Studies in Normative Ethics*, *Journal of Moral Education*, and several edited collections. His first book, *Buddhism, Ethics, and the Good Life*, is scheduled for publication by Routledge in fall 2020.

Paul Condon is an Assistant Professor of Psychology at Southern Oregon University in Ashland, Oregon. His research examines the social and relational processes that contribute to health and well-being, and how those outcomes may be facilitated by compassion and mindfulness meditation. His research on meditation is informed by collaboration with scholars of Buddhist philosophy. At SOU, he teaches courses in Health Psychology, Mindfulness and Compassion, History of Psychology, Statistics, and General Psychology. He also teaches meditation through the Foundation for Active Compassion. He completed his PhD at Northeastern University in Boston, Massachusetts, and his BA at Gonzaga University in Spokane, Washington.

Peggy DesAutels, PhD, is Professor of Philosophy at the University of Dayton. Her publications have focused on moral psychology, virtue theory, and feminist ethics. Her books include *Feminists Doing Ethics*; *Moral Psychology: Feminist Ethics*; and *Social Theory* and *Global Feminist Ethics*.

Colin G. DeYoung is Associate Professor of Psychology at the University of Minnesota, in the area of personality, individual differences, and behavior genetics. He researches the structure and sources of psychological traits, using neuroscience methods to investigate their biological substrates. He developed a general theory of personality, Cybernetic Big Five Theory, which identifies psychological functions associated with major personality traits as well as their connection to other elements of personality and various life outcomes, including mental illness. He won the Tanaka Dissertation Award from the Association for Research in Personality and the SAGE Young Scholar Award from the Foundation for Personality and Social Psychology. He has published more than 100 scientific articles, and his research has been supported by the National Science Foundation, the National Institutes of Health, and the Templeton Foundation.

John Dunne, PhD (1999, Harvard University), serves on the faculty of the University of Wisconsin—Madison, where he holds the Distinguished Chair in Contemplative Humanities, a newly endowed position created through the Center for Healthy Minds. He also holds a co-appointment in the Department of Asian Languages and Cultures. Previously he was an Associate Professor in the Department of Religion at Emory University, where he co-founded the Collaborative for Contemplative Studies.

His work focuses on Buddhist philosophy and contemplative practice, especially in dialogue with Cognitive Science and Psychology. His publications appear in venues ranging across both the Humanities and the Sciences, and they include works on Buddhist philosophy, contemplative practices, and their empirical examination and interpretation within scientific contexts. His current research focuses especially on the varieties of mindfulness and the contemplative theories that inquire into the nature of mindfulness. He speaks in both academic and public contexts, and he occasionally teaches for Buddhist communities. In addition to serving as a faculty member for the Center for Healthy Minds, he is a Fellow of the Mind and Life Institute, where he has previously served on the Board of Directors.

Ricca Edmondson holds an undergraduate degree in philosophy with political theory (Lancaster, UK); this was followed by a PhD in the theory of the social sciences, emphasizing the ways rhetoric and communication impinge on social-scientific argument (Oxford, UK). She did postgraduate research at the Max Planck Institute for Human Development (Berlin, Germany) in rules and norms in the sociology of organizations. She was subsequently employed to teach sociology, ethnography, and political theory at the National University of Ireland—Galway, where she is Professor in the School of Political Science and Sociology. She is also co-editor of the *European Journal of Cultural and Political Sociology* and visiting professor at the University of Tampere, Finland. Her recent research has focused on developing ethnographic and sociological/theoretical methods for studying culture and cultural change, including the use of rhetorical analysis; aging and the life course; and wisdom.

Michel Ferrari has an undergraduate degree in Liberal Arts, with a minor in Ancient Greek language (Concordia University, Montréal, Québec); and an MA and PhD in Developmental and Educational Psychology, using statistical analyses of group differences (Université du Québec à Montréal [UQAM], Montréal, Québec). He is a postdoctoral associate with Robert Sternberg, researching Psychological Test Development and Gifted Education using statistical techniques (Yale University, Connecticut). He is a research associate with Michelene Chi and Kurt VanLehn, studying computer simulations as training for the workplace using thematic analyses, and with Rosa Pinkus, studying case-based ethical reasoning in engineering education (LRDC, Pittsburgh, Pennsylvania). Dr. Ferrari is currently Professor in the Department of Applied Psychology and Human Development at the University of Toronto's Ontario Institute for Studies in Education (OISE). He is Director of the Wisdom and Identity Lab, which explores understanding and teaching personal wisdom at different ages, in special populations (such as people with autism), and in different countries, using a mixed-methods approach with a particular interest in person-centered methods.

Blaine J. Fowers, PhD (1987, University of Texas—Austin), is Professor of Counseling Psychology and Chairperson of the Department of Educational and Psychological Studies at the University of Miami. He is a Fellow of the American Psychological Association. His primary scholarly interest is exploring the moral dimension of psychology, both in research and practice. His current scholarly work is centered on the contributions of virtue ethics to a richer understanding of research and clinical practices in psychology. His empirical work has been devoted to clarifying the role of cultural values in marriage and the family, including positive illusions about marriage and parenting. He has also written about the centrality of practical wisdom for theory, research, and applied practices. He is currently directing the Constitutive Goals Project, which is focused on documenting the existence and functioning of higher-order goals and investigating the links between pursuing inherently valuable goals and human flourishing. He is the author of *Virtue and Psychology* (American Psychological Association, 2005) and *Beyond the Myth of Marital Happiness* (Jossey-Bass, 2000), and a co-author of *Re-envisioning Psychology* (Jossey-Bass, 1999). Fowers has published numerous peer-reviewed articles on virtue and practical wisdom in psychology, including *The Virtue of Multiculturalism* (*American Psychologist*, September 2006).

Javier Gomez-Lavin is currently a Provost Postdoctoral Fellow at the University of Pennsylvania, working closely with Professor Lisa Miracchi on topics at the intersection of philosophy and cognitive science. His work also extends to the social domain, and integrates findings from moral and aesthetic psychology in an attempt to provide a more holistic model of agent-based cognition.

Warren Herold received undergraduate degrees from Oberlin College and the Oberlin Conservatory of Music. He received his MSc and MA from University College—London and his PhD from the University of Michigan—Ann Arbor. He is currently an Assistant Professor of Philosophy at the University of Arkansas.

Ethan Kross received his BA from the University of Pennsylvania and his MA and PhD from Columbia University. He is currently a Professor in the Psychology Department at the University of Michigan and the Director of the University of Michigan Emotion and Self-Control Laboratory.

Dawne Moon is an Associate Professor of Sociology at Marquette University who uses qualitative methods to study gender, sexuality, religion, and culture. She has published in such journals as the *American Journal of Sociology, Theory & Society*, and the *Annual Review of Sociology*. With Theresa W. Tobin, she has published research findings from their Self, Motivation, and Virtue Project–funded research on the conservative Protestant LGBTI movement in *Hypatia*, the *Journal of Moral Education*, and *Political Power & Social Theory*.

Darcia Narvaez is Professor of Psychology at the University of Notre Dame. She focuses on moral development and flourishing from an interdisciplinary perspective. Dr. Darcia Narvaez's current research explores how early-life experience and societal culture interact to influence virtuous character in children and adults. She integrates neurobiological, clinical, developmental, and educational sciences in her theories, research and writing about moral development, parenting, and education. She is a fellow of the American Psychological Association and the American Educational Research Association. Author of papers, she has authored or edited more than 20 books. Her recent books include: *Indigenous Sustainable Wisdom: First Nation Know-how for Global Flourishing* (edited with Four Arrows, E. Halton, B. Collier, & G. Enderle); *Basic Needs, Wellbeing and Morality: Fulfilling Human Potential*; and *Embodied Morality: Protectionism, Engagement and Imagination*. One of her recent authored books, *Neurobiology and the Development of Human Morality: Evolution, Culture and Wisdom*, won the 2015 William James Book Award from the American Psychological Association and the 2017 Expanded Reason Award. She writes a popular blog for *Psychology Today* ("Moral Landscapes") and hosts the webpage EvolvedNest.org.

Shaun Nichols is currently a Professor of Philosophy at The University of Arizona, and will be Full Professor at Cornell University's Sage School of Philosophy in fall 2019.

Jesse Prinz is a Distinguished Professor of Philosophy and Director of the Committee for Interdisciplinary Science Studies at the Graduate Center of the City University of New York.

Robert Roberts is Distinguished Professor of Ethics, emeritus, at Baylor University. His most recent books are *Emotions in the Moral Life* (Cambridge, 2013) and *The Moral Psychology of Gratitude* (Rowman and Littlefield, 2019; edited with Daniel Telech). Recently he wrote a series of essays on the ethics, epistemology, and spirituality of humility. He is at work on a book titled, *Kierkegaard's Psychology of Character*.

Nancy E. Snow is Professor of Philosophy and Director of the Institute for the Study of Human Flourishing at the University of Oklahoma. She is the author of *Virtue as Social Intelligence: An Empirically Grounded Theory* (Routledge, 2010) and more than 45 papers on virtue and ethics more broadly. She has also edited or co-edited seven volumes. She is currently revising a monograph on hope, writing one on virtue ethics and virtue epistemology, and co-authoring a book on virtue measurement. She is the series editor of "The Virtues," a 15-book series published by Oxford University Press featuring interdisciplinary volumes on virtues or clusters of virtues. The first volume in this series, *Justice*, edited by Mark LeBar, was published in 2018.

Walter Sowden received his BA from South Dakota State University; MA from Teachers College, Columbia University; and MS and PhD from the University of Michigan—Ann Arbor. He is a past Director of Behavioral Biology in the Center for Military Psychiatry and Neuroscience at the Walter Reed Army Institute of Research, Silver Spring, Maryland. As of July 2019, he became the Director of Research, Department of Behavioral Health at Tripler Army Medical Center, Honolulu, Hawaii.

Michael Spezio is an Associate Professor of Psychology and Neuroscience at Scripps College in Claremont, California, where he mentors undergraduate scholars in the Laboratory for Inquiry into Valuation and Emotion (The LIVE Lab), and is a Visiting Researcher at the Institute for Systems Neuroscience at the University Medical Center Eppendorf (UKE) in Hamburg, Germany. He has worked with l'Arche USA and with l'Arche Communities and La Ferme in France, thanks to funding from the John Templeton Foundation, the Templeton Religion Trust, and the Self, Motivation, and Virtue Project. He is grateful for the generosity and kindness of Jean Vanier and of all the Core Members and Assistants who contributed to the projects. He gratefully acknowledges the friendship and scholarly contributions of Robert C. Roberts, Gregory Peterson, Sister Anita Maroun, and all of those who worked together on the research. He has co-edited *Habits in Mind* (Routledge, 2017) and *The Routledge Companion to Religion and Science* (2012).

Nina Strohminger is an Assistant Professor of Legal Studies and Business Ethics at the Wharton School. Professor Strohminger's research approaches key questions in business ethics through the lens of psychology. She holds a BA in Cognitive Science from Brown University and a PhD in Psychology from the University of Michigan. She has held postdoctoral fellowships at Duke University and Yale University.

Moin Syed is an Associate Professor of Psychology at the University of Minnesota—Twin Cities. His research is broadly concerned with identity and personality development among ethnically

200 Contributors

and culturally diverse adolescents and emerging adults. He is co-editor of the *Oxford Handbook of Identity Development*; the editor of *Emerging Adulthood*, the official journal of the Society for the Study of Emerging Adulthood; and is past-President of the International Society for Research on Identity.

Valerie Tiberius is the Paul W. Frenzel Chair in Liberal Arts and chair of the Philosophy Department at the University of Minnesota. Her work explores the ways in which philosophy and psychology can both contribute to the study of well-being and virtue. She is the author of *The Reflective Life: Living Wisely with Our Limits* (Oxford, 2008); *Moral Psychology: A Contemporary Introduction* (Routledge, 2015); and *Well-Being as Value Fulfillment: How We Can Help Each Other to Live Well* (Oxford, 2018). She has published numerous articles on the topics of virtue, well-being, and the relationship between positive psychology and ethics, and has received grants from the Templeton Foundation and the National Endowment for the Humanities.

Theresa W. Tobin is Associate Professor of Philosophy at Marquette University where she also currently serves as Associate Dean for Academic Affairs and Student Development in the Graduate School. She researches topics in practical and theoretical ethics and feminist philosophy, with a focus on moral emotions and virtue ethics under conditions of oppression. Her recent collaboration with Dawne Moon works to clarify the nature of gender-based spiritual violence and examine its impact on moral and spiritual agency.

Christine D. Wilson-Mendenhall is an Associate Scientist at the Center for Healthy Minds, University of Wisconsin—Madison. She draws on training across multiple disciplines (e.g., cognitive science, affective science, systems neuroscience, philosophy of mind) and in multiple scientific methodologies (e.g., behavioral paradigms, mobile experience sampling, self-report, neuroimaging) to study how the mind works and how psychological patterns underlying suffering and flourishing emerge. Her work includes peer-reviewed theoretical and empirical articles on cognition, emotion, and well-being. She received her PhD in Cognitive Psychology from Emory University where she conducted research as a National Science Foundation Graduate Research Fellow. She completed her Postdoctoral Fellowship in the Interdisciplinary Affective Science Lab at Northeastern University and the Martinos Center for Biomedical Imaging. There she studied the nature of human emotions in collaboration with scientists and scholars funded by her advisor's National Institutes of Health Pioneer award. Building on her interdisciplinary training and collaborations with contemplative scholars, Dr. Wilson-Mendenhall's research program currently focuses on bridging basic and translational science to investigate psychological well-being as multi-faceted and skill-based.

Index

admiration 85, 89–90, 92–101, 103–106
aesthetic self (selves) 31, 34, 39
altruistic motivation 78–82
Apostle Paul 95, 103
Aristotle 52, 97, 127, 136
atheist 168, 177
Ayduk, O. 75

basic humanity 88, 98, 101, 106
behavior 14–15, 52–57, 64–65, 70, 76–82, 114, 130, 136, 176, 178, 184
benevolence 71–75, 82
Big Five (personality traits) 14, 18, 56, 129
Bleidorn, W. 55
Bobocel, D. R. 78–79
Boyle, G. 85, 90, 100–102, 106
Brienza, J. P. 78–79
Bronfenbrenner, U. 139
Buber, M. 154
Buddha 115–117
Buddhism 110–111, 115, 119
Buddhist 110–118, 120–121, 168, 173, 177
Buddhist philosophy 112–114, 118
burdened virtues 130

Callard, F. & Fitzgerald, D. 169, 171, 186, 189
Card, C. 149
caring 113, 120
character 39, 55, 63, 67, 70–71, 74, 87–88, 91–92, 95, 97, 99, 103, 132, 134
characteristic adaptations 13–14, 16–19, 129–130

Christian 147–154, 156–157, 161–162, 168, 171, 173, 177–179
Christian love 147, 152, 154
Christian virtue ethics 149, 158
circumstances 63–66, 69–70, 73–74, 77, 79, 82
cognition 13–14
cognitive-based compassion training 119
co-location 186–187
communicative styles 184
compassion 14, 86, 89–90, 92–93, 98, 100–101, 105, 113, 115–116, 118–119, 129, 182–183
Condon, P., Dunne, J., & Wilson-Mendenhall, C. 118
conduct 63–64, 67–68, 71–74, 81–82
Cooley, C. H. 8
core self 112–113, 120
cultural master narratives 132, 134–135, 137–139, 142
cultures of reasoning 168, 183, 185, 188, 190

deep integration 8, 18, 109–111, 118, 120–122, 169, 172
Denissen, J. J. A. 55
density distribution approach 53–54, 59
development 130–132, 137–138
developmental psychology 9, 11, 12, 20
DeYoung, C. G. 15, 20
diachronic identity 27–28
direct interaction 186
disposition 50–52, 54, 57, 87, 95, 97, 104, 117, 149–153, 156
Dranseika, V. 29

Index

ecological fallacy 54
ecological model of development 139
Edman, E. M. 153
emotion 13–14, 36, 70, 75, 82, 88–89, 92–93, 95, 99–100, 106, 111, 114, 148, 150–151, 153, 155–156
emotional reactivity 65–66, 74–75, 77
empirical approach 109, 120, 122
empirical investigations 45, 51, 53
empirical methods 46, 53
emulation 89–90, 92, 94–95, 103–104
epistemic preferences 184
epistemological 169, 184–185
Erikson, E. 11–12
ethnographic 170–171, 173–174, 177–178, 181
eudaimonia 43–44, 52, 56, 128, 136–138
eudaimonic growth 128, 132–134, 136, 138, 140, 142
eudaimonic virtues 128, 132, 138, 142
evaluation 91, 95
executive function 36
exemplar 85–96, 98, 100, 106
exemplarism 85, 90–91
exemplarity relation 85, 88–89, 106
exemplary 168, 177
experience sampling research 53–54
experimental philosophy 26, 29, 32, 39

faith 148, 152, 159, 162
feelings 63–65, 68, 70, 74–77
feminist 148–149, 157
feminist affect theory 150
feminist philosophy 127
feminist virtue ethics 158
Flanagan, O. 45
flourishing 109–110, 112–119, 134, 140, 149–150
Fowers, B. J. 54
framework of personality 7, 16–17, 21
framework of self 7, 13, 16–17, 21
Frankfurt, H. 63

generosity 172, 174
global self-report scales 52, 54
gratitude 174
Griswald, C. L. 64
Grossmann, I. 78–79
Grounded Theory approach 178
group-based identity 136
group membership 11, 12, 176

happiness 66–68, 70–72
hermeneutic 178, 185, 188
Hume, D. 8, 16, 19
humility 147, 150, 152–153, 155–156
humility-pride 156

identity 7–13, 15, 17, 19–21, 25–31, 34–40, 113–114, 137–138, 151, 156–157
individual selves 64, 74
influence 86–88, 90–91, 94–96, 99
inspiration 85, 87, 94, 97–98, 106
interdisciplinarity 168, 170–171, 189–190
interdisciplinary cooperation 168–169, 175, 189
interdisciplinary research (IDR) 46–50, 59, 167, 189
interdisciplinary team 167–169
interpersonal relationship 176
interpretation 178–179, 181, 185–187
intersectional justice 147

James, W. 8–9, 10–12
Justice Sensitivity scale 57–58

Kierkegaard, S. 99
knowledge 10, 21, 37, 44, 47–48, 50, 52, 57, 59, 73, 77, 111, 121–122, 158–159, 169–170, 184, 188
Kross, E. 75, 81

Leary, M. R. 9–10, 12, 16
LGBTI 147, 150–154, 156–157
LGBTI Christians 154
life narratives 13, 15–16, 17–18
life stories 127–128, 130–143
Locke, J. 27
Lockean memory approach 30
love 68, 70–71, 92–93, 95–100, 103, 116, 131, 147–148, 150, 152–155, 161–162

MacIntyre, A. C. 55
McAdams, D. P. 13, 129, 131
McAdams, D. P. 13–14, 17–18
McLean, K. C. 131
Mead, G.H. 8
meaning 171–178, 181, 187–188
methodological 169, 175, 190
methodologically conservative 169
Mischel, W. 75
Mollica, C. O. 54
moral change 28–30, 37, 39

moral continuity 28
moral development 45
moral effect 89–90
moral exemplars 177, 179, 181, 185
moral formation 95, 106
moral improvement 29
moral influence 86–87, 92, 94, 106
moral injury 37
morality 25–26, 28, 31, 34–36, 40, 148
moral motivation 44, 148–149, 151
moral norm 30, 37
moral psychology 44–46, 91
moral quality 86
moral self 25–26, 29, 36
moral self-effect 29, 31, 35–36
Moral Self Hypothesis 26, 29, 34, 36
moral sentiment 97
moral transformation 28–29, 36
moral values 26, 28, 30–31, 36–37, 156
motivation 7–8, 13–14, 17–19, 21, 43, 51–57, 64, 74, 78, 81–82, 94, 127–128, 131, 142, 148–149, 152–154, 159, 161, 167, 169, 176, 178
motivational concordance 54
motive 129–132, 142, 171
multidimensional scaling 30, 32
multi-disciplinary 109
Muslim 168
mutual value 50–51, 58

narrative 128–130, 132, 134, 137–138, 141–142
narrative psychology 15, 128
narrative self 128–130, 132, 138
Neo-Aristotelian 148–149
Newcomb, T. 38
Nisbet, R. 134
Nussbaum, M. C. 136

open-mindedness 48, 50, 174, 189–190
openness 109, 129, 149, 153–154, 156

Pals, J. L. 13–14, 17–18
patience 109
perfectionism 138–140
personal identity 10–12, 26–30, 37
personality 7–9, 12–21, 26, 32, 36, 38, 129–131, 138, 142
personality traits 7, 13–14, 21, 53, 129
personal projects 20–21

personhood 25, 129
personological model of personality 129
philosophical anthropology 176
phronesis 52
physiological synchrony 118
plasticity 14
positive illusions 114–115, 121
positive psychology 111–112
pride 150, 152–153, 155–156
Procacci, E. N. 54
prosocial behavior 78–80
psychoanalytic theory 12
psychological realism 45, 51, 58
psychological science 112, 116, 118

queer pride 153

reconciliation 147
redemption 134–135
reflexive thinking 9
relationship 20–21, 50, 55–56, 58, 79, 81, 86, 89, 91, 103, 106, 109–110, 112, 114–121, 131–133, 138–140, 148, 150–157, 176
respect 88, 94–95, 97, 104, 111, 113, 116
responsibility 28–29, 39
responsiveness 113, 120
Roberts, R. C. 149
role-sensitive 51, 58

sacramental shame 147, 150–152, 156, 160–161
scalar traits 51, 58
Scripture 154, 157–159
self 7–14, 15–21, 25–28, 31, 63, 67–71, 74–81, 99, 105, 109, 113–114, 118–119, 122, 128–131, 134, 137, 148, 150–154, 167
self-concept 10, 148, 156
self-concordance 55
self-consistency 53–56
self-control 9–10
self-development 127
self-distancing 64–66, 68–70, 73–82
self-esteem 9, 17
self-expressiveness 55
selfhood 148
self-identity 129, 136, 138
self-narration 132
self-regulation 9–10
self-report 120–121, 181
sentiment 63–64, 74
sexuality 148, 155–157

shame 147, 150–157, 159–160, 162
situational factors 52, 57–58
situationist critique 128
Slote, M. 90
Smith, A. 63–75, 78, 80, 82, 93, 97
Snowden, W. 81
social 8, 11–12, 14, 16, 19, 38, 47, 54–55, 94, 97, 104, 116, 127–129, 130–132, 134, 136–138, 142, 148–150, 155, 159, 161, 167, 169, 171, 176–177, 185–188
social context 9, 13, 82, 127, 149–150
social ecology 130, 133
social emotion 151
social identity 10–12
social identity theory 10
social justice 131, 148, 157, 177
social psychology 9–12
social sciences 8
spiritual formation 151, 159
spiritual self 150
spiritual violence 147, 150–152, 159–161
stability 14
stories 114–115, 119
STRIVE-4 Model 51–53, 57–58
Syed, M. 17–18

Tajfel, H. 10–11
Tangney, J. P. 9–10, 12, 16
tentativeness 179, 184–185, 188
Tessman, L. 149
Three-Dimensional Wisdom Model 182
Three-Dimensional Wisdom Scale 180
three levels of personality 129–130
tolerance 129
trait 30–32, 39, 50–54, 56–59, 87–88, 94, 105, 113–114, 119, 129–130, 149–150

trait-situation interaction 52
trust 111

understanding 113, 120

validation 113, 120
values 10, 16, 19–21, 27, 30, 32, 35, 36–37, 38, 50, 52, 68–69, 78–79, 81, 92–93, 97, 99, 104, 113, 119, 129–134, 136, 138, 155, 159, 184
Vanier, J. 85, 90, 96–98, 105–106
virtue 7–8, 14, 17–19, 21, 43–46, 49–59, 64–65, 70–74, 81–82, 86–89, 92–93, 97–98, 100–101, 104, 106, 109, 112, 117, 122, 127–132, 134–135, 138, 140, 142–143, 147–150, 152, 154, 156, 158, 161, 167, 169–174, 177–178, 180–181, 185, 187
virtue development 149–150, 159
virtue ethics 90, 127–129, 150
virtue of care 134
virtuous motivation 64, 74, 81–82
virtuous motives 129, 142
virtuous self-development 127, 131, 137

Watson, G. 90
Weidman, A. C. 81
well-being 7–8, 19–21, 67, 112–113, 115, 119–120, 132, 142
Williams, B. 26
wisdom 113–116, 118–119, 128–129, 132–133, 142, 167, 170, 172, 174–175, 179–183, 185, 187
Wolf, S. 87

Zagzebski, L. 89, 94

Printed in the United States
by Baker & Taylor Publisher Services